ON HARPE

ON HARPER'S TRAIL

ROLAND MCMILLAN HARPER,

PIONEERING BOTANIST OF THE

SOUTHERN COASTAL PLAIN

Elizabeth Findley Shores

THE UNIVERSITY OF GEORGIA PRESS

Athens & London

© 2008 by the University of Georgia Press
Athens, Georgia 30602
All rights reserved
Designed by Kathi Dailey Morgan
Cartography by David Wasserboehr, Flying W Graphics
Set in Galliard by BookComp, Inc.
Printed and bound by Thomson-Shore
The paper in this book meets the guidelines for
permanence and durability of the Committee on
Production Guidelines for Book Longevity of the
Council on Library Resources.

Printed in the United States of America
12 11 10 09 08 C 5 4 3 2 1

Library of Congress Cataloging-in-Publication Data
Shores, Elizabeth F.
On Harper's trail : Roland McMillan Harper, pioneering botanist
of the southern coastal plain / Elizabeth Findley Shores.
p. cm.
Includes bibliographical references and index.
ISBN-13: 978-0-8203-3100-3 (hardcover : alk. paper)
ISBN-10: 0-8203-3100-7 (hardcover : alk. paper)
1. Botanists—United States—Biography.
2. Naturalists—United States—Biography.
3. Botany—Southern States.
4. Harper, Roland M. (Roland McMillan), 1878–1966.
I. Title.
QK31.H26S56 2008
580.92—dc22 [B]
2007045064

British Library Cataloging-in-Publication Data available

For Anne Findley Shores

CONTENTS

ACKNOWLEDGMENTS

The first persons, other than my mother, Anne Findley Shores, who told me stories about Roland McMillan Harper were my grandfather, Judge Herbert Lyman Findley Sr.; my uncle, Dr. Herbert Lyman Findley Jr.; Dr. Walter B. Jones of the Alabama Geological Survey; Dr. Harper's widow, Mary Sue Wigley Harper; Tom Dodd Jr.; and David DeJarnette. Much later in my search for stories, Roland Harper's nephews, Robin Harper and David Bartram Harper, and niece, Lucy Harper Traber, were very helpful.

I could not have done this research without the unfailingly cheerful and knowledgeable help of the entire staff, particularly Merrily Harris and Jessica Lacher-Feldman, of the W. S. Hoole Special Collections Library at the University of Alabama, as well as the interlibrary loan staffs of the Central Arkansas Library System and the University of Arkansas for Medical Sciences. I am also deeply indebted to the staff of the University of Georgia Press, particularly the director, Nicole Mitchell, and the editors Jon Davies and Patrick Allen; to Barb Wojhoski, who copyedited the book; and to the anonymous reviewers who commented on the manuscript.

Across the southern coastal plain, many naturalists, scientists, and other students of Roland Harper went to considerable trouble to share their knowledge and escort me to locations in the field. Christopher T. Trowell and Frankie Snow of South Georgia College in Douglas, Georgia, took me to Broxton Rocks and to meet Milton Hopkins of Osierfield, Georgia; Chris Trowell also took me into the Okefenokee Swamp and gave me copies of the many primary source documents he had obtained from the W. S. Hoole Special Collections Library and other libraries. Louise Kirn of Apalachicola National Forest took me to the type locality for Harper's beauty. Jim Moyers and Thomas Estes of St. Joe Timberland Company allowed me and my husband to visit the Bay County site of Harper's beauty in the company of Moyers and Edwin J. and Lisa Keppner of Panama City, Florida. Todd Engstrom, then of the Nature Conservancy, arranged for me to interview Angus Gholson, Wilson Baker, and Leon Neel, who was present at Harper's address to the first Tall Timbers Research Station fire ecology conference. This interview took place at historic Greenwood Plantation in Thomasville, Georgia, and afterward Leon and Julie Neel entertained us at their fascinating home in a longleaf forest. Baker organized our June 22, 2004, expedition to historic Aspalaga Landing, the site of Harper's 1909 camping trip on the Apalachicola River in Gadsden County, Florida. Gholson led that foray, which also included Gil Nelson and Mark Ludlow.

Several scientists and historians also took the time to review draft sections of this book. I particularly thank Wilson Baker of Tallahassee, Steven Noll of the University of Florida, and Edward J. Larson of the University of Georgia for this assistance, as well as the four anonymous reviewers who made many helpful suggestions. These scholars are not responsible for any of the mistakes that remain.

I also thank Hazel R. Delcourt of the University of Tennessee and G. Ward Hubbs of Birmingham-Southern College for giving me their personal collections of Harper reprints and monographs; Daniel Erlandson of Little Rock, Arkansas, for his insights and kind help; David Avant and George Avant of Tallahassee, Florida, for telling me what they remembered of Harper; Alfred E. Schuyler of the Academy of Natural Sciences in Philadelphia for corresponding with me about his contacts with Harper and reviewing successive drafts of my passage about the complicated genus *Scirpus*; Robert Thorne of Rancho Santa Ana Botanic Garden; Clermont Lee of Savannah, Georgia; and Professor Emeritus Cornelius van Bavel of Texas A&M University. Professor van Bavel graciously examined Hugo de Vries's account of his 1912 visit to Alabama, written in Dutch, for details about the pilgrimage to the type locality for largeflower evening primrose. For this help, and for his very useful monograph, *Hugo de Vries: Travels of a Dutch Botanist in America, 1904–1912*, I am grateful.

Rusty Russell, the collections manager for the Department of Botany at the Smithsonian Institution, spent several hours locating Harper holotypes and isotypes and other specimens in that collection and allowed me to examine them. Stella Sylva, administrative curator of the herbarium of the New York Botanical Garden, arranged for me to examine its Harper specimens and answered many questions. Barbara Thiers and William R. Buck of the NYBG also were very helpful. Wendy B. Zomlefer, curator of the University of Georgia Herbarium, provided me with valuable information about a trip that Harper made with Wilbur H. Duncan. I also thank the archivists at the Botany Libraries of Harvard University and the Wilson Library, University of North Carolina at Chapel Hill; Marvin Goss of the Georgia Southern University Special Collections; the Redwood City, California, Public Library; Dwayne Cox and the Draughon Library Special Collections at Auburn University; Earle E. Spamer and the library of the American Philosophical Society; Amy Crumpton at the archive of the American Association for the Advancement of Science; Carol J. Armstrong and J. Douglas Calman of the Florida Geological Survey; Jim Pate and Yvonne Crumpler of the Linn-Henley Research Library, Birmingham Public Library; and Margaret Morrissey of the Jacob Edwards Library in Southbridge, Massachusetts.

Richard Wunderlin, Bruce Hansen, and all the people at the University of South Florida who created and maintain the online atlas of Florida vascular plants have my sincere gratitude. Their atlas is a phenomenal resource; one can search for plants by common and scientific names and by individual county; for example, when I could not decipher Harper's handwritten diary entry about the hour he and his brother Francis spent on Santa Rosa Island in 1939, I could search all known species in Santa Rosa County and match scientific names to Harper's partially legible abbreviations. The online collections of historic maps of Alabama and Florida, maintained by the University of Alabama and the University of South Florida, also were invaluable.

I am grateful to the publishers of, and all the contributors to, the delightful magazine *Alabama Heritage*, particularly Larry Davenport, whose column "Nature Journal" I always read first.

I have many friends and family members to thank. Melissa Macdougall traveled with me to Okefenokee, Broxton Rocks, and Greenwood Plantation in Georgia. She also read the entire manuscript and offered many very good suggestions. Jane and Jim Beachboard cheerfully listened to many updates on my research and provided innumerable meals and refreshments after I spent long days at my desk. Bob and Robin Devan shared their house on St. George Island in Florida with us two summers in a row; Bob also restored and framed a print of a painting, by Robert Thom, of Henry Rusby, that was a reliable source of inspiration. Stephen Recken encouraged me to write this book; C. Fred Williams encouraged me to become a historian. I thank Louis Hedgecock and Jerry Croghan for their hospitality in New York; the late Marion Molnar of Little Rock and Indianapolis, who gave me her copies of Rickett's *Wildflowers of the United States* and Steyermark's *Flora of Missouri*; the amazing Cathy

Grace, who respected my need to write this book, and Charles Grace, who gave me a place to lay my head; my aunt and cousins, Margaret Findley, Lynn Findley, and Louise Findley Labosier of Tuscaloosa, Alabama; my brother, James Layet Shores III, with whom I played with the pasteboard houses; and my sons, Findley Shores Johnson and Layet Spigner Johnson, for their love, support, and encouragement.

This project would not have been possible without Finos Buford "Buddy" Johnson Jr., my husband and the love of my life, who accompanied me on many field trips around the Southeast, providing wonderful company and invaluable help. He has always supported my odysseys and tangents and has been my beloved traveling companion for more than twenty-five years.

A NOTE TO READERS

Unless otherwise noted, the diaries of Roland M. Harper are the source for events described here and the source of unattributed quotations of Harper. The diaries, letters, and photographs cited here are found in the W. S. Hoole Special Collections Library at the University of Alabama. Letters are to and from Roland M. Harper unless otherwise noted. Unsigned materials accessed online are noted but are not included in the list of works cited.

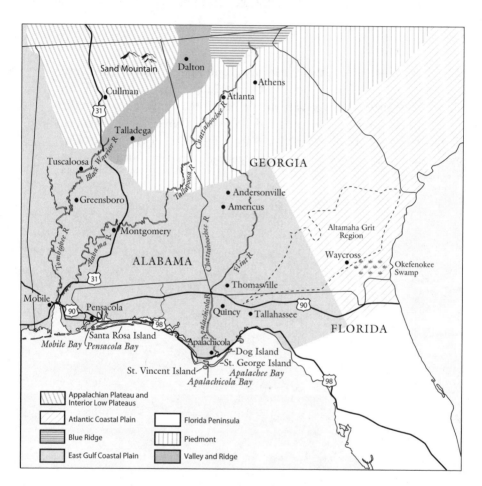

The Southern Coastal Plain

PROLOGUE

There was an odor of lumber that had been heated by the summer sun and cooled each winter, dry as a bone, for decades, as I ascended the narrow, steep staircase to my grandfather's attic. I went up to the attic many times as a child, searching for new old books to read during our visits to the house on University Boulevard in Tuscaloosa, Alabama. I lived for most of my childhood in Birmingham, sixty miles to the northeast in the foothills of the Appalachian Plateau, but Tuscaloosa, on the edge of the great southern coastal plain, with giant oaks and pecans above me and red dirt beneath my feet, was my first and real home and 329 University Boulevard was where my heart beat fastest, where every family story stirred my imagination and I awoke each day asking to hear the stories again. The front bedroom, where I slept in the four-poster bed, with a burnished green music box on the dressing table and the solemn ringing of the university carillon, Denny Chimes, to keep me company during the dark nights, was for a time during the Great Depression rented space to Annie Laurie, a laundry worker in town whom my mother remembered fondly. The second bedroom, with the pineapple bed and a fireplace, where the stairs to the attic began, was Roland Harper's room in those years, when his and Annie Laurie's rent payments helped the family, when a judge's salary was not enough. I already knew that Dr. Harper, a botanist with an office in Smith Hall at the University of Alabama, named the hybrid camellia that grew beside the breezeway for us, for the Findleys, and that Mrs. Harper still lived in their small house just a block away. My mother's pastel portrait of Dr. Harper hung in our house in Birmingham, and I had known for longer than I could tell that although he looked like a grandfather, he was not; he was the family friend known in the formal way of a vanished time as "Dr. Harper," and he was somehow special to us and part of our story.

That day I passed the turkey caller hanging on a hook, the mounted deer head, the cedar chest, and the hatboxes, to see what was stacked at the far end of the attic, beside the window that overlooked the backyard.

There I found them, coated with decades of dust but with their colors still evident, strange and amazing, wonderful cardboard models, with details carefully drawn and painted, of a plantation house, a cabin, and a weird conical tower with shuttered windows—like dollhouses, but better, artworks, unique and handmade. I took them down the stairs one at a time, brought them to my mother, and asked, "What are these toys?"

"Oh, those are some of Dr. Harper's pasteboard houses," she said. "He made those for me and Lyman." I felt our family's story become more fantastic and mysterious. It was as if my life had changed, as if Denny Chimes were ringing in my chest or the strange scent of the sweet shrub outside the sun porch wafted through my mind; Dr. Harper was no longer a solemn stranger who had rented a room in our house, whose expression could not really be considered a smile in the portrait my mother copied from a photograph. He was different from that. My first idea of him had been wrong. He was someone who made toys by hand for my mother and her brother when they were children. "He made a lot of those pasteboard houses. We have a photograph of them somewhere," she said, and my heart beats faster even now as I remember my anticipation—there was more to see, another clue to the story of who we were, of who I was. The photo she found, one I now know Dr. Harper took himself, shows my mother, Anne, at about six, her expression reserved, sitting on the unpainted back-porch steps to the left of an array of pasteboard houses, the tower with a trough for marbles to roll down, cabins, a two-story house with columns, a barn, small beds, a castle, a church, an odd house with shutters hinged above the windows, and, largest of all, a round structure with a peaked roof. Her brother, my Uncle Lyman, about eight, stands to the right. Both children gaze solemnly at the pasteboard houses.

After I found the pasteboard houses, I often rode my bicycle from 329 to the campus quadrangle to hide beneath a giant tree in front of Gorgas Library and watch the students and professors walking to and fro, imagining the scene as Dr. Harper walked to and from his office in Smith Hall. My mother took me to visit his widow, who read aloud to us from the memoir she was writing. I wanted to find out more about his life as a scientist, so my mother found the address for Walter B. Jones, a past director of the Alabama Geological Survey, who had known Dr. Harper, and I began writing to him. He wrote back to me that Dr. Harper visited the same places in the landscape again and again, could remember plants he had found many years earlier, and could find the very same spots to view them again. Wanting to be like Dr. Harper, I bought my own copy of *Wildflowers of Alabama and Adjoining States* and began exploring the first field that was open to me, the southern side of Red Mountain in Birmingham. I tramped the same trails repeatedly, discovering one-flowered cancer root (*Orobanche uniflora*) and wild petunia (*Ruellia strepens*). Dr. Jones pointed me to others who remembered Dr. Harper, and I wrote to them, too—to the president of the university, Joab Thomas; to David DeJarnette, the director of Moundville State Park; to Tom Dodd Jr., a nurseryman in south Alabama. I pursued the story of Dr. Harper off and on for years. My mother took me to Moundville and Dodd Nursery in 1975 to interview DeJarnette and Dodd—our trip was my first experience at highway driving—and Dodd gave me photos of himself with Dr. Harper standing in a field somewhere on the coastal plain.

Dr. Harper was an eccentric character. Everyone recalled, with affection and humor, his disdain for women with "bobbed" hair, his objection to income taxes, his constant newspaper clipping. But I knew something most of them didn't. He had made pasteboard houses for a little girl and her brother, even though he wasn't their father. He had read cartoons to them and drawn cartoons for them; he had devoted his time to them. There was a kindness beneath the quirks that I felt driven to understand. What had inspired him to do those things for Anne and Lyman?

Almost thirty years after I found Dr. Harper's pasteboard houses, I watched a television program about Edward O. Wilson, the Harvard University entomologist who is from south Alabama, and realized he might have known Dr. Harper. I wrote to him, as I had written to others who knew Harper. Professor Wilson called to say yes, he remembered Roland Harper. He remembered his notoriety for making plant observations from the windows of moving cars and trains. He told me that Harper was considered old-fashioned for his dedication to making notes in the field, that Harper's life harkened to the pioneer naturalists, to William Bartram—but that he, Wilson, had made the same kind of exhaustive notes when he explored New Guinea because no one had investigated the area before and it was all new. Professor Wilson encouraged me to write about Harper and his place in the grand history of explorer-naturalists.

I realized that Dr. Harper's story was more than the story of a kindly old gentleman who had spent some time with a shy little girl.

Harper began saving material in a collection he referred to as his library—and began misplacing the material—at a young age. He apparently attempted to save every letter and document he ever obtained. He also saved first drafts or carbons of many of his outgoing letters. He kept a daily journal in which he recorded his activities, including to whom he wrote and what letters he received. He also collected newspapers in order to clip articles, some of which he mailed to friends, relatives, and colleagues, but many of which he saved.

The W. S. Hoole Special Collections Library at the University of Alabama in Tuscaloosa holds a massive collection of Harper's letters, field notebooks, diaries, photographs, newspapers, pamphlets, clippings, and manuscripts. Occupying 144 linear feet of shelving, it is the largest single collection at Hoole, and in 2003, almost forty years after his widow donated it to the library, it was not yet completely processed. The first time I visited Hoole was around 1974. A young graduate student, Guy Hubbs, who was interested in Harper himself, permitted my mother and me to enter the sanctum where the boxes were stacked on shelves to the ceiling. The second time I visited was in the early summer of 2003, before going to St. George Island, a barrier island near Apalachicola Bay in Florida. That time, I asked an archivist, Merrily Harris, if it was possible to determine if Harper had ever visited the Apalachicola area. Harris queried the photo database for all the photographs Harper had made in Florida, sorting them by year and county, and gave me a printout of the report. The printout was eighty-six pages long. Using the dates of the photographs as a guide, I began reading excerpts of Harper's diaries for his times in the port town of Apalachicola, finding his succinct, intriguing account of making a pilgrimage to "Chapman's grave" and copying the epitaph. I didn't know who Chapman was, but I had a place to start.

Harper was one of the last explorers of the virgin forests and undisturbed swamps and bogs of the southern coastal plain. Within a small circle of scientists, he is legendary for his sweeping, detailed knowledge of the plants and geography of the region and for his remarkable treks over the countryside. The great mystery of Harper's life is why, beginning in the 1920s, he gradually spent more time studying sociological issues and left undone the phytogeography of the southern coastal plain that his friends and admirers expected him to write.

Another puzzle is why he avoided forming a family. A handsome and, as he matured, charming man, with classic features and striking blue eyes, he was gregarious and nurtured many friendships, writing thousands of letters to friends, acquaintances, and relatives and saving thousands that he received. He would walk for hours on dirt roads, in cold, heat, or rain, to call on an old friend. Yet he lived most of his life alone, in rented rooms. He was clearly fond of children, and although he perhaps avoided fatherhood to remain financially independent, he had the example of his brother Francis, whose wife cheerily lived in near-impoverished circumstances, raising their four children virtually on her own, so that Francis was free for his scientific and sociological quests. Despite overtures by interested women, matchmaking help from his friends, and his mother's brutal nagging to marry, however, Roland remained single until he was sixty-five years old and never had children.

A third mystery emerged as I followed Harper's trail, on a day with two unexpected discoveries. My husband and I were exploring the Gulf resort town of Lanark Village, Florida, looking for buildings that were there when Harper passed through. We stopped to question a woman who was standing in her front-yard garden. She suggested we consult the couple who ran the Gulf Specimen Marine Laboratory in the coastal town of Panacea, to the east and around Bald Point. We found the marine laboratory, and I discovered that the proprietors were Jack and Anne Rudloe, he the author of a book I owned, *The Wilderness Coast: Adventures of a Gulf Coast Naturalist*. Jack was not there, but Anne stopped her work to talk with me. When I explained that I was looking for sites that Roland Harper had visited, she asked, "Is the *Harperocallis* named for him?" I wasn't familiar with the genus, so she explained, "It's an endemic lily in this area."

Later the same day, Buddy and I had supper in a small, old café in Sopchoppy, a few miles to the northeast, on the other side of St. Marks National Wildlife Refuge. A pleasant instrumental music was playing on a compact disc player, and a few couples and families sat around the small dining room. After we ordered, I walked across the room to admire a print of a painting of a wild turkey. A man sitting nearby volunteered, "That fellow right there painted that!" and pointed to a man at the table on the other side of ours. He added, "And he wrote that book!" pointing to a stack of books on a shelf of merchandise. The painter and author wore a camouflage cap and jeans; the book was *Illumination in the Flatwoods*, by Joe Hutto (Lyons Press, 1998). "And that fellow with him recorded that music they're playing!" my new friend added.

Hutto recognized that he was the subject of conversation and turned to introduce himself; his wife, Claudia Zahuranec; the musician, Sammy Tedder; and Tedder's wife, the flutist Sandy Tedder. I explained our mission, and Hutto responded simply, "Oh, yes. Harper." I was puzzled;

could this stranger actually know about Roland Harper? "Perhaps you're thinking of his brother Francis Harper, who annotated the *Naturalist Edition* of Bartram's *Travels*?" I asked.

"Oh, no," Hutto replied. "Roland Harper is an icon around here." He described how two generations of botanists in north Florida were familiar with Harper's pioneering work in the Panhandle. For the second time in one day, I encountered someone by chance who gave me valuable information about Harper. We bought a copy of Hutto's book and a copy of Tedder's compact disc, *From the Land of Many Rivers*, a set of original compositions that combine his improvisational jazz with recordings made in the Apalachicola National Forest and other wild areas, some of the recordings by Hutto.

Driving on to St. George Island that night, Buddy and I listened to the CD, and I was enchanted by Tedder's saxophone and the sounds of frogs, insects, birds, and water. As we followed Highway 98 west along the edge of the land, the sun was low and struck the trunks of the pines. The storm clouds from earlier were gone; cumulus clouds had taken their place. We reached the coast, and the water and sky seemed to blend and shimmer. Pines towered a few yards from the edge of the bay. Passing this way ninety-three years earlier, Harper had noted that "the long narrow islands or barrier-beaches a few miles offshore seem[ed] to be mostly wooded with pine, sometimes such a narrow and low strip that trees appear[ed] to be standing in a single row in the water." Buddy and I reached Eastpoint and took the bridge to St. George Island. People and great blue herons were standing near each other in the shallow water of the bay.

As I learned more about *Harperocallis*, I realized that the third mystery I needed to solve was how, despite his perseverance in searching for new botanical species, Harper missed discovering an entirely new genus, a beautiful endemic lily that grew in the very ecological niche he covered most minutely, the pitcher plant bogs in longleaf pine woods, in one of the regions he explored repeatedly, the Apalachicola River basin of Florida.

CHAPTER ONE

To Be Forever Famous

On an early fall day in 1898, twenty-year-old Roland McMillan Harper set out on what he thought of then as the "greatest walk of [his] life," heading thirty-three miles north from Southbridge in south-central Massachusetts to Wachusett Mountain. It was an impulsive foray, and he left without enough food or money. He walked alone, carrying only his botany box and something for lunch. He felt lonesome, as he often did on solitary rambles, wishing one of his boyhood friends were with him, but he told himself he wasn't really alone because Worcester County was "thickly settled." Roland walked from Southbridge to Charlton, crossed the Worcester and Stafford Turnpike, turned east at Charlton Depot, turned north at Rockdale, and followed the road through Leicester, Paxton, and Holden. At Leicester, he may have passed the factories that manufactured hand cards, tools used in textile mills, or the Unitarian church where the Reverend Samuel May harbored runaway slaves on the Underground Railroad. Between Holden and a point slightly west of Princeton, he apparently walked along the track of the Barre and Gardner Railroad.[1] He turned north again at Princeton. Roland reached Asnebumskit Hill, twenty miles from Southbridge, by midday and stopped to eat his lunch and enjoy the fine view of Paxton and Worcester. Later, he carefully noted that Asnebumskit was 1,407 feet high and Worcester's population was about one hundred thousand. Continuing down the northern side of Asnebumskit toward Wachusett, he may have passed the two-hundred-acre farm of Thomas and Margaret Aheard, immigrants from Ireland who had bought an apple orchard in Paxton in 1866 and gradually expanded their farm to a variety of crops. After lunch, he passed the brand-new Massachusetts Hospital for Consumptive and Tubercular Patients, a state prison camp and hospital, and several small private tuberculosis sanitariums in Rutland.

The country he walked through that day had gone through two cycles of logging and reforestation, the region's first farmers having cleared the woods to plant orchards and crops. Many of those farmers' descendants left for factory jobs in booming New England towns and cities, for new farmland in the Midwest, or for the allure of gold in the West. After white pines grew up to cover their old fields, a new generation of loggers cut them down. Young Roland found the twice-cutover land excellent for botanizing.[2]

At sunset, he was still two miles from his destination and probably did not have money for a room in one of the summer hotels in the area, so he slept on the top of Little Wachusett, huddling under some bushes through the chilly night. The next morning, he began gathering plants before the sun was up; took a photograph of his destination, Wachusett Mountain; and resumed walking at daylight down Little Wachusett to the southern base of the larger mountain. Hiking up the southeastern side of Wachusett, he passed through old-growth forest, including two-hundred-year-old red oaks (*Quercus rubra*) near the summit. He reached the top of the bigger mountain, a bare granite outcrop (elevation 2,006 feet), by seven that morning. Except for a cleared space of an acre or two at the top, the mountain was still covered with woods. Roland had hiked through one of the oldest forests in southern New England, with maples, birches, and red oaks, some more than three hundred years in age, saved from early farmers' hatchets and from the loggers' removal of second-growth forest in the mid-nineteenth century by their inaccessibility on the steep sides of the mountain. Yet it seems that no one recognized just how old the woods on the slopes of Wachusett Mountain were because they were not dramatically tall. Even a half-century later, describing his Wachusett Mountain trek in *Nature Outlook*, a periodical of the Worcester Natural History Society, Harper did not explicitly note that the trees on Wachusett Mountain were virgin timber, although he observed that the mountaintop trees were stunted: "I found Mt. Wachusett covered with forest, except for an acre or two at the top, and the lack of trees there was probably not due to clearing for the hotel, for the trees nearest the summit were quite stunted, presumably by cold winds and ice in winter."[3]

After descending Wachusett Mountain, Roland rode the Fitchburg and Boston and Albany Railroads back to Southbridge. At the time, Roland was working fifty-eight hours per week at Southbridge's American Optical Company, one of the world's leading manufacturers of eyeglasses. He spent his spare time during the growing seasons gathering plants on solitary walks such as the one described here and on bicycle rides out from Southbridge, climbing hills and mountains to survey the views of Massachusetts, Connecticut, and New Hampshire.

Roland described his hike to Wachusett Mountain in a letter on March 26, 1899. A handwritten first draft of the letter survives in the W. S. Hoole Special Collections Library at the University of Alabama. Fourteen pages long, including a detailed account of his family's move from Georgia to Massachusetts in 1897 as well as a nearly step-by-step report of the trek to Wachusett Mountain, it is a typical letter in the collection. From letters written by his childhood friends in Farmington, Maine; Southbridge, Massachusetts; and Dalton and Americus, Georgia, it is clear that as a young boy Roland was fascinated by many things: trains, engines, magnets, stamps, travel. Called "Roli" by his family, he was a playful child. A letter from a small friend in Farmington to seven-year-old Roland hinted at happy times: "Didn't we have a nice time last summer when we went up in the back attic and played with those horrid . . . iron shovel handles and . . . that tiny bit of a stove? Didn't we have a nice time racing in the rain, Roli, Otto and Mondi? . . . We had a good time eating ginger snaps and raisins." When Roland was ten, his maternal uncle, Otto Tauber, wrote, "Can you swim? Can you run fast? Can you clime [sic]? Can you skate on rollers? Can you turn a summer-sault [sic]?" Roland dreamed of being a sailor, like Uncle Otto, and later of being a chemist, perhaps at his father's urging. His eventual inclination for botany could have come from his father, who was a science teacher, or his mother, who had made beautiful, detailed paintings of flowers when she was a girl in Germany and took her children hunting for violets along the roadsides.[4]

Whatever field Roland chose, he was likely to be a scholar. The Harper family ethos consisted of caring for one's own, studying and exploring, and teaching and writing, with a streak of religious fervor. Roland's father, William Harper, was born to a pioneer family in Ontario, Canada, the second of nine children and the oldest son. When he was thirteen, his mother died, and William inherited much of the responsibility for seven children, yet he advanced quickly enough in school to begin teaching at the age of sixteen. He entered a seminary in Evanston, Illinois, at age twenty-two and transferred to Albion College the following year, doing farmwork to earn the money for tuition. After receiving a bachelor's degree, he became a Methodist minister in 1870 and was assigned to a tiny church in "one of the outposts of civilization in the pine region of the northern half of the Lower Peninsula" of Michigan. But ministry didn't satisfy him. Two years later, William moved to Germany, considered to have the greatest universities in the world at the time, and enrolled in the University of Munich, where he spent three years studying the natural sciences. He supported himself by writing for American newspapers. At thirty-one, still single, he made a walking trip around Switzerland—an adventure his children memorialized after his death. In Munich, William met Bertha Tauber, the daughter of a painter, and they were married in 1875. After returning to the United States with his new wife, he lived in Michigan for a brief time before he took a job teaching science at Western State Normal School in Farmington, Maine, in 1877. Throughout his teaching career in New England, New York, and the South, William Harper wrote steadily for religious, educational, and scientific publications. An advocate of the temperance movement, he turned to sociology in his forties and worked on a manifesto about church and society.[5]

William and Bertha's first child, Herman, lived only about a year and died in 1877. Roland was born in Farmington on August 11, 1878, followed by Hermina in 1880, Otto in 1882, and Wilhelmina in 1884. Bertha and William usually spoke German at home, and Roland learned that language before English. The family attended a Methodist church. Community life was rich and interesting during the years when the family lived in Farmington. By 1885, the Center Village area of town had two shoe stores, three clothing stores, three candy stores, two pharmacies, three dry-goods stores, five groceries, two jewelry stores, two millinery shops, two stores selling musical instruments, and three hardware stores, among other retail businesses. There were also several major events: a total eclipse of the sun (1878); a lecture by Henry Ward Beecher, a prominent Congregationalist minister and writer who preached on the compatibility of Christianity and Darwinian evolution; a visit by General James A. Garfield; a comet appearing in the heavens (1882); a hurricane that did great damage to timberland throughout the state (1883); a temperature of thirty degrees below zero on December 27, 1884; and many fires.[6]

William Harper was at the center of a local controversy in the spring of 1883, when he and two other instructors walked out of Farmington Normal School in a dispute over the administrative practices of the school principal. Despite wide public support for the principal, William survived the controversy and got a better job, as principal of Farmington High School, the same year. Years later he was remembered in Farmington as "an earnest advocate of temperance and always interested for the public good."[7]

The family moved to Southbridge, Massachusetts, in 1885 for William to become its superintendent of schools. Fifty-five miles west of Boston, Southbridge was on a bend in the Quinebaug River, which originates a few miles northwest near the historic town of Sturbridge. The youngest Harper child, a son named Francis, was born there. When Roli was nine, the family moved again for William's new job as superintendent of schools in Dalton, Georgia. William preceded his family to secure a new home for them; when Bertha and the children arrived, she was relieved to find a few "good German families" nearby. The townspeople soon invited William to deliver a series of scientific lectures in the hall; he began with a talk on astronomy. He came to be admired for establishing the public school system and as "an ideal Christian gentleman."[8]

For many dedicated New England teachers of the period, going to teach in the South, where poverty and economic depression following the Civil War had done nothing for public education, was a crusade. Dalton, originally known as Cross Plains, was one of the early southern railroad towns. The Western and Atlantic Railroad extended its track to the community in 1847 and built a depot there in 1852. As northern investors pushed into the southern interior after the war, the railroad boom linked Dalton to much of the region and the nation. By the time the Harpers got off the train at Dalton, one could travel from there south to Rome, Georgia, and northwest to Chattanooga, Tennessee, by rail, making the town an important hub in the northern part of the state. The railroads had made possible a burgeoning textile industry in northern Georgia. In the years since the war, Georgia had tripled its cotton mill production; the Crown Cotton Mill, with an unusual belfry and a one-hundred-foot chimney, opened in Dalton, right beside the Western and Atlantic track, in 1885, just two years before the Harpers arrived. Business and civic leaders promoted Dalton as a new industrial and cultural center. Many traveling entertainers performed at the Dalton Opera House. Dewey Grantham describes southern economic boosters who espoused the New South creed of "industrialization, urbanization, and economic diversification. The vision . . . gave rise to an elaborate myth of southern potential and success [and a] new urban business class rose in the late-nineteenth and early-twentieth centuries that did much to direct the modern South."[9]

Although railroads and the textile industry seemed to promise a New South, the Old South and the Civil War were still vivid memories in Dalton when the Harpers arrived. The screams of injured soldiers, hospitalized after Civil War battles in some of Dalton's antebellum houses, probably still seemed to echo around the town. Both armies had set up field hospitals in nearby houses to treat injured soldiers; seriously wounded men were shipped from the depot to hospitals in Marietta and Atlanta.

Most dramatically, there was the story of Dalton's teenage hero of the Confederacy, seventeen-year-old Edward Henderson, who worked in the local telegraph office and helped stop the Union hijacking of a Confederate train, the General, in the famous Great Locomotive Chase on April 12, 1862. Union raiders had cut telegraph lines along the track of the Western and Atlantic, and young Henderson ventured south from Dalton on foot to determine why the telegraph to the south wasn't working. The General's conductor, William Fuller, commandeered another train, the Texan, to overtake the raiders and the General; when he spotted the boy, he pulled him onto the train. Fuller moved the Texan fast in reverse in an attempt to catch the raiders and regain control of the General. He wrote a warning to Confederates in Chattanooga: the raiders had the General and were destroying tracks and telegraph wires as they steamed north! Young Edward jumped off the Texan as it rolled through Dalton and raced to the telegraph office, where he sent the message to Chattanooga. Confederate General Danville H. Ledbetter received the telegram and led some of his troops down the track toward Ringgold's Gap, where the General ground to a halt and the Great Locomotive Chase ended.[10]

While the Harpers were living in Dalton, Roland received a copy of Jules Verne's popular novel for schoolboys, *The Mysterious Island*. Verne's heroes were manly and adventurous and possessed vast knowledge on a wide range of subjects. They had no need of women and, most importantly, were able to survive in the wild. Their leader, Cyrus Harding, was an engineer. His closest associate was Gideon Spilett, a newspaper reporter who took constant notes. Pencroft was a sailor who had seen the world and was afraid of nothing. Neb was Harding's devoted former slave. Finally, there was Herbert, Pencroft's teenage ward, "a young boy [who] was well up in natural history." Verne's story began as the five heroes escaped from a Confederate prison camp in a balloon. They were blown off course by a storm; the balloon crashed; and they found themselves on an island, seven thousand miles from their country, in "an unknown region." After Harding disappeared in the surf, the rest of the group feared they had lost their leader. "[I]f Cyrus Harding had been with them, if the engineer could have brought his practical science, his inventive mind to bear on their situation, perhaps all hope would not have been lost. . . . The engineer was to them a microcosm, a compound of every science, a possessor of all human knowledge. It was better to be with Cyrus in a desert island, than without him in the most flourishing town in the United States." Back in Farmington, Roland's friend Clarence Hinckley

Knowlton had read the book too. He wrote, "Isn't it splendid? I like to read it over about once in three months. I think the first two parts are the best."[11]

In 1892, a few months after receiving *The Mysterious Island*, Roland moved with his family again so that William could become superintendent of schools in Americus in southwestern Georgia. Americus was only ten miles from the Confederate prison camp—like the one in Verne's novel—at Andersonville, Georgia, where more than forty-five thousand Union soldiers had been confined and almost thirteen thousand had died in hideous conditions. The east-west Savannah, Americus and Montgomery Railroad and the north-south Central of Georgia Railway intersected at Americus. A second-story turret distinguished the Central passenger depot; the older Central depot on McGarrah Street was by then used for freight.

Having completed the eleventh grade in Dalton, and with no twelfth grade available in the Americus school, Roland needed a job. He worked in the railroad offices in Americus, earning ten or fifteen dollars per month for ten-hour days, six days a week. It was probably here that he began collecting the railroad timetables he saved throughout his life. He also collected stamps and exchanged them with collectors in California and Moscow. He corresponded about electrical experiments with Clarence, who was two years older than Roland and by then a student at Farmington Normal School, and began corresponding with a friend in Dalton, who discussed the construction of hollow balls, the use of lead versus Babbitt metal in engines, the use of a lathe, and stamp collecting.[12]

In 1894, at age sixteen, Roland entered the University of Georgia at Athens, where he shared a room in a boardinghouse with two other boys. His landlady wrote to Bertha that he was "a quiet nice little gentleman." William wanted Roland to take a heavy load of courses, perhaps to compress the undergraduate years and keep college expenses to a minimum. A university administrator warned William that the schedule he requested could be too much. "You have laid out a pretty heavy programme for the boy. . . . Consider this, please, and let us avoid the danger of too much hurry," she wrote the week before Roland arrived on campus. Just two days before he was to arrive, she wrote again, "Dear Mr. Harper: It will hardly be possible to work in all that you propose, but we will do our best to carry out your wishes. We will do our best to help your boy to become a *man* in every good meaning of that word."[13]

Walking to and from his boardinghouse, Roland probably passed by the Arch, a large iron gateway built with proceeds from the university's sale of its botanical garden, that stood at the Broad Street entrance to the campus, directly across from the town's business district, but according to custom he would not have walked through the Arch during his freshman year. He may have attended some classes in the deteriorating Old College, built in 1806 and originally called Franklin College, and he probably took his engineering classes in Moore College, a practically brand-new building where technical and scientific classes were held. The cadet corps drilled and intercollegiate football and baseball games took place on a field south of Moore. The Demosthenian Literary Society met in Demosthenian Hall, a two-story brick building constructed in 1824, and students enjoyed long, heated debates and discussions there. However, fraternities were beginning to usurp Demosthenian and other literary societies as the centers of student social life; while Roland was at the University of Georgia, its trustees repealed a requirement that students participate in literary societies. During Roland's undergraduate years, the university's trustees also considered recommendations in favor of a faculty chair in biblical studies and against student dances but, true to the separation of church and state, declined to establish such a chair or to prohibit dances. Thomas Walter Reed, a long-time registrar at the university, recalled standing in the street outside the open windows of the university library in June 1896 and listening to a trustee who "was on hand as usual with a tirade against dancing and an additional attack on intercollegiate athletics. . . . Every word the old gentleman said could be heard plainly down on the street, and what he said was full of eloquence, [but] his resolutions were not passed."[14]

Two of Roland's close friends joined both literary societies and fraternities. Robert J. H. DeLoach of Statesboro, Georgia, was a year ahead of Roland. Alfred Akerman, two years ahead of Roland, was primarily interested in forestry. Another friend, J. Walter Hendricks, was an aspiring orator.[15] These chums became devoted friends of Harper. Charles Cotton Harrold, a friend in Americus whose father, Uriah Harrold, was a railroad executive, entered the university the year after Roland.[16] Ulrich Bonnell Phillips, a serious young history student from LaGrange, Georgia, was another acquaintance.[17]

Roland's younger brothers wrote to him from Americus while he was away at college. Eight-year-old Francis was most interested in collecting toy figures of the popular "Brownies" from the children's books by Palmer Cox (the same comic characters with which the Brownie camera was marketed to children). "Dear Roland: the names of the brownies what Mamma is going to get me are Brer Rabbit, soldier, Sailor, Dude, Policy, Baby, Uncle Sam, Mischief, Indian, Thomas, Esquimau, Rats." Francis also asked Roland to bring him a chipmunk. "I wish you would bring me a chipmunk when you come home at Christmas." Perhaps he meant a specimen of a real chipmunk, which was probably more common in the deciduous forests around Athens than the piney woods of Americus. Otto was a budding farmer who delivered the *Evening Herald* for fifty cents a week to pay his garden expenses. He wrote to Roland, "I am going to have all the garden this year except the strip next to the cow lot; that is Booie's [the family nickname for Francis]. I am to pay all the expenses, buying seeds, paying papa 50 cents rent, and paying for plowing." Their mother looked forward to mail from Roland. After she received one of his letters, Otto wrote, "Your picture came yesterday and when I came back from getting the mail, Mamma and the rest of the children had gone to walk and I went and caught them near the Central Railroad. When I brought the mail to Mamma she sat down on a cross-tie and opened your letter and showed your picture to us." Bertha and the children often walked in the countryside to look for flowers. Otto wrote, "We walked on down the railroad and then turned down the creek. There was a funny little tree at the edge of the water full of blooms. The tree was about the size of a small willow. I will send you a few of the flowers and maybe you can analyze them." He added that Wilhelmina, Francis, and a friend, Lily Thompson, had gone flower hunting "and found a few little white violets."[18]

Roland had begun his own botanizing in the Piedmont region around Athens by the spring of 1895. Throughout his years at the university, he made frequent treks along the banks of the Oconee River. He also hunted for plants on campus and along railroad tracks and explored nearby fields, using a copy of the second edition of Alvan Wentworth Chapman's *Flora of the Southern United States* as his field manual. In the fall of 1896, he collected a specimen of Bosc's pigweed (*Chenopodium boscianum*) "in dry open woods on the university campus in Athens," later proudly observing, "it does not seem to have been reported from Georgia before." As he collected plants, Roland categorized them as being in primeval or second-growth forests. He observed, "The original forest is now mostly confined to the steep sides of the valleys, while the second-growth is found on the more level land along the ridge-tops."[19]

Clarence Knowlton, writing from Farmington, may have been the first to encourage Roland to pursue botany. In the summer after Roland's freshman year, Clarence wrote: "Botany is a fine study and I am glad you are so much interested in it. Your list shows that you have done good work since you started." He made a long list of plants for which he wanted Roland to send him specimens. Instructing Roland on the fine points of botanical collecting, Clarence wrote, "I have received both of your letters and the plants you sent me. I was glad that you sent larger specimens than before. A botanical specimen should show as much of a plant as possible." Clarence had begun corresponding with Merritt L. Fernald, a young assistant at Gray Herbarium at Harvard University whose father was president of Maine State College of Agriculture and Mechanic Arts. Clarence wrote to Roland regarding the younger Fernald, "[He] has been revising a list of Maine Flora and wanted a list of the plants I know. I sent it and one of them, an aster, he said was new to the state."[20]

Clarence feared his preparation in the Farmington schools qualified him for nothing more than the local normal school and a career as a teacher, but he took the entrance examinations at Harvard in June 1895, was admitted, and enrolled in the summer term. As an undergraduate at Harvard and an acquaintance of Fernald, Clarence offered Roland entrée to the world of academic botany in the Northeast. He sent a tantalizing description of the botanical community in Cambridge: "Harvard is a great place to study botany, and I hope to find many new plants in this vicinity next spring. . . . There is a large botanic garden here, founded in 1806. [Gray] Herbarium here is the largest in America. They have approximately 250,000 named species in their collection, not to mention varieties and duplicates. . . . It was there that Asa Gray lived and did most of his great work. If at any time you are in doubt about any plant you have analyzed, if you send a specimen here to the 'Gray Herbarium, Cambridge' they will gladly identify it for you, if the specimen is complete enough for them to compare with what they have."[21]

In Americus with his family in the summers during college, Roland explored the pine barrens of southwestern Georgia. The town was located on Muckalee Creek, about twenty miles west of the Flint River in the East Gulf Coastal Plain, in the Black Belt, where cotton flourished in the soil of an ancient ocean bed. He collected specimens of *Sarracenia*, the intriguing pitcher plants that grow in sunny bogs, and sent some to Clarence. Pitcher plants were particularly interesting to Roland for several reasons. They are highly unusual in appearance, with leaves in the form of hooded, hollow tubes that stand erect or, in the case of the parrot pitcher plant (*S. psittacina*), recline on the ground in a basal arrangement. The translucent leaves are brilliant shades of chartreuse, yellow, pink, and burgundy, the veins in vivid contrast. Most unusual of all, pitcher plants are carnivorous. The "pitchers" are traps for insects that fall or slide to the bottom and cannot crawl back up to escape tiny pools of rainwater. Roland may have sent Clarence a specimen of the rare parrot pitcher plant, which still grows in the vicinity of Americus. With maroon and green umbrella-like flowers that bloom on tall stalks, the parrot grows in areas prone to flooding and even captures small aquatic insects. (The French naturalist André Michaux first described it in 1803 after exploring southern Georgia and northern Florida.) Or Roland might have sent Clarence a sample of the whitetop pitcher plant (*S. leucophylla*), which also grows around Americus and today is even rarer than the parrot pitcher plant. The early American naturalist and explorer of the Southeast William Bartram described the whitetop, and Constantine Samuel Rafinesque named it in 1817. Its hoods are erect, with frilly edges, white and veined with red and purple. Roland searched unsuccessfully for the purple pitcher plant (*S. purpurea*), which grows in an arrangement resembling a circle of small green and purple urns.[22]

The pitcher plants of southern Georgia thrive in sunny bogs, so collecting them was more arduous than simply walking along a country road. One's feet could sink into the sucking muck of peat and standing water. The dominant trees, longleaf pine (*Pinus palustris*), grew far apart and provided little shade. Mosquitoes could be prolific. The pitcher plants grew among a community of grasses and other low plants that sometimes hid them when they were not blooming. Snakes were a constant concern, and slender glass lizards, odd, legless lizards that looked just like snakes, might lie coiled at the edge of a path. Two-toed amphiumas, a type of large salamander capable of inflicting painful bites, burrowed in the mud at the edge of creeks.[23]

While Roland went on long summer hikes in the countryside, braving the pine-barren bogs, William Harper kept up the pressure for him to excel academically and physically during the school year, urging him to join the college YMCA so that he could use its gym. The Harpers sent money to their son whenever they could, but it was not always enough. In February 1895, William enclosed $15.50 with a short note on the back of an old letter: "I hope you will continue to do well in all respects." He chastised Roland in a letter the next month for requesting more money and for not inquiring about the family. In March, he sent one dollar and berated the boy for making a poor grade in physics. "It is of much greater importance than I imagine you think. For you to have the reputation of not doing well in such an important branch is no trifle. . . . Remember you are making your reputation as a scholar now and it will go with you through life," he wrote. He told Roland he was going to contact the professor himself to find out what Roland had missed on a test. That winter, he sent Roland lists of books to read in his spare time, with the reminder, "[M]ake your Saturdays and Sundays count from now on. You cannot afford not to." The pressure worked: at the age of nineteen, Roland completed a bachelor's of science in engineering, like Captain Cyrus Harding of Verne's *Mysterious Island*.[24]

Engineering was a booming profession in the late nineteenth century. Roland took the civil service exam in Atlanta in April 1897 but may not have been too disappointed that he did not score high enough to merit an immediate job offer. In the final weeks before commencement in 1897, it was botany, not engineering, that motivated the young naturalist. He made collecting treks on May 5, 6, 23, and 28 and collected plants on the campus on May 27. Tramping through the marsh beside the Middle Oconee River a few miles west of town with Alfred Akerman on May 23, Roland made his first original plant discovery, Georgia bulrush (*Scirpus georgianus*).[25] Botany had become his passion.

At the time Roland walked to the top of Wachusett Mountain in 1898, his family had moved back north to be near friends in Southbridge. With William unable to find a job, Roland and Otto worked in the optical factory. Roland was unhappy about having to help support the family instead of entering graduate school and vented his anger and depression in a letter to his mother while she visited her sister, Franziska Tauber, in Milwaukee. Bertha shared the letter with her sister, who wrote to Roland, "You are the oldest of the children, you should be as manly as possible, you owe this to your mother." She wrote again the following day, adding, "That you are under pressure I understand, but you must not consider work such a misfortune, nor should Otto either. How many thousands of boys have to perform much more?"[26]

To briefly escape the drudgery of his factory job, Roland visited Clarence in Cambridge two or three times, meeting Merritt Fernald and the director of the Gray Herbarium, B. L. Robinson. He tried to get hired for a botanical expedition to Puerto Rico, but the job did not materialize. During the long winters of 1898 and 1899, when he could not go on botanical tramps, Roland studied in the Southbridge public library, reading Charles Darwin's *Origin of Species.* Darwin proposed three revolutionary principles of evolution: variation, inheritance, and selection. First, organisms in nature vary, and natural selection is the process of some variations becoming dominant. Second, the variations *that can be inherited* are factors in evolution. Accidental variations, such as a foot damaged in a rockslide, play no role in evolution. Third, some variations are multiplied in successive generations because they support survival or reproduction, so the individuals with those variations are able to produce more offspring. This idea of natural selection was controversial among scientists of the time as well as among fundamentalist Christians. The premise that species changed over time was believable, but the concept of natural selection—that nature brutally winnowed less-desirable traits from a population—was harder to accept because it conflicted with the deeply held belief in a Supreme Being who watched over every tiny sparrow. Even Henry Ward Beecher, who generally supported Darwinism, stopped short of endorsing the theory of natural selection. Darwin's notion of "blended inheritance" also was problematic. Scientists who attempted to analyze inheritance of particular traits could not explain how red hair or blue eyes, for example, appeared and disappeared from generation to generation in a family. Darwin's theory was nowhere more controversial than in the South, where in the 1870s, 1880s, and 1890s, leaders of Baptist, Methodist, and Presbyterian colleges repeatedly attacked public universities for teaching the scientific theory of evolution.[27]

Roland also read books by Henry David Thoreau; works by the New England botanical illustrator and landscape painter William Hamilton Gibson, including *Camp-Life in the Woods* and *Highways and Byways, or Saunterings in New England*; and *Wake-Robin*, a collection of essays about birds by John Burroughs. During the same period, Lucius E. Ammidown, of the local family that owned the eyeglass factory, showed Roland a flora, or manual of vascular plants, for Worcester County, Massachusetts, by Joseph Jackson.[28]

Perhaps Roland also pulled out his copy of *The Mysterious Island* and reread it. It is not hard to see parallels between Verne's heroic retelling of the Robinson Crusoe legend and young Roland's account of his great walk to Wachusett Mountain. Like the steely-eyed engineer Captain Harding, Roland set his sights on climbing the tallest mountain and reached a penultimate point at nightfall. Like plucky young Herbert, who found a safe refuge among the rocks where the adventurers spent their first night

on the island, Roland created a rough shelter in some bushes. Like Verne's
hardy band, he observed stunted old-growth trees that were bent but not
broken by high winds from the sea. Roland was Harding and Herbert and
Spilett and Pencroft all in one.

> The engineer was not a man who would allow himself to be diverted from
> his fixed idea. It might even have been said that he did not observe the
> country at all . . . his great aim being to climb the mountain before him,
> and therefore straight towards it he went. At ten o'clock a halt of a few min-
> utes was made. On leaving the forest, the mountain system of the country
> appeared before the explorers. . . . The distance, increased by detours and
> obstacles which could not be surmounted directly, was long. . . . At twelve
> o'clock, when the small band of adventurers halted for breakfast at the
> foot of a large group of firs, near a little stream which fell in cascades, they
> found themselves still half way from the first plateau, which most probably
> they would not reach till nightfall. . . . Towards four o'clock the extreme
> zone of the trees had been passed. There only remained here and there a
> few twisted, stunted pines, which must have had a hard life in resisting at
> this altitude the high winds from the open sea.[29]

Even as his followers prepared to rest, Harding pushed on, climbing even
higher to get a glimpse of the surrounding territory in the moonlight.
Similarly, young Roland rose before dawn to get a first look as soon as
possible at his ultimate destination. He wrote, "The night was rather cool,
but there was no dew at that elevation, and I got up before daylight feeling considerably rested. While waiting for the sun to rise I looked at the
landscape and gathered a few plants, and when it got light enough I took
a picture of the big mountain."[30]

Charles Morton Strahan, Roland's civil engineering professor at Georgia,
contacted him in 1898 to tell him he had met Lucien M. Underwood, a
botanist at Columbia University and editor of a botanical journal, the
Bulletin of the Torrey Botanical Club. Roland quickly located copies of the
journal and was fascinated by articles about southern plants by another
New York botanist, John Kunkel Small. Around that time he also learned
that Columbia offered scholarships to graduate students in botany, and
his next step became clear. Accepted by the graduate program at Columbia University, tramping the fields and mountains of Massachusetts, and
wishing he could further explore Georgia, Roland became fixed on the
goal of immortality through exploration of the southern coastal plain.

Verne observed near the conclusion of *The Mysterious Island* that man's heart beats with "the desire to perform a work which will endure, which will survive him." Roland wrote, "One who does not know the plants he sees misses half the pleasure of life. Besides that, a botanist in such a little-explored place as Georgia has a good chance to make himself forever famous by discovering new plants."[31]

CHAPTER TWO

Wonderful Country

Roland's father worried that the young man would be lonely at Columbia and encouraged Lucius Ammidown of Southbridge, the retired business-man who had befriended Roland, to write to him. Ammidown obliged, telling Roland in a letter, "I think most fellows feel a little bit lonesome the first few months away from home. I know if I were away I should be glad to hear from most anybody in Southbridge, black or white, Yankee, French, Irish or 'heathen Chinese,' so long as it only came from home. So you see I'm just going to follow the Golden rule."[1]

Harper probably was lonely, but at the same time, New York was a thrilling place for an aspiring young botanist. Columbia had opened its new campus beside the Hudson River in Morningside Heights two years before Harper arrived. The enormous columns and dome of the university library must have quickened the heart of the young man who had re-lied on the Southbridge public library. Massive Schermerhorn Hall, where he took science classes, was quite a contrast to the crumbling Old College in Athens. The botanical explorers whom he met surely dazzled Harper. Marshall Avery Howe took him to the New York Botanical Garden in nearby Bronx Park on Harper's first day at Columbia, October 2, 1899.[2] Still under construction, the Garden covered 250 acres with woods, meadows, and bogs, all on a convenient railroad stop. The conservatory, which would formally open in June 1900, was a fantastic "crystal palace" of eleven connected pavilions, whose iron framework supported seventeen thousand panes of glass. As curator of Columbia's herbarium, Howe was supervising the transfer of the collection, including a half million speci-mens and a library of five thousand volumes, to the new Garden. Harper wrote to Clarence about the outing with Howe and still remembered it forty-six years later. "When we called on [Nathaniel Lord] Britton, we found him and Mr. [George Valentine] Nash making a list of plants in the Garden that had been killed by a freeze the night before. Somewhere in the wooded part of the grounds, in or near the hemlock grove, Dr. Howe showed me how the ripe fruits of [jumpseed] *Polygonum virginianum* jump several feet from the plant when loosened by a touch; something I had never seen before."[3]

At the turn of the century, Britton's research program and his fantastic new botanical garden were part of Columbia's attraction for graduate students from across the nation. The Garden—as well as the research opportunities at the New York Public Library, the Metropolitan Museum, and the American Museum of Natural History—drew so many students that Columbia was rapidly becoming the country's largest graduate school. Harvard had Asa Gray's herbarium and a fifty-year advantage over Columbia in botany, but Britton was building a program that would surpass Harvard's and match those in Cambridge and Berlin within fifteen years. A small man with dark hair and a prominent nose and ears, Britton had earned a degree in geology from Columbia and worked as a geologist for five years as a young man, until his involvement in the Torrey Botanical Club inspired him to return to the college and teach botany. Britton's constant companion was his wife and colleague, Elizabeth Gertrude Knight Britton. An avid naturalist, she was renowned as a fieldworker, collecting plants in the Adirondack and Appalachian mountains and areas of Canada and the Caribbean Islands. Two decades earlier, as a young teacher at New York's Normal School, Elizabeth Gertrude Knight had discovered the fruit of the moss *Eustichium norvegicum* and a rare curly grass fern, *Schizaea pusilla*, in Nova Scotia. She published a list of the mosses of West Virginia in 1892 and considered compiling her research in a comprehensive handbook of mosses of eastern America. She didn't complete that project but instead wrote hundreds of shorter papers. Even before marrying Britton, she was every bit as influential in New York botanical circles as he. When the couple visited Kew Botanical Garden in England in 1888, they were inspired to establish a similar institution in New York. Nathaniel and Gertrude worked side by side to promote their vision of the New York Botanical Garden, which became the gathering place for New York's leading botanists as well as graduate students, amateur naturalists, and scientists in related fields.[4]

U.S. District Court Judge Addison Brown was an important supporter of the movement to create the Garden. An enthusiastic naturalist who collected plant specimens that sprouted in the piles of ballast dumped from ships in New York's harbors, he joined the local Torrey Botanical Club in the 1870s and was president when Harper arrived. This club began as a small circle of admirers of the New York physician and botanist John Torrey. Brown also financed publication of his and Britton's book, *An Illustrated Flora of the Northern United States and Canada*.[5]

There were many other interesting scientists for Harper to meet: Lucien Underwood took him on a ferry outing to the rocky woods of Fort Lee, New Jersey, and became his dissertation advisor.[6] Charles Arthur Hollick, a constant presence at the garden, was a paleobotanist and instructor in geology at Columbia, a close friend of the Brittons, and one of the principal illustrators of Britton and Brown's *Flora*.[7] The garden's curator, John Kunkel Small, shared Harper's interest in southeastern plants and completed his doctoral dissertation, published as *Flora of the Southeastern United States* in 1903, while Harper was still at Columbia.[8] Willard N. Clute published the *Linnaean Fern Bulletin* and founded the American Bryological and Lichenological Society, initially called the Sullivant Moss Chapter of the Agassiz Association, with Elizabeth Britton and A. J. Grout in 1898. Jean Broadhurst was a fellow graduate student in 1902–3 and earned a master's degree in morphology. John Hendley Barnhart was a young employee of the Columbia library, organizing the library of the New York Academy of Sciences, which he recalled later was "then stored in utter confusion in an upstairs room accessible only through the herbarium." Henry Allan Gleason, another of Harper's fellow graduate students, also had become interested in botany as a teenager.[9]

The most dashing scientist whom Harper encountered upon entering graduate school was Henry Hurd Rusby, who presided over the first meeting of the Torrey Botanical Club that Harper attended. One of the Garden's honorary curators, a physician by training, and a member of Columbia's College of Pharmacy, Rusby had arranged for that college's herbarium and botanical library to be transferred to Columbia's new botany program and to be housed at the New York Botanical Garden. Rusby was a heroic figure who had spent eighteen months botanizing in Texas and New Mexico on behalf of the Smithsonian Institution and the years 1885–87 collecting in South America, traveling down the Amazon for the pharmaceutical firm Parke, Davis, and Company. Rusby's intrepid field research became a model for the faculty members and adjunct collectors of the New York Botanical Garden.[10]

When Harper first visited the Columbia herbarium, or plant repository, he found approximately 400,000 specimens, including the collections of John Torrey and Chapman, the author of the field manual Harper used as an undergraduate.[11] Seeing Torrey's and Chapman's specimens, some with the naturalists' own names incorporated into the plants' scientific names, preserved for botanists to study as long as the samples were conserved, surely inspired young Harper to add his own discoveries in Georgia to the great collection.

B. L. Robinson, who assisted Merritt Fernald in editing the botanical journal *Rhodora*, encouraged Harper to submit articles as well as botanical specimens. When Harper made his first submission to the journal, around the time he entered Columbia, Robinson wrote, "Fernald and I have looked over your paper and find it a very welcome piece of material for *Rhodora*. . . . We shall always be glad to [receive] articles upon rare and unrecorded plants from you. Articles from one to five pages of print are most easily handled. Brief notes are also always in demand. I hope that you will have a very pleasant year at Columbia."[12] This seemed to be a promising start to a long scientific relationship. Harper could not have known that Fernald would become something of a botanical antagonist in years to come.

Harper was keenly interested in the Rochester Code, a set of rules for botanical nomenclature that Britton and others established in 1892. Britton emphasized the "concept of 'type,' a herbarium specimen with which a name is permanently associated, and a rigid system of assigning priority of names to botanical entities." Roland also was intrigued by the emerging concept of habitat groups, which he learned about in his independent reading in the university's botany library. He immediately began interpreting his collections in ecological terms and had two articles based on his Athens and Americus botanizing published in the Torrey Club's *Bulletin* in 1900. The following year his article "Synonymy of *Burmannia* and *Gyrotheca*" appeared in the first issue of the new journal *Torreya*; it was the first of at least eighty articles by Harper to be published in that journal.[13]

Considering a minor in zoology, Harper attended a few lectures at Columbia by the biologist Edmund B. Wilson, whose recent book *The Cell in Development and Inheritance* (1896) earned him a reputation as a leader in the new scientific field of cytology. Wilson's students included W. S. Sutton, who established important concepts in genetics while at Columbia by studying the chromosomes of grasshoppers. Sutton showed that the mix of genetic contributions from each parent is random, that the individual parent's genetic makeup is not bound to be repeated. But Harper disliked laboratory work. He wanted to be a field scientist like Darwin, who took extensive field notes, sought out older scholars while he was a university student to learn informally from them, and participated in the natural history society in Cambridge.[14] The subject of genetics did not yet interest Harper.

During Harper's second year at Columbia, however, three European scientists caused a seismic wave throughout the international scientific community—a breakthrough that undoubtedly was the topic of much discussion at the Garden and in the herbarium room of the Columbia University library. Working independently, Hugo de Vries of the Netherlands, whom Harper would later meet, Karl Correns of Germany, and Erich von Tschermak of Austria each found and cited long-overlooked papers by the Austrian monk and scientist Gregor Mendel. (De Vries actually ignored Mendel's work in the original French publication of his article, but cited the monk in a German edition after Corren criticized his omission.) Working almost four decades earlier, Mendel had conducted methodical experiments with pea plants and from them developed what he called the laws of segregation and independent assortment. Mendel had uncovered the basics of genetics—that an organism inherits traits variably from its parents, with some traits dominant and others recessive. When the younger scientists acknowledged Mendel's breakthrough in separate papers in 1900, the Austrian monk's scientific discovery received international attention.[15]

Mendel's theory of heredity seemed to explain perfectly the mystery of appearing and disappearing traits in Darwin's process of evolution. The issue became complicated again in 1903 when de Vries followed up with a book, *The Mutation Theory*, arguing that the slow process of variation was not the only way that species adapted to challenges in the environment. He speculated that "new species could originate in a single generation through the occurrence of large-scale variations, called 'mutations'"—an idea that ultimately was proven incorrect. It was a fascinating, confusing time to be a young scientist studying at Columbia.[16] Harper did not yet know it, but the question of inheritability would become the central issue of his professional and personal life.

The collecting seasons in 1900–1904 were intense periods of exploration and discovery for Harper, who was anxious to search unexplored areas of the coastal plain. He traveled by train from one depot town to another, closely scrutinizing the vegetation along the tracks, and then hiked back along the same routes to examine plants he had seen from the moving trains, following the example of his professor Lucien Underwood, who based his own doctoral thesis in geology at Syracuse University on the geologic formations he had studied along the Syracuse and Chenango Railroad. The New York Botanical Garden provides extensive clues about

Harper's forays during his years in graduate school. Its online virtual herbarium lists 576 plant specimens that Harper collected for the Garden over the years, with images of many actual specimen sheets, including Harper's handwritten notes and sometimes his photographs of the type localities, the places where he discovered new species.[17]

Addison Brown, the New York judge and financier of Britton's flora, lent Harper two hundred dollars for a research trip in Georgia in 1900. On the train ride south, Harper made a running list of trees and plants he saw from the window, noting that colonies of yellow pitcher plant (*Sarracenia flava*) grew in the sandhill region, beginning one mile south of Lemon Springs, North Carolina, and extending all the way to Aberdeen in that state. The class of 1897 had a reunion dinner at the Commercial Hotel, where Hendricks had warned Harper he might be called upon for a speech. "If you have no subject in mind, I would suggest the following: 'What I did for greater New York.'" Harper omitted any account of the dinner in his diary but carefully recorded that he and Alfred Akerman found pale meadowbeauty (*Rhexia mariana*), bulrush (*Scirpus*), and Virginia buttonweed (*Diodia virginiana*) in their rambles along the Oconee River.[18]

Harper stayed in Georgia from June 15 until at least September 24, 1900, collecting plant specimens in many counties. Collecting plant specimens was painstaking work. He placed each specimen between sheets of newspaper, carrying them in his botany box until he could get back to a campsite or his desk, where he transferred the specimens to layers of blotting paper and a portable dryer heated by kerosene or gas. Once they were dry, he attached labels with notes about the location, date, and circumstances of the collection. He concentrated on tramping along the swampy banks of sluggish rivers of the East Gulf Coastal Plain, which flowed south toward the Gulf of Mexico, and rivers of the Atlantic Coastal Plain, which flowed southeast to the Atlantic Ocean. He explored the edges of the Kinchafoonoo, Muckalee, Flint, Ochlocknee, Ocmulgee, and Oconee rivers and many smaller creeks in the southern half of Georgia.[19] Hunting in an area of moist pine barrens at Tifton in Tift County (formerly part of Berrien County), Harper collected a sedge that he later determined to be a new species, *Rhynchospora solitaria* (onespike beaksedge).[20] He also discovered a new species of the disk flower *Balduina*, one with crimson rather than yellow petals, that eventually received the name *Balduina atropurpurea*, or purpledisk honeycombhead. He photographed a patch of the showy flowers near a split-rail fence, using a folding Pocket Kodak he had bought with part of the loan from Judge Brown. "That such a common, conspicuous and unmistakable plant should have been overlooked until the end of the nineteenth century is a striking illustration of how little the interior of south Georgia has been explored by botanists," he wrote.[21]

Returning to Georgia in 1901, Harper went to Savannah and then west, riding the Georgia and Alabama Railway across the southern part of the state, through the pine barrens of Tattnall, Telfair, Dodge, Wilcox, and Dooly counties. He visited Walter Hendricks, who was living in Bloys in Bulloch County, and the two went hiking in the nearby woods. Hendricks plucked a sprig of gorgeous white flowers from a bush and asked Harper to identify it. Harper was stumped until he consulted his copy of Chapman's *Flora*, which he had left at Walter's house. The shrub was Georgia plume (*Elliottia racemosa*), a member of the heath family that had not been found in the wild for a quarter century. He wrote to Small in New York, who replied that coincidentally he was writing an article about the "long-lost *Elliottia*."[22]

The pine barrens that Harper explored were vast open areas of longleaf pine with virtually no understory except grasses and forbs; the trees were so far apart that in many places one could drive a wagon between them. Although longleaf occurred in some upland areas of northeast Alabama and northwest Georgia, it was primarily a species of the coastal plain flatwoods. A British traveler who passed through a similar forest in 1838 remarked, "The eye was bewildered in a mass of columns receding far back and diminishing in the perspective to mere threads, till they were lost in the gloom. The ground was everywhere perfectly flat, and the trees rose from it in a direction so exactly perpendicular, and so entirely without lower branches, that an air of architectural symmetry was imparted to the forest, by no means unlike that of some gothic cathedrals."[23]

When botanizing in longleaf woods, Harper may have heard the loud "Kent! Kent!" of an ivory-billed woodpecker and spotted it swooping from pine to pine.[24] Perhaps he was startled by northern bobwhite quail, or by grasshoppers that suddenly flew up from the wiregrass (*Aristida stricta*), making a sound like wooden paddles, or by the crash of an enormous longleaf cone hitting the ground. Looking outward, through a quarter mile or more of uninterrupted pine savanna, he might have seen white-tailed deer grazing in the distance. Maybe he heard the chattering of red-cockaded woodpeckers and watched them moving in step with each other up the opposite sides of longleaf trunks, or the "Pee pee pee / three! / pee pee / pee / three!" of the palm warbler, or the high-pitched "Zeet-zeet-zeet-ZEET" of the prairie warbler. Undoubtedly, Harper observed scarred pines that had survived lightning strikes and noticed that hardwood saplings, wax myrtle (*Morella cerifera*), huckleberry bushes (*Gaylussacia*), and blueberry bushes (*Vaccinium*) only grew in sunnier spots where old trees had been killed by lightning. He would have noticed the circles of slender young longleaf trees that surrounded old longleaf stumps like courtiers. But at the time of his first botanical forays into longleaf woods, Harper was most interested in the rich diversity of grasses, ferns, and blooming plants of the forest carpet. He was intrigued by the narrow wetland zones that hugged the edges of tiny streams, following imperceptible declines in the surface of the earth, with water lilies (*Nymphaea*) growing in the water, and Spanish moss (*Tillandsia*) festooning understory branches that leaned over the streams.

In 1902, his third year of collecting in Georgia for the New York Botanical Garden, Harper remained in the South from June until mid-November, beginning and ending his sojourn at Augusta. Roaming pine barrens near Moultrie in southern Georgia, he found and described a new species of the native perennial grass dropseed, which he named *Sporobolus teretifolius*. He spent a week in adjoining Berrien County studying the habitat groups of the Altamaha Grit, a sandstone formation distinguished by cliffs and flat outcrops. While collecting near Ellaville in Schley County, Harper found what he thought was a new variety of wild carrot (*Ptilimnium nodosum*), which he sent to the authority on that genus, Joseph Nelson Rose, a former assistant curator of the United States National Herbarium. Rose determined that Harper's find was a new genus and in 1905 named it for him, first calling it *Harperia nodosa*; after learning that name had been simultaneously given to an unrelated genus in Australia, he renamed it *Harperella nodosa* in 1906 and naming a related species that Harper found in Alabama *Harperella fluviatilis*. Harper was proud that *Harperella* was "one of the only two or three genera of flowering plants discovered in the eastern United States in the last three quarters of a century."[25]

William and Bertha Harper and their youngest child, Francis, continued to live in Southbridge until 1901. Hermina moved from Southbridge to Boston to attend a deaconess school, a school for women chosen to assist in church ministry, before enrolling in Boston University. In the summer

of 1901 she worked for a charitable agency's summer program for children
and wrote to Otto, "I am having a fine time this summer with the slum
children." Harper wondered if she was on the brink of marriage, and
she replied, "I am not such a fool as that. I expect to study for years and
years. But in the mean time I intend to have as many 'student-preacher'
friends as I want. . . . You must remember that there are about 175 students every year in the [Boston University School of Theology] so you
see a girl who lives in Boston has a chance to make lots of acquaintances
and friends among the 'student preachers.'" In light of her later marital
troubles, Hermina's final comment is chilling: "I certainly hope I have
sense enough to know enough not to go crazy and make a fool of myself
and get married."[26]

Hermina missed her brothers. Urging Otto to transfer to a college
in Boston, she wrote, "[I]t would be nice if you could . . . go to B.U.
with me."[27] She also encouraged Roland to visit her. "Can't you come to
Boston to see me when you return from the South? I have not seen you
for a long time, and if I should go home in September you would not be
there then. Doesn't your business ever take you to Boston now? Didn't
you use to belong to some sort of a society here, or go to see some sort
of a Mr. Fernald? It seems as if you ought to have business here once in
a while"—but Roland apparently did not miss his sister, for he declined
her invitations to visit her in Boston, even when he went to Cambridge
to see Fernald and Robinson at Gray Herbarium. Again in October 1901
she pleaded with Roland to visit her, promising to take him to church, to
B.U., and to the Italian neighborhood in the North End. She guessed,
however, that even if Roland should come up to Boston, he would spend
little time with her. "I suppose you would be so busy going to see your
botanists," she pouted.[28]

The Harpers lived briefly in the Bronx, where Bertha had a job, but in
1901 William finally secured a position as superintendent of the Conrad
Poppenhusen Institute, a private academy in College Point, a section in
north central Queens County, New York. The family moved to Northern
Boulevard in College Point, into a new clapboard house with three stories, a basement, and front and back porches that was next to an almost
identical house in what appears to have been a new subdivision. Roland
moved into the new house and commuted by ferry across the East River
to the Bronx and then by train to the Garden.[29]

By 1903 Harper had decided to focus his dissertation research on the
flora and geology of the Altamaha Grit Region, now known as the Al-

tamaha Formation. In rolling wiregrass country south of the Fall Line, the boundary between the Piedmont and the Coastal Plain, the Altamaha is a sandstone formation covered by a layer of Pleistocene deposits in most places; here and there, however, the sandstone is evident at the surface—often in the longleaf pine barrens, where it may form cliffs or flat outcrops. Early in his fieldwork in Georgia, Harper had noticed habitat groups on the sandstone outcrops that resembled the plant communities on granite outcrops north of the Fall Line, yet were disjunct, or isolated, within the coastal plain. He wondered how the outcrop plants came to grow in these spots. To Harper, it was virgin territory—his dream come true. He believed his work was pioneering: "Very little work has been done in the region by other botanists, and published references to it are scarce." However, he was careful not to claim too much for his own explorations in the Altamaha Grit; he searched the herbarium at the Garden to find clues of earlier naturalists' explorations of the region and acknowledged "the younger Bartram and the elder Michaux," the eighteenth-century Georgia naturalist John Abbot, the botanist Thomas Nuttall, and the pioneer Florida naturalist Hardy Croom, but suggested that none had fully investigated the area. "It is not surprising, therefore, that I should find new species in that region nearly every season."[30]

Harper eagerly explored the Altamaha Grit, finding it "one of the most interesting (from a phytogeographical standpoint at least) and extensive (covering at least 11,000 square miles) geological formations in the state." Starting his 1903 field trip at sunrise on June 12 in Effingham County, "where the Seaboard Air Lines crosses the Savannah River," he walked a few miles down the river to Sisters' Ferry. William Bartram had crossed the river there in April 1776, and André Michaux and his son had done so in April 1787. Harper collected specimens of eastern leatherwood (*Dirca palustris*) and mountain laurel (*Kalmia latifolia*), species that Bartram and André Michaux found there, but acknowledged later that he had overlooked other Michaux plants because he was not yet aware of Michaux's travels in Georgia. Despite the brutal southern heat, the young botanist waded into shallow lagoons of the Canoochee River in Bryan County to collect specimens of yellow pond-lily, which he sent to Fernald at Harvard, who named it *Nymphaea fluviatilis*, distinguishing it from a similar plant Small had found in Lake County, Florida, in 1894. (Botanists eventually decided the two plants were the same species, which they currently call *Nuphar advena*.) Crossing the river sound at Darien on a steamboat, Harper observed that this was "where the Bartrams, father and son, crossed in the eighteenth century, and discovered that now long-lost tree, *Franklinia alatamaha*." Still collecting specimens and data on the Altamaha Grit region in 1904, Harper recorded that he used three cameras to make 250 photographs and calculated that he rode trains for 2,500 miles through the region. It was a "wonderful country."[31]

Although he was thrilled to be describing unexplored territory, Harper had trouble writing his dissertation. He joked to a friend in December 1904, "I am at last about to begin work on my thesis, or at least I am fixing to think about trying to begin preparations for starting to write it. I have some hopes of finishing it by next June." But his first draft was unwieldy with lists and details. Underwood repeatedly urged Harper to trim the manuscript. He wrote to him in May 1905, "You will remember that the one repeated criticism I have given you through the years of your residence here is on the subject of diffuse writing and the introduction of irrelevant and unnecessary detail in your contributions." Extraneous material made Harper's paper more like "a school-boy essay" than a scientist's dissertation. Underwood added that he had consulted Nathaniel Britton, who agreed: the dissertation was unacceptable without significant revisions. After Harper made the changes Underwood demanded, the chairman accepted the paper, and Harper's doctoral work was complete. The university conferred the degree in 1905, and his dissertation was published in the annals of the New York Academy of Sciences in 1906.[32]

Harper explained in his dissertation that several methods had been employed in the past for subdividing the flora of temperate eastern North America, including political boundaries, parallels of latitude, altitude, temperature, drainage basins, and geological formations, but maintained that geology was the best classification system. He recognized his predecessors—"The same principles have been recognized by Hollick on Staten Island and elsewhere in that neighborhood, Gattinger in Tennessee, Smith in Alabama and Florida, and Hilgard in Mississippi"[33]—yet boldly suggested that his work broke new ground: "Several other botanists and geologists have noted the intimate relations between botany and geology in a superficial way, but there have been comparatively few attempts in this country as yet to generalize observations of this kind or to explain them." There were, he explained, four effects of geology on vegetation: physical, chemical, topographical, and the passage of geological time. "Most of the papers hitherto published on the subject deal only with the more immediate and obvious effects of geology on vegetation, acting mainly through the physical and chemical composition of the soil. The more remote and subtle—but no less important—effects of topography and geological history have not attracted so much attention, but it is one of the purposes of this thesis to discuss some of them for the region under consideration." He also identified the frequency of fire as an environmental factor that could affect local diversity of vegetation. Concerning the habitat groups he described in the Altamaha Grit region, Harper cautioned, "It should be borne in mind that Nature draws few hard and fast lines, and the nearest we can get to her methods is only an approximation. I may have drawn the limits of the different habitat-groups too far apart in some cases and too closely in others, but further study will always bring us nearer the truth."[34]

Exploring between Peacocks and Harrison in the Altamaha Grit during the summer after he completed his dissertation, Harper discovered a vine climbing on rayless goldenrod (*Bigelowia nuttallii*). He sent a sample to Small at the New York Botanical Garden, who established that it was a new species in a genus of parasitic vines called dodder and in 1913 named it *Cuscuta harperi*. Harper's specimen sheet in the Garden's herbarium has "This is a type!" handwritten at the bottom and several other notations concerning its status as a type, or new discovery.[35] Today the plant is known as Harper's dodder, Harper's strangle-weed, and Harper's love-vine.

CHAPTER THREE

A Pioneer or Transient Type

Harper went to Tuscaloosa, Alabama, in late 1905 to work for the Alabama Geological Survey, following the example of Nathaniel Britton, who began his career by working for the Geological Survey of New Jersey. The Alabama survey office was on the campus of the University of Alabama. At the time of Harper's arrival, the university was still rebuilding after the devastating damage inflicted by the Union Army, which in 1865 had burned many of the university's buildings and destroyed the collections of its Alabama Museum of Natural History. University president John William Abercrombie was erecting a "Greater University" with reorganized schools and colleges. Harper's new employer was the survey's director, Eugene A. Smith, a widely admired geologist who had spent three decades exploring Alabama's woods and evaluating the state's mineral resources. An Alabamian and a graduate of the University of Alabama, Smith had earned a doctorate from the University of Heidelberg in 1868 and became an assistant professor of chemistry at the University of Mississippi, where his mentor was Mississippi's state geologist, Eugene W. Hilgard. Smith returned to the University of Alabama in 1871 as a professor of chemistry and mineralogy; two years later, the Alabama legislature appointed him state geologist and director of the geological survey. Smith was responsible for discovering fields for economic exploitation; his focus was the rich veins of minerals in the mountains of north-central Alabama. He traveled often through the state with his assistant, a former slave named Jeff Jackson, carrying a glass-plate camera with which he took almost a thousand photographs between 1885 and 1910.[1]

During the 1880s, iron-ore mining in Alabama had increased tenfold, to more than all the other southern states combined, with mining companies building railroads and spurs as fast as possible to move the ore to their foundries. G. Ward Hubbs writes that the university town on the southern edge of the iron and coalfields enjoyed "unprecedented and uninterrupted growth. Mining, machinery, and transportation improvements revolutionized the county's economy. Electricity, clean water, and other conveniences . . . made urban life a pleasure." Steamboats were still an important form of transportation when Harper arrived, but railroads carried people and goods across more of the interior between rivers. In 1903, the Central Iron and Coal Company built a foundry, with a blast furnace and 150 coke ovens, on the Black Warrior River at the community of Holt. There were many small homes for foundry workers nearby. The Tuscaloosa Belt Railway, a small steam locomotive called a "dummy line," ran east from town out to Riverview and Holt on the Mobile and Ohio Railroad. The dummy was Tuscaloosa's public transportation from 1888 to 1915. A horse-car line also operated on the route for a few years.[2]

Because it is on the Fall Line, Tuscaloosa was the northernmost point where nineteenth-century cotton dealers and coal miners could load their products and ship them down the Black Warrior, Tombigbee, and Mobile rivers and into Mobile Bay. Mine owners in Tuscaloosa County and other parts of north-central Alabama wanted to reduce their costs by loading their ore on barges north of the Fall Line. Economic boosters in Tuscaloosa, dreaming that their city could become an industrial center, were happy to help and began campaigning in 1885 for federal funding for construction of locks and dams to make the river above the Fall Line navigable for steamboats and barges. By 1897, three locks were complete, and the U.S. Army Corps of Engineers built nine locks and dams on the Tombigbee and the Warrior between 1888 and 1915. Although Tuscaloosa was experiencing some of the economic benefits of the coal industry, the region's small farmers were not so lucky. The postwar industrial boom did not reach most of Alabama or the South. Cotton was the dominant crop, and in the decade before Harper arrived in Tuscaloosa, "self-sufficiency steadily declined among southern farmers, the average size of farms in the region drifted downward, and the rate of tenancy surged upward." Wartime destruction, abandoned fields, livestock losses, and insect scourges pushed many Alabamians into jobs in the timber industry and mines, where they labored for low wages to extract Alabama's natural resources and ship them to manufacturers out of state. In what C. Vann Woodward called "the persistence of the plantation pattern," families of tenant or sharecropping farmers, rather than gangs of slaves, worked portions of large farms, living in poverty. The rate of tenancy in Alabama was near 60 percent; sharecropping, an even less economically stable form of farm employment, accounted for almost one-fourth of farmers.[3]

Harper undoubtedly soon realized that the Black Warrior River, which drained Alabama's mountainous region of rich coal and iron deposits, dropped about four feet at Tuscaloosa, falling onto the northern edge of the East Gulf Coastal Plain. The historian G. Ward Hubbs describes the Fall Line and the woods: "Beyond the falls (at the present site of the cities of Northport and Tuscaloosa), early visitors would have seen the river spread and meander through the softer sediments, finally entering a broad valley of swamps, terraces, and hills before it emptied into the Tombigbee. . . . Punctuating the hardwood forest were extensive tracts of large long-leaf pines." Not long after arriving in Tuscaloosa, Harper took a long hike along the eastern bank of the Black Warrior, following the tracks of the Mobile and Ohio northeast about eight miles into the coal country around Holt, on a day when "there was a heavy frost in the morning, some of which remained on the ground all day in shaded places." He came to some cliffs about five miles upriver, at the mouth of a tributary, the North River, where he noticed Jersey pine (*Pinus virginiana*), a type of pine never reported so far south or at so low an altitude. "I stopped to examine the flora of the cliffs more minutely." Among the ferns and sedums and showy oakleaf hydrangea (*Hydrangea quercifolia*), he found the rare Alabama snow-wreath (*Neviusia alabamensis*). Harper described this "December ramble" the following year in *Plant World*, as usual carefully acknowledging the naturalists who went before him: "The *Neviusia* was discovered somewhere near this spot about fifty years ago by Drs. Nevius and Wyman, and was known nowhere else until Mr. [Thomas Grant] Harbison found it a few years ago on Sand Mountain in the northern part of the state." Reuben D. Nevius, rector of Christ Episcopal Church in Tuscaloosa, and William Stokes Wyman, a professor of Latin at the university who later became its president, had found the plant on a sandstone slope. Unable to identify it, Nevius sent a specimen to Asa Gray at Harvard, who determined that it represented a new genus in the rose family. Nevius also sent specimens to the herbaria at Columbia College and Princeton University; the former became part of the New York Botanical Garden's collection.[4]

Hiking farther upstream, Harper found a new location for red elm (*Ulmus serotina*), a tree discovered in the Alleghenies a few years earlier by Charles Sprague Sargent of Harvard's Arnold Arboretum. Another surprise: basking in the winter sunlight of an exposed cliff near the riverside railroad, white Canada violets (*Viola canadenis*) bloomed. And just before he turned to retrace his steps, the most thrilling find of the day: the rare and subtly beautiful Alabama croton (*Croton alabamensis*), which Eugene

Smith had discovered growing on shaded limestone rocks along the Cahaba River in adjoining Bibb County a generation earlier, and which was known nowhere else. Harper reported, "At the new station its habitat is on steep sandstone cliffs, well exposed to the afternoon sun."[5]

The young botanist felt fortunate to be in a place where the mountains and the coastal plain met: "[N]early everywhere east of here the coastal plain is bordered by ancient crystalline rocks . . . and west of Alabama there happen to be very few important towns along the fall-line. Here the relations between the geology and flora are very striking." He believed that most of the upland plants he had identified on his ramble that December day did not occur in the coastal plain. "The reasons for this are mostly too complex to be discussed here, but are all originally dependent on geological history." Harper described the outing again in 1922, adding that he had revisited the river bluffs "at all seasons of the year, [taking] several visiting scientists along the same route." By then he had explored "the more or less celebrated bluffs on the east side of the Apalachicola River in Middle Florida," but still considered the Black Warrior bluffs to be truly remarkable for their rich flora. "The two places have several species in common . . . and the two endemic trees of the Florida bluffs, [the stinking cedar (*Torreya taxifolia*) and the Florida yew (*Taxus floridana*)] are no more remarkable than the shrubs *Croton Alabamensis* and *Neviusia*, which are not known outside Alabama."[6]

Still interested in exploring locations that no other botanists had studied, Harper noted that Charles Mohr seemed "to have done very little field work in this neighborhood, having depended mainly on Dr. Smith for information about the flora of Tuscaloosa County." Mohr's seminal monograph, *Plant Life of Alabama*, had appeared in 1901, two weeks after his death, and Harper often sought to fill gaps in that work. Sometimes accompanying Smith on geological reconnaissance, he explored mountainous areas of the Appalachian Plateau and the Piedmont region, noting when he found coastal plain trees and plants in locations above the Fall Line. He found his own *Harperella nodosa* along with the aquatic golden club; the bog plant dwarf milkwort (*Polygala nana*) in full bloom; the tiny carnivorous sundew (*Drosera brevifolia*); and zigzag bladderwort (*Utricularia subulata*), another carnivorous bog plant, in DeKalb County in November 1905. Limestone County, on the Cumberland Plateau, also had coastal plain plants. He found a stand of longleaf pine in Walker County, part of the Cumberland Plateau, in April 1906 and remarked, "[T]here is little or nothing in the picture to distinguish it from some places within a few miles of the coast."[7]

Wondering how pine barren species came to grow above the Fall Line, Harper duly acknowledged predecessors who had noted the wandering coastal plain plants. "The unusual occurrence in the Cumberland plateau region of Alabama of quite a number of species . . . rarely met with outside of the coastal plain has been mentioned in the last few years by [Thomas H.] Kearney, Mohr and Harbison, but the subject is by no means yet exhausted, as recent investigations have shown." Considering the succession of habitat groups on the steep slopes of Bald Knob in Elmore County, Alabama, at the upper edge of the coastal plain, he speculated that Henry C. Cowles, one of the earliest ecological theorists, was correct that vegetation was related more to processes of geologic change than to soil composition or climate: "[I]t is pretty evident that . . . the summit flora must be gradually giving place to that now inhabiting the dry slopes, and the latter to that of the ravines, thus furnishing an excellent example of natural succession. . . . The vegetation of the pine-barrens represents a pioneer or transient type, while that of the much older metamorphic region approaches the 'mesophytic climax' condition described by Dr. H. C. Cowles and subsequent writers." Harper saw the issue of how these species reached the mountains as a promising field of research. "It is most singular that many of the coastal plain plants . . . even the rock-loving ones, seem to be confined in the mountains to the immediate vicinity of the larger streams. When this is satisfactorily explained we will perhaps have the key to the whole situation. But a great deal more careful field work has got to be done before this and analogous problems in other parts of the world can be solved."[8]

Although the geological survey's responsibility was to explore the mineral regions, Harper ventured to Alabama's central counties in the coastal plain whenever he could during this first period in Alabama. A few weeks after starting his job in Tuscaloosa, he accompanied Smith to a conference of the American Association for the Advancement of Science in New Orleans. As Smith had done for twenty years, Harper took photographs of the landscape. He used Smith's system of noting "the exact location of each photograph, the direction of the shot, time of day, weather conditions, exposure time, and lens opening," and also like Smith, he observed the cultural or sociological factors in the countryside. Smith, who was a vice president of the association and chairman of its section on geology and geography, gave a major address at the conference in Gibson Hall on the Tulane University campus, alluding to the Altamaha Grit in a discussion of geological formations in the coastal plain. In another presentation that no doubt interested Harper, B. L. Robinson of Gray Herbarium, who was the chair of the botany section, referred to the classification of the intriguing genus *Hexastylis*, the group of ginger plants that occurs in the southeastern coastal plain and in Asia. After the trip, Harper submitted an account of his train-window observations and some brief comments about cypress swamps near New Orleans to *Torreya*.[9]

The Tuscaloosa job was temporary, and in July 1906 Harper headed back to New York. Traveling through Georgia, he hired a wagon and driver to take him to Broxton Rocks, an Altamaha Grit outcrop in Coffee County where the Ocmulgee River once flowed and Rocky Creek now falls about ten feet into a pool surrounded by rocks. The outcrop is the largest and most extensively weathered Altamaha Grit formation in southern Georgia. Hiking down a gently sloping path through longleaf pine woods, Harper found a twenty-five foot precipice. He observed that groundwater from the pine barren seeped and dripped over the walls, replenishing mosses, ferns, and green-fly orchids (*Epidendrum conopseum*) flourishing in "gloomy crevices" that could be twenty degrees cooler than the woods above. The spot, a popular destination for countryside day trips, reminded him of the sandstone plateaus he had explored in Alabama. He borrowed a camera from the train station agent at Broxton to take a single photograph of the falls, which contemporary scientists believe is the only natural waterfall in Georgia's Atlantic Coastal Plain.[10]

Harper planned the train trip from the South to New York so that he could observe as much of the coastal plain as possible during daylight. Still a collector of railroad timetables, he meticulously recorded his route in his diary: "From Augusta to Yemassee and Charleston on the afternoon of July 25th, from Charleston to Florence, South Carolina, the next afternoon, from Florence to Wilmington, North Carolina, and Wrightsville Beach on the 27th, from Wilmington to Rocky Mount and Tarboro, North Carolina, and Norfolk, Virginia on the 28th, and from Norfolk to Petersburg, Richmond, and northward on the afternoon of the 30th. By this zigzag route I crossed the coastal plain several times while working gradually lengthwise of it, thus obtaining a broad view of it which could hardly be surpassed in so short a time." As the train rolled along, Harper scrawled a running record of trees and plants he observed from the window. He later copied and condensed his notes into a diary.

Harper initially found the terrain of the Carolina plain monotonous in comparison to Georgia's and wondered how one could interpret the plant associations there. On reflection, however, he concluded that the Carolina bays, shallow depressions and ponds that dotted the plain, particularly in South Carolina, were distinct ecosystems within the coastal plain that needed ecological analysis. "At present they do not seem to be as well known to botanists as they are to ornithologists, but they should be most interesting places for ecological study." He observed the loss of longleaf pines in the region. "I do not remember seeing a single mature and round [i.e., unboxed] longleaf pine in either state, though this may be partly explainable by the fact that all the railroads I traveled on after leaving Georgia are comparatively old."[11]

Back in New York, he began an enjoyable routine of transcribing and organizing his field notes, reproducing photographs, preparing batches of plant specimens for herbaria, and visiting the New York Botanical Garden. He quickly produced at least seventeen articles for the *Bulletin of the Torrey Botanical Club, Torreya, Rhodora,* and *Plant World.* He went to Boston to see Robinson and Fernald at Gray Herbarium and attend a meeting of the New England Botanical Club. With Nathaniel Britton's help, he may have gotten a temporary job writing labels for the herbarium of the American Museum of Natural History. Harper also was enjoying the first reactions to his dissertation. Several friends and acquaintances praised it. The botanist Forrest Shreve reported Harper's study at a journal club meeting at Johns Hopkins University and in a letter to Harper complimented him for having "refrained from manufacturing a lot of associations, societies or whatnot"—a clear criticism of Frederic Edward Clements, the author of the new text *Research Methods in Ecology.* Roland's old friend Clarence Knowlton was impressed, although he thought Harper's view of weeds was "a little harsh." The geologist Hilgard, by then at the University of California, told Harper, "I am glad indeed that you have undertaken to call attention to the phytogeographical aspects so strongly, for as you say that embraces many points still [to] be investigated and settled." Harper sent reprints of his dissertation to William Trelease, director of the Missouri Botanical Garden, and other leading figures in botany circles, including Cowles, who wrote a brief review of it for the *Botanical Gazette.* Cowles complimented Harper's "scheme of annotated bibliography, and of giving the location of reviews as well as original papers." He told Harper that the prominent botanist and ecologist E. N. Transeau also admired the work.[12]

The winter was sad. A young woman whom Harper liked moved to Mexico to become a teacher, and Walter Hendricks hoped Roland was not too shaken by the loss: "I am glad to see that you do not allow your equilibrium to be disturbed by any such matters," he wrote ten days before Valentine's Day in 1907. Then came a blow that would reverberate through Harper's life for years: his father died of pneumonia on February 11. Snow fell soon after his body was buried in Flushing Cemetery, and a family member wrote that it was "emblematic of the pure, white life gone from [them]." Eight months later, Roland lost a second father figure when Lucien Underwood—who had given him a clerical job that made graduate school affordable, done field research in Alabama, addressed Roland as "my dear Harper," and kindly but firmly insisted that Roland revise and condense his dissertation to eliminate unnecessary detail—committed suicide on November 16, 1907.[13]

The Harpers could not get by without William's income from Poppenhusen Institute, so Roland took over his teaching and administrative duties for the remainder of the term. Despite College Point's name, it was a company town, the location of Conrad Poppenhusen's hard-rubber factory and the houses for his workers. A German immigrant himself, Poppenhusen established the academy in 1868 as a place where immigrants could learn English and trades and receive an introduction to the liberal arts. The five-story Victorian building towered over the modest houses surrounding it and became the center of the community and home at various times to a Congregational church, a bank, and the nation's first free kindergarten. Harper loathed teaching; in his free time, he explored the woods and swamps on Long Island, and he relinquished the teaching position at the end of the term. The family then had no income, and Francis had to withdraw from Cornell and take a job at a publishing company in New York. Francis's sacrifice contrasted with Roland's behavior; Bertha said later that Francis "gave up his studies and took a position with the American Book Company. He remained there six years."[14]

Forrest Shreve, who was teaching in Baltimore, visited Roland at College Point in the fall of 1907, while Roland was unemployed. Shreve had published an article about carnivorous plants in *Popular Science* in 1904, alluding to Roland's 1902 discovery of the giant variety of hooded pitcher plant in Okefenokee Swamp. Analyzing the ecology of pitcher plants, Shreve drew heavily from Darwin to explain morphological adaptations of the plants that enable them to trap insects. "How could such peculiar adaptations arise?" he asked. What purpose do they serve? In his raising such questions, Shreve's interest in traditional botany was yielding to the exciting new field of plant ecology. After completing his dissertation on pitcher plants at Johns Hopkins University, Shreve had made an eight-month collecting trip to Jamaica in 1906 for the New York Botanical Garden. While visiting Roland, Shreve probably talked about exploring the virgin forests of Jamaica on horseback and on foot, as he described in an article in *Torreya*: "Now walking, now sliding, clutching blindly for support at the spiny trunks of tree-ferns, we soon reach the river. Standing at the edge of the stream we find ourselves amid surroundings of indescribable beauty."[15] If Roland worried that his own railroad treks were not as heroic as Shreve's jungle botanizing, he did not make a note of it.

Shreve found one of Roland's sisters attractive and after returning to Baltimore, wrote to Roland that he hoped he had made a good impression on her. But while Shreve had women on his mind, Harper was interested in the "peculiar distribution of certain coastal plain plants." Shreve mentioned that he had found water cowbane (*Oxypolis filiformis*) on the Potomac River near Hancock, Maryland, but Harper told him that the plant was more likely his own *Harperella nodosa*. Harper had only found *Harperella* in Georgia's coastal plain and in Alabama's coal region, "but the Alabama localities were along streams in the Cumberland Plateau, which is a direct continuation of the mountains of western Maryland, and a great many species of plants are common to the mountains of these two states." Harper asked Shreve to send him a specimen of the Potomac bank plant, so after returning to Baltimore, Shreve sent him one he had collected the previous summer. Harper deposited the specimen in the Botanical Garden's herbarium and compared it to specimens of *Oxypolis filiformis* collected in Virginia. He also wrote to Rose at the United States National Herbarium, asking him to visit the locality of Shreve's find on the Potomac. Harper submitted a rather breathless update of the *Harperella* situation, including Shreve's and Rose's parts in the story, to *Torreya*. He reported that Rose had "found a small patch of [*Harperella*] just above high-water mark on the bank of the Potomac near that place, and collected flowering and fruiting specimens." Harper noted, "He finds it very similar to my specimens from the mountains of Alabama, but is not sure now that those are identical with the original material from the coastal plain of Georgia. This implies that there may be two species of *Harperella* instead of one."[16]

Harper longed to return to the coastal plain, unfettered by family or financial responsibilities, and wrote to acquaintances to inquire about possible jobs. W. L. Sherwood of Highlands Biological Station, a research station of the University of North Carolina, wrote that there might be some temporary work for Harper "attending to the few visitors" and in the herbarium "mounting, determining (if necessary), and making notes of possible discoveries," but it does not seem that Harper went there. Harper applied for a job with Georgia's Second District Agricultural College in Tifton—at the time, these agricultural experiment stations offered some of the best opportunities in the South to pursue biological research, as there were few doctoral programs in the basic sciences in the region—but was turned down despite efforts on his behalf by his college friends Walter Hendricks and R. J. H. DeLoach, who was working as a botanist for the station. Even more demoralizing, his younger brother Otto was offered a job there thanks to DeLoach's intervention. DeLoach tried to encourage Roland: "I have long cherished the hope that you and I would be associated in work at this Station, but in as much as it seems impossible to have things this way, I am willing to accept the will of the fates." He urged his friend to make "a brave stand."[17]

Henry Cowles, the botanist at the University of Chicago, urged Harper to attend upcoming scientific meetings in Chicago. "I am very anxious to meet you and talk things over. . . . Clements, Adams, Transeau, and others of ecological bent will be there, and we can have a fine time 'chewing the rag' together." But Harper apparently did not attend, probably because he could not afford it. Transeau later wrote that he regretted not seeing Harper in Chicago. Transeau was busy analyzing the relationship of evaporation to plant societies and wanted to debate geographic differences in bog societies with Harper. Referring to Harper's article about New England coastal plants in the April 1905 issue of *Rhodora*, he commented in January 1908, "The point I have in mind is that the bogs of the southern coastal plain bear the same relation to the southern conifer forest that the northern bogs bear to the northeastern conifers." The same month, another leading botanist sought Harper's company. Charles Sprague Sargent of the Arnold Arboretum at Harvard invited Harper to accompany him on a collecting trip to Augusta, Georgia, but without a salary Harper could not afford to accept the invitation.[18] It must have hurt deeply to miss an opportunity to escort Harvard's arboretum man through Harper's own territory in the coastal plain of Georgia.

At least three friends offered Harper temporary or permanent jobs in February 1908 alone, but he turned them down. Edward W. Berry at Johns Hopkins told him about a temporary position studying Maryland's swamps. Shreve, who planned to work at the Carnegie Institution's desert research laboratory in Tucson, offered to recommend Harper for his teaching job at Woman's College in Baltimore. Roland's college chum Alfred Akerman suggested that they collaborate on a book about Georgia forests, with Harper doing the botanical material and Akerman the economic. Trelease could not offer Harper a contract or a permanent job at the Missouri Botanical Garden immediately but wanted Harper to help him analyze the region where the Ozark Mountains overlapped the Gulf swamp region. It was a "particularly pretty field for such analytical work as [Harper had] demonstrated a faculty for doing."[19]

By the summer of 1908, Harper's choosiness about jobs was enraging his family and must have mystified the friends who tried to help him find work. This time, Harper forfeited a position at the country's first forestry school, on the estate of George Vanderbilt in extreme western North Carolina. The job was not perfect. It involved teaching, which Harper did not like, and was located in the Blue Ridge Mountains, not on the coastal plain. It also required horseback riding up and down curving, slippery trails and roads, and Harper does not appear to have ever ridden a horse on a botanizing expedition. The offer was to teach a summer course at Biltmore Forestry School as a way of trying out for a permanent position as a lecturer, to succeed C. D. Howe. Akerman, by then professor and head of the new forestry school at the University of Georgia, had spent time at Biltmore and recommended Harper for the job. He wrote to Harper on May 27, 1908, urging him to apply for the position. Carl Alwin Schenck, director of the forestry school, followed up on May 30, inviting Harper to apply for a position as lecturer, adding that the successful applicant would be paid one hundred dollars per month plus fifteen dollars toward maintenance of a horse. "The lecturer is compelled to use a horse continuously, owing to the large distances which he has to cover on the Biltmore Estate," he explained, adding, "Biltmore is a lovely place. Forestal work at Biltmore is fascinating and, if you love nature, as well as work, a life at Biltmore may involve for you that chance at getting happy, which every one of us covets." Schenck may have sensed or learned that Harper was reluctant, or perhaps Schenck heard something about Harper that caused him to have second thoughts about offering him a permanent position without meeting him first. A week later he wrote again, inviting Harper to accept a trial position teaching a summer course in August. "This short stay would enable you to get acquainted with the Biltmore School and the work on the Biltmore Estate. For me your visit would involve the advantage of a personal acquaintance with your good self. It seems to me well for us to be mutually acquainted before we enter into an agreement, which, I hope, will live a long time to mutual advantage. The Biltmore School would be glad to defray your traveling expenses and to pay you at the rate of $25 a week for such lectures as you might be will-ing to give on the following topics: Mosses and Ferns, or Seed Plants. . . . Should you have any other topic you would *prefer* to lecture on, I would be glad to obtain your suggestions."[20] Akerman encouraged Harper to accept the offer.

Harper responded to Schenck with an offer to teach a class on the coastal plain, but Howe, the departing lecturer, intervened, insisting in a letter to Harper on June 17 that the students needed instruction on seed plants, not coastal plants. Was this a sticking point? Possibly. However, Harper apparently announced to several people that he had accepted the job. Otto wrote, "I am glad you are going to North Carolina and am sure you will like it there." Edward Berry wrote from the Maryland Geological Survey and Johns Hopkins University, "I am glad you are going down to Biltmore. Hope that you can make something permanent out of it." Wil-helmina notified their uncle, J. R. Harper of Oconalufty, North Carolina, that Roland would be moving near him, and the uncle wrote to Roland, "My Dear Nephew, Wilhelmina has written to Edith that you think of coming to North Carolina to be located on the Vanderbilt Estate at Bilt-more and I am very glad indeed that we may expect a visit from you." Uncle John wrote again a few weeks later with directions to his home.[21]

Harper spent some time that summer in North Carolina, collecting plant specimens in Transylvania County on July 29, but ultimately did not take a job at Biltmore. On August 1, Bertha wrote, furious that Roli had declined a permanent position at Biltmore. "I cannot understand you! . . . You must be crazy!" She had counted on Roland contributing to the family's income so that Francis could return to college. She told Roland that Booie felt "awfully downhearted [and] disgusted. The poor boy shall have the greatest burden to bear of all of you." Otto added to the pressure. "I was glad and very much relieved to know that you seemed about to get a pretty good place and at last help Sis and Booie and me in contributing to the support of the family and getting long standing debts paid off and send Booie back to college if possible. . . . Your income is needed badly. . . . Please make a move to stay where you are, at least for the time being."[22]

Perhaps Harper learned that in an earlier position as director of the forestry division of the United States Department of Agriculture, Schenck had actually advocated clear-cutting virgin longleaf forests as quickly as possible, and this fact made Schenck an unappealing colleague. Perhaps Forrest Shreve's tales of riding horses in the Jamaican mountains made him nervous about riding. News of an acquaintance's death also could have made him apprehensive about solitary horseback riding on rough terrain: a month before Akerman first reported the Biltmore job possibility, Harper learned that Eugene Smith's daughter, Julia, had drowned in Hurricane Creek near Tuscaloosa while riding alone. She had stopped to gather some laurel and "somehow she lost her footing and fell in the creek." Or perhaps Harper simply wanted to get back to the coastal plain. H. D. House, who was scheduled as the other August guest lecturer, wound up in the permanent position, and Harper told his mother that House needed the job more because he had a wife. However, House was concerned about what Harper would do next. He wrote to Harper from Biltmore in October, "I am most anxious to know—Have you landed a permanent and well paying job along your line?"[23]

Britton, Rusby, and other botanists at the Garden may have been concerned about Harper's prolonged unemployment, too. In February 1908, they asked him to chair a subcommittee on local flora for the Torrey Botanical Club. Rusby had been urging club members to do more local floristic study, perhaps seeing this as a way to engage members and motivate them to make financial contributions to the club's endowment. "All that is needed is a leader, and this is the point of difficulty. He must be a capable botanist, and he must give practically his whole time to the work." But who could be the leader, when the club lacked the funds to pay a salary? Rusby's manifesto on behalf of local flora appeared in the July 1906 issue of *Torreya*, just before an article by Harper, "Some More Coastal Plain Plants in the Palaeozoic Region of Alabama." Seeing Harper's article may have reminded Rusby of the southerner who liked field research so much and yet was without a job. Probably at Rusby's request, Harper gave a talk on how to conduct local floristic study at the April 1908 club meeting. He sent a copy of his paper to Shreve, who wrote with encouragement: "I read your New York paper . . . with a great deal of interest. It must have opened the eyes of some of those old museum specimens who think it has all been done. . . . Keep it right up, old man, the science of botany is suffering more today from the influence of crystallised people than from any other one thing." He hinted that Harper might occupy himself with a more thorough study of the New Jersey pine barrens. "If I had stayed in Baltimore I think I should have got busy with the New Jersey pine barrens, turned them upside down and inside out. There is material there for an extremely interesting phytogeographical and ecological study. The soils ought to come in for a large share of attention, and by extending the work down the coast in its later stages it ought to be possible to explain a good deal that now seems mysterious."[24]

Although Shreve was complimentary and encouraging, Fernald at Harvard was not so kind. Responding to letters from Harper in May 1908, the assistant professor insinuated that Harper's inquiries were not important enough for his attention. "[U]nless letters are strictly urgent they have to wait or be indefinitely side-tracked; and this condition is so generally understood by my friends that I was surprised to have you say in your recent letter that you felt that your numerous inquiries offended me. They do not, merely I have to decide from all the letters which ask for answers which it is most imperative to answer at once. As most of your inquiries are such as you can with a little effort answer yourself, I am sure, it has seemed to me that they could wait until I could catch a moment's breathing space." Harper had written to question Fernald's repetition of a particular fact in a journal article. Fernald responded, "It was absolutely intentional, for the simple rhetorical effect of making my point more clear to the minds of people who would not remember all that they had read before." Again, Fernald hinted that Harper's questions took time from more important matters: "Now I must get back to work."[25]

Akerman continued trying to help Harper; he published an article Harper wrote, although he gently requested some editorial improvements, including deleting Harper's discussion of whether trees are observable from moving trains. "This is interesting to you and me, but probably not to [readers]. Do you give me this permission? I would also like to strike the expression of grief over the advent of turpentining. . . . I am mighty glad to get the manuscript and want to print it, but I think these few changes would improve it."[26]

The job that Roland finally got was another temporary position, this one collecting specimens for the Georgia Department of Agriculture. DeLoach may have landed the work for him, prevailing on the department to hire Harper for a few weeks. Harper was probably very glad to be back in Georgia, but Bertha was not happy; she thought the Biltmore position would have been a good place "to break [him] in pleasantly into dealing with people and with students." Relinquishing the Biltmore job was a "gross blunder." Furthermore, she added in a series of letters that amounted to a tirade in August and September 1908, no one in the family was going to help him financially any longer. Francis wanted to return to college, and Otto was already burdened by having to support Hermina, who had been teaching in Dalton, Georgia, but spent the summer writing a book and wanted Otto to support her while she typed it and searched for a publisher. Bertha told Roland she thought Hermina was unbalanced—and implied that she thought Roland was, too. More horrifying, she wrote with no apparent guilt that she wished Hermina were dead: "I doubt that such a creature as she can write anything that will be read. I wish she were where Papa is, instead of Papa; it would be best all round. I never dreamed I would have to worry so over my two oldest and from the start most promising children!"[27]

Eugene Smith of the Alabama Geological Survey came to the rescue in August 1908 with an invitation that allowed Harper to temporarily escape his mother's harping. Smith proposed that Harper join him and several other geologists on a trip down the Black Warrior River. Mourning the death of his daughter Julia a few months earlier, Smith wanted to make the river trip by houseboat to view the "exceptionally complete geological sections displayed in the river-bluffs between Tuscaloosa and Mobile." He offered to pay Harper's travel expenses and commented, "I would like to have a discussion of our botanical matters with you."[28] Harper said yes.

Smith assembled a research party of seven other geologists, including Gilbert Harris, T. H. Aldrich, William F. Prouty, and Elias Howard Sellards; Harper as botanist; an authority on mollusks, H. E. Wheeler; a navigator; and a cook. They traveled on a houseboat fitted with a twenty-horsepower gasoline engine and on a smaller launch boat during the second week of October 1908. The river trip took a week, as the houseboat chugged slowly through the flat plain, past the Mississippian mounds in Hale County and many small-town landings and cultivated fields on terraces or "second bottoms" just out of reach of flooding. With each bend in the broad river, there were new plants and microenvironments to see, as "the different bluffs face all points of the compass."[29] Bright blue belted kingfishers probably swooped from perch to perch along the banks, calling in a loud, high-pitched rapid rattle before taking flight.

Harper made running notes of the plants he saw and compiled them later in a list with subheadings for each named landing, bluff, and creek they passed. "As we usually kept near the middle of the river, and no one had thought to bring along a field-glass, my notes made on the boat were chiefly confined to trees, shrubs, and vines. But our frequent stops at the bluffs, lasting from half an hour to several hours or all night, gave me opportunity to note many herbs and check up on my identifications of woody plants, and to do a little collecting." At White's Bluff, fifty-two miles south of Tuscaloosa, Harper got off on the low side, and the geologists disembarked on the bluff side. From across the river, he took two photographs to capture a wide view of the geologists, most dressed in dark suits, examining the variously colored clays of the bluff. At Beckley's Landing in Marengo County, he and one companion set out on foot and walked about nine miles, through the town of Myrtlewood and on to the Naheola ferry, where they rejoined the boat crew.[30]

Harper spotted only a few longleaf pines on ridges in Choctaw and Clarke counties. Black willow (*Salix nigra*) and sycamore (*Platanus occidentalis*) were the most common trees on the banks. Spanish moss hung from tree branches. Sprays of white and pink calico aster (*Aster lateriflorus*) hung down from the bluffs; purple American bellflower (*Campanula americana*) bloomed at the foot of St. Stephens Bluff in Washington County. Burr cucumber vines (*Sicyos angulatus*) climbed on every bluff and every type of tree, their pale-green flowers still blooming. Extending and correcting Mohr's pioneering work, Harper recorded narrowleaf paleseed (*Conobea multifida*), a delicate nonnative herb, and long-leaved loosestrife (*Ammannia coccinea*), which Mohr had only recorded in Mobile County. He saw Vahl's fimbry (*Fimbristylis Vahlii*) growing on damp, loamy banks near the water's edge, where it coped with frequent submersion by producing multiple generations of seed stalks each growing season.

Smith's crew spent each night at a bluff. Seminole bats likely left their nests in clumps of Spanish moss to flit overhead at dusk, and the scientists must have heard the strange barking of barred owls, the whistles of bird-voiced tree frogs, and the phenomenal nasal quacking of hundreds of male green tree frogs clinging to the stems of vegetation a foot or two above the water. Harper enjoyed talking with the shell man, H. E. Wheeler, who like Harper's father was a Methodist minister as well as a man of science. Waiting for sleep in the cramped space of the houseboat, anchored each night at the foot of bluffs as much as two hundred feet tall, often with no lights but the stars, Harper may have fancied that he was exploring a riverine wilderness as Rusby had on the Amazon and Shreve in Jamaica.

The group of scientists concluded the boat trip at Jackson and the headwaters of the Tombigbee River. Once the adventure was over and he was back at his mother's College Point apartment, Harper wrote letters to friends and acquaintances about the Black Warrior trip. He began a correspondence with Wheeler that continued for at least thirty-five years. Characterizing their trip in an article for the *Bulletin* of the Torrey Botanical Club, Harper likened it to the exploration by the nineteenth-century naturalist Thomas Nuttall. "Since Nuttall's memorable journey of exploration on the Ohio, Mississippi, and Arkansas Rivers in the years 1818 to 1820, probably very few botanists have traveled any considerable distance by daylight on any of the navigable rivers of our coastal plain." He wrote a report of the trip that was primarily a list of the plants he saw, categorizing the plants in the Cretaceous or Eocene formations and as trees, shrubs, or herbs and providing a lengthy explanation for his list-making system. Counting about forty species of "weeds" on the riverbanks, he speculated that they had migrated to the Black Warrior's banks from fields and settlements and then traveled downstream, for "a river is an excellent highway for plants to travel."[31]

Harper also described economic activity along the river. "The cultivated fields visible from a boat are mostly in the 'second bottoms,' just above the reach of floods. And such locations are not considered very healthy to live in, consequently not many houses are to be seen. Cotton warehouses, with inclined tracks leading down to the water, are frequent on the bluffs of the lower Tombigbee, but rare or absent on the Warrior." They had motored downstream past the sites of future locks No. 2 and No. 3. Harper acknowledged the "economic necessity" of locks to facilitate river transport of heavy freight such as coal and cement, but said the locks were "a detriment to science in more ways than one. In the first place, [the system] seriously interrupts the normal life-history or physiographic development of the rivers, and, what was of more concern to [their] party, it ha[d] permanently covered the lowest few feet of one of the most important bluffs with an opaque screen of muddy water."[32]

Although Harper's dissertation and other articles drew compliments, not everyone was encouraging about his work. Clements, author of the widely read book *Research Methods in Ecology* and an associate professor of plant pathology at the University of Nebraska, was frankly dismissive of what he called "descriptive ecology." He could have been referring to Harper's numerous brief published articles about summer fieldwork in Georgia when he wrote in *Research Methods* that mere inventories of plant diversity—the type of lists in which Harper found so much meaning—lent themselves with "insidious ease to chance journeys or to vacation trips." "While there is good reason that a record should be left of any serious reconnaissance, even though it be of a few weeks' duration, the resulting lists and descriptive articles can have only the most rudimentary value, and it is absurd to regard them as ecological contributions at all." Clements was one of the earliest ecologists and seized the opportunity to define the field, arguing that plants existed in discrete "associations." Although Forrest Shreve praised Harper for not employing Clements's approach, another member of the Carnegie Institution staff, George Shull, warned Harper against writing too many articles based on car-window observations. "I believe you run a great risk when you write a paper of considerable length on what you can see from a car-window. I happen to know that Dr. [John William] Harshberger did himself more harm than good by his ecological study of Mt. Katahdin, the result of a day's trip or such a matter. Students engaged in fields in which it is absolutely necessary to work for months before they can publish anything are sure to accord small credit to work which costs so little."[33]

Discouraged about finding a job that didn't require teaching or experimental research and would leave him free for botanical exploration, Harper sought advice from Shull, whom he probably had met in 1901 when Shull was a botanical assistant at the United States National Herbarium. Shull was blunt in his reply: Harper needed to be friendlier to other botanists. When they were both at the conference of the American Association for the Advancement of Science in New Orleans in 1905, Shull was not the only scientist who had noticed that Harper seemed to shun the meetings and presentations in favor of roaming the country around New Orleans. "I fear you are making a mistake by avoiding the scientific meetings. At the New Orleans meetings, you made it clear that the associations offered by the meeting meant almost nothing to you. You might now be reaping a reward quite satisfactory to yourself if you had found it possible to go to the Philadelphia meetings, and when there had cultivated the acquaintance and friendship of others who were in attendance." He advised Harper to be less prickly. "I think you are too sensitive, and assume that people are slighting you or overlooking you or slurring you, when they have not the least intention of doing so and you should carefully guard your expressions from every hurt that you feel so." Harper had apparently expressed disdain for the ecological research of some botanists, and Shull urged him to avoid criticizing others in the new scientific specialty. "I think you have made a great mistake at times by saying that you do not know what 'ecology' is. A man working in your particular field ought to be in a position to explain to the rest of us what ecology is. Of course, I understand your intention in expressing it so, but by putting it in this way you deliberately stepped off of a very important bandwagon of present day scientific effort. If ecology is not now what you think it ought to be, proceed to make it mean what you think it ought to mean, but don't refuse to talk in the language of contemporary science."[34]

Considering the source, these were strong words. Shull was working on the edge of contemporary science and was about to publish results that would truly revolutionize American agriculture. He was part of the original staff of Cold Spring Harbor Laboratory, a genetics research facility that the Carnegie Institution of Washington established on Long Island in 1904, which was the center of genetic research at the time. In fact, Hugo de Vries, one of the three European scientists who rediscovered and built on Mendel's work in 1900, participated in the laboratory's formal opening. Shull used Mendel's techniques to analyze the inheritability of various traits of corn, particularly the number of rows of kernels on an ear. He found that when he cross-pollinated two strains that had been self-pollinated, the resulting strain was superior. A young scientist, only four years older than Harper, Shull was conducting breakthrough science.[35] Harper meanwhile clung to his self-concept as a naturalist explorer searching the southern coastal plain for new species, a pursuit that many of his contemporaries probably saw as quaint and outdated.

Harper found it very hard to adopt anyone else's perspective, and in a reply to Shull, defensively argued that he could not attend scientific meetings because he had no money for travel expenses. Shull replied again, in a sixteen-page handwritten letter. "I see I have not made my point clear. When funds are lacking one is always justified in staying away, but when you *can* attend, it is certainly advantageous," he wrote. "You preferred to go exploring to gather up data for a little article, to showing the courtesy that was due to those who had come hundreds or thousands of miles to read a paper. . . . If you want to be appreciated, don't be scant in your appreciation of others." Harper had dismissed ecology as a "fad," and Shull warned him that he risked seeming irrelevant. True, the field was young, but it was "one of the most fundamental phases of biological research." To be taken seriously, Harper needed to broaden or deepen his own research goals beyond the discovery of new species. "You seem to think you are not getting the recognition due you from ecologists, [but] your writings make very little attempt to aid in the solution of the fundamental ecological problems, such as adaptation, response to environment, the nature of competition, causes of the success or failure of vegetation types, mutualism, the causes of the different types of association and succession, etc.," Shull wrote. A self-made man who had worked his way through school, Shull urged Harper to get a job. "Think a little less of your capacity to occupy a *particular* position or type of position, and accept whatever work comes to hand that you are capable of doing, always 'keeping an eye out' for a position which more nearly meets your ideal." At the time Shull wrote this letter, less than a year had passed since William Harper had died. The members of the Torrey Botanical Club had gathered only a few days earlier to pay tribute to Lucien Underwood, and Roland no doubt was bereft.[36] "My dear friend," Shull told him tenderly, "[w]hile I can not assume a father's place and give you the helpful results of long years of experience, I would be only too glad if I could be of some service to you, such as an older brother might render."[37]

Near the end of 1908, Roland received an invitation to return to the coastal plain. Elias Howard Sellards, one of the scientists he had met on the Black Warrior boat trip, wanted him to survey peat deposits in Florida. Harper left for Tallahassee at the end of November.[38]

CHAPTER FOUR

In the Footsteps of Croom and Chapman

The periods that Harper spent in Florida during 1909 and 1910 were rich in discoveries: He found a sponsor in the Florida Geological Survey that would be important for the next two decades. He made long treks through swamps and bogs in the heat of Florida summers, earning a reputation as a field botanist of extraordinary stamina and keen eyesight. He walked in the footsteps of the pioneering botanists Hardy Croom and Alvan Wentworth Chapman.

Harper posed for a photograph in March 1909 at a campsite with Elias Sellards and Herman Gunter, geologists with the Florida Geological Survey. The other men sat on campstools, while thirty-one-year-old Harper, with a trim dark moustache, wearing a suit, vest, and brimmed hat, stood, a small satchel over his shoulder. Their tent was pitched beside a split-rail fence, probably near the ferry operator's house at the top of Aspalaga Bluff. They had a fine view of the fast, muddy Apalachicola River and Jackson County stretching flat and densely wooded to the west. The river had carved its way through the limestone formations, creating rocky bluffs where a distinct community of trees and plants thrived in the steamy shade of giant sweet gum (*Liquidambar styraciflua*) and American beech (*Fagus grandifolia*). The tops of the bluffs were longleaf-wiregrass communities; *Torreya*, magnolias, and oakleaf hydrangea grew on the slopes. At the base of the bluffs, the river floodplain supported loblolly (*Pinus taeda*), spruce pines (*P. glabra*), and enormous hardwoods. The three men camped at Aspalaga March 5–9 to study the area's limestone outcrops and associated vegetation. The weather was cool and the sky cloudy; one night it rained. Campfires warmed them in the mornings. A wide road, lined with cultivated pink-flowering crepe myrtles (*Lagerstroemia indica*) that the ferry operator or one of his predecessors had planted, led down the steep hillside to the alluvial plain, the sandy riverbank, and a dock. Mules pulled wagons loaded with pine resin to the dock for shipment upstream to River Junction and transfer to trains that carried the resin on to Jacksonville, Pensacola, and Savannah.[1]

Harper and the geologists used a small boat to explore the base of the bluff and found the current in the shallow river very swift. With Gunter, Harper hiked up and down the eastern riverbank in the area north of Aspalaga Landing on March 6 and in the area to the south on March 8, through the muddy, swampy floodplain and up several small streams, sometimes seeing steamboats pass by on the Apalachicola. Golden silk spiders probably waited for flying insects to become trapped in enormous webs they spun between trees, while cardinals, Carolina wrens, red-bellied woodpeckers, and hooded warblers busied themselves in the trees. The men may have noticed deer trails in the switch cane (*Arundinaria tecta*) along the streams that rushed through limestone chutes. Making constant notes as he tramped through the river bottoms, Harper found croomia (*Croomia pauciflora*), a small plant of the forest floor with tiny greenish-yellow flowers nodding underneath its leaves, just beginning to bloom in two spots. Hardy B. Croom, a North Carolina planter who had bought and leased property at Aspalaga Bluff in the 1830s, discovered the species near Aspalaga. Although an earlier naturalist collected *Croomia* in Wilcox County, Alabama, in 1821, Croom's was the first Florida collection of the plant. Croom was a serious botanist who contributed articles to the *American Journal of Sciences and Arts*. In 1836, a year before he died in a shipwreck, Croom explored the Aspalaga area with another young naturalist, a physician in nearby Quincy, Florida, Alvan Wentworth Chapman, who wrote to John Torrey that Croom "belonged to that class of wealthy and intelligent southern gentlemen."[2]

Harper found that another of Croom's discoveries, the stinking cedar (*Torreya taxifolia*, known then as *Tumion taxifolium*), was "common all over the bluff, from end to end and from top to bottom," some specimens forty feet tall. He had first searched for the rare tree on a side trip to River Junction, Florida, in 1903, hoping to see the stinking cedar "in its native haunts." On that expedition, he hiked for thirty miles up one of the Apalachicola's tributaries, the Flint River, hoping to discover the tree above River Junction, but did not succeed.[3] Hiking with Gunter on this, his second visit to *Torreya*'s type locality, Harper recorded that the *Torreya* grew in company with beech; tulip tree (*Liriodendron tulipifera*); sugar maple (*Acer floridanum*); red oak; oakleaf hydrangea; red-flowered buckeye (*Aesculus pavia*); the yellow Florida flame azalea (*Rhododendron austrinum*); red-flowered Florida anise (*Illicium floridanum*); Adam's needle (*Yucca filamentosa*); eastern leatherwood, a handsome understory shrub with a graceful form and distinctly bendable branches; tinted woodland spurge (*Euphorbia commutata*); and bloodroot (*Sanguinaria canadensis*).[4] He noted two species of trillium: the longbract wakerobin (*Trillium underwoodii*), which Lucien Underwood and Franklin Sumner Earle had discovered in Lee County, Alabama, in 1896, and the lanceleaf wakerobin (*Trillium lancifolium*), which the Florida botanist and collector A. H. Curtiss had found near Chattahoochee in 1901. He also noted the wild plum (*Prunus americana*); smooth Solomon's seal (*Polygonatum biflorum*); and false garlic (*Nothoscordum bivalve*), a tiny lily whose white flowers open in the afternoon. He speculated that the calciferous limestone of Aspalaga and nearby Alum Bluff was the ecological factor that allowed *Torreya* and other endemic plants to flourish.[5]

On their last full day in camp, Harper and Gunter struck out to the south along a high sandy ridge and hiked about four miles to Cooper's Point at the mouth of Rock Creek, where they ate lunch and observed the steamboat *W. C. Bradley* make a stop. Returning upriver, Harper admired giant sweet gums that were four feet in diameter. Back at camp in the afternoon, he collected a few bluff plants before Sellards rejoined them, bearing groceries and the mail, including letters for Harper from Shreve and John William Harshberger, a botanist and ecologist at the University of Pennsylvania. The next morning, March 9, the three men hauled their gear back to River Junction, hiking along a rugged ridge for seven or eight miles. Harper noted that the *Torreya* disappeared after they crossed Flat Creek. At River Junction, the trio took a train for Tallahassee, but Harper wanted to "trace some of the creeks to their sources on the plateau and study the difference in vegetation," so he got off at the Quincy depot and walked back toward Gretna. He found magnolias, spruce pine, beech, and tulip tree in the creek bottoms. Florida anise bloomed luxuriantly along a branch of Quincy Creek, along with mountain laurel, sweet bay (*Magnolia virginiana*, then known as *Magnolia glauca*), tupelo (*Nyssa biflora*), American devilwood (*Osmanthus americanus*), and sourwood (*Oxydendrum arboreum*). Sweet Pinxter azalea (*Rhododendron canescens*, which Harper knew as *Azalea nudiflora*) grew along the creek's edge and may have been in bloom, in which case the showy pink flowers were a fragrant and lovely sight in the early-spring woods. Longleaf pine grew on the plateau along with wiregrass and many oaks. "Going upstream [on Quincy

Creek,] this ravine becomes wider and shallower, passing by insensible gradations into pine-barren branch-swamp." After reaching Gretna, he walked another five or six miles along the railroad and arrived at Quincy around 7 p.m.—for a total hike of about twenty miles that day.[6]

Harper took another short walk east from Quincy the next day before catching a train to Havana, a few miles to the northeast; he made car-window notes during the rail trip. His connection to Tallahassee was late, so he took the opportunity to walk two miles north up the railroad track past Hinson and back. The train ride to the station in Tallahassee was only thirty minutes, and he reached the capital in time to stop by the office of the Florida Geological Survey and look through his mail, which included the February issue of the *Bulletin* of the Torrey Botanical Club, a copy of Torrey's *Florida Sketchbook*, which Francis had sent to him, and letters from his mother, his uncle John Harper, and Henry Rusby.

When Harper conducted the statewide survey of peat deposits for Sellards in 1909, he made Tallahassee his base of operations, working out of the geological survey's office and renting a room in town. In June 1909, Harper took a train southwest from Tallahassee toward the town of Apalachicola at the mouth of the Apalachicola River on the Gulf of Mexico. Making car-window notes as usual, he recorded that longleaf pine was "common nearly all the way." His first sighting of the yellow pitcher plant was at Arran in Wakulla County, within the present Apalachicola National Forest. From the town of Sopchoppy to the Ochlockonee River bay, he found snakeroot-leaf aster (*Aster eryngiifolius*) blooming along the track. From Lanark to the fishing village of Carrabelle, the train took him within view of the Gulf and Dog Island. He spent the night at Carrabelle, where he walked on the beach before dark. The next morning he set out on foot again, walking east about seven miles along the railroad track to a point about a mile east of Lanark Springs; there he found a spot in the shallow surf that was "sufficiently secluded to take a bath." The pines grew in belts there, with slash pine (*Pinus elliottii*) closest to shore, longleaf behind it, and sand pine (*Pinus clausa*) on higher ground. Collecting peat samples and pausing once to photograph a chuck-will's-widow's nest on the ground, Harper missed two trains that day and twice had to go back to pick up samples he had placed on the ground and forgotten. He made it back to his hotel at almost 6 p.m. and spent a second night there.[7]

After collecting a few more peat samples the next morning, Harper took the steamboat *Crescent City* to Apalachicola, along the way passing through St. George Sound and into Apalachicola Bay.[8] He made notes about the barrier islands and an uncharacteristic ornithological observation, writing that he saw "several pelicans . . . in the sound [but] no other birds." After arriving at the shipping and fishing town of Apalachicola, Harper checked into the elegant, two-year-old Franklin Inn, which had clear views of the bay from wraparound porches on the first and second floors.

He spent June 11, a hot cloudless day, hiking in the pine barrens, marshes, swamps, and hammocks near the mouth of the Apalachicola River, even wading into the river to photograph the Apalachicola Northern Railroad drawbridge four miles above the bay. The drawbridge, completed two years earlier, had a fifteen-horsepower engine, the first of that kind he had seen. Walking upriver another mile, he found a large sawmill and turned west toward Lake Wimico. He passed through stands of virgin longleaf in higher, dryer spots. Ogeechee lime (*Nyssa ogeche*) grew at the edges of the marshes, cabbage palm (*Sabal palmetto*) on the shell hammocks. Along shallow freshwater branches, he found titi and spotted the showy pale pink bracts of the uncommon and lovely Georgia bark or fever tree (*Pinckneya bracteata*, then known as *Pinckneya pubens*). Here he found the striking corkwood (*Leitneria floridana* Chapman), one of Chapman's Florida discoveries, growing in shallow cypress ponds. This was a momentous find for Harper, since he had searched for corkwood on the lower Altamaha River in Georgia and because Chapman's book, *Flora of the Southern United States*, was one of his first field guides.

Passing "first through several hundred acres of low pine-barrens with very dense growth of *Pinus elliottii*, never lumbered or turpentined," he found sweet bay magnolia and the variety of bald cypress that Croom had earlier observed in pine barren ponds and swamps (*Taxodium distichum* var. *imbricarium*, now known as *Taxodium ascendens*) common, and cabbage palm scattered. He described a dense groundcover of shrubby peelbark St. John's wort (*Hypericum fasciculatum*), more corkwood, and various irises and sedges. "Farther away from [the] river the pine-barrens become more open and park-like, lumbered a little and turpentined considerably . . . and with some [longleaf] in drier spots." Where the ground was a few inches lower, he slogged through "an intricate maze of shallow cypress sloughs or very irregularly shaped ponds, none containing much standing water just [then]." Particularly beneath the cabbage palms, he noted smallhead doll's daisy (*Boltonia diffusa*), bighead rush

(*Juncus megacephalus*), irises, Baldwin's milkwort (*Polygala balduinii*), needlegrass rush (*Juncus roemerianus*), marsh fimbry (*Fimbristylis spadicea*), fewflower milkweed (*Asclepias lanceolata*), stiff bluestar (*Amsonia rigida*), and star grass (*Dichromena colorata*, later renamed *Rhynchospora colorata*). Harper probably saw bald eagles and ospreys soaring over the marshes or diving for fish. It is likely that he walked near female alligators guarding their nests in the marshes, but if so the great reptiles watched him go by without making themselves known. Harper wrote in his diary that he "wandered around this trackless wilderness an hour or two, striking Huckleberry Creek once, but couldn't get near Lake Wimico." He reached the bed of an unfinished railroad at 2:39 in the afternoon and walked two miles along it to St. Joseph's Bay, and then along the bay through "two or three titi swamps with water about a foot deep." A train ride took him from St. Joseph's Bay back to Apalachicola.

He had supper with an acquaintance from college, Charles Henry Bourke "Harry" Floyd, a local lawyer and an erratic, brilliant character who was at various times a justice of the peace, a tax assessor, and a member of the Florida legislature. The next morning, June 12, after writing a letter to Shreve and shipping another peat sample, Harper walked around town with Floyd on streets paved with oyster shells. The port had recovered from two fires in the 1890s that had destroyed the heart of the town and was again a bustling commercial and shipping center, with large businesses, a bank, an electric-light plant, and telegraph service. Harper and Floyd visited Chapman's grave in Chestnut Street Cemetery, just behind Chapman's imposing two-story house.[9]

Leaving Floyd in Apalachicola, Harper departed on a typical train-window botanizing trip up the eastern side of the Apalachicola River basin. He recorded everything he saw, collecting the raw data of phytogeography. Crossing territory that is largely in the present Apalachicola National Forest, through swamps and pinewoods and past small sawmill communities situated near the tracks, he made constant notes, including mile markers along the track for reference. Longleaf pine and yellow pitcher plant were the most common species he recognized from the train window. "Hammocks and hills begin about first crossing of Telogia Creek, and continue with some interruptions for twelve or fifteen miles, often with pretty good Tifton topography." There were "a good many cultivated fields." The train entered the Altamaha Grit plateau at Greensboro, "a fine neat new town," and after another five miles, began a steep descent through ravines and hammocks to River Junction, the staging area for his

March camping trip with Sellards and Gunter. Harper summarized his sightings of "species of special interest" on this train trip: Ogeechee lime four or five times in Franklin County and once more a mile or two north of the line; southern magnolia absent in fifty miles of low country; sand pine only near Apalachicola. Slash pine and sweet bay were "nearly always in sight." He saw bald cypress only in river swamps between the fourth and ninth mileposts, and "not very abundant." In delta bayous and in a creek near Sumatra, he found yellow pond-lily, the plant he described after discovering it in shallow lagoons of the Canoochee River in 1903. Georgia bark was frequent except in flatwoods, snakeroot-leaf aster common except in the two hammock belts bordering the plateau. The bright pink flowers of savannah meadowbeauty (*Rhexia alifanus*) were very abundant in the ditches in the pinewoods. Golden crest (*Lophiola aurea*) was a common sight all the way from the river to Telogia Creek. Yellow pitcher plant flourished from mileposts nine to fifty-two, but he spotted it only twice between Hosford and Sedalia. He began to see pond pine (*Pinus serotina*) near Liberty; titi about a mile north of there; tulip tree just above Telogia; loblolly, spruce pine, and sweet gum near Telogia Creek; upland willow oak (*Quercus cinerea*) and southern red oak (*Quercus falcata*) just beyond the creek; and devil's walkingstick (*Aralia spinosa*) at Hosford. Harper made some notes of wildlife and agriculture: he first saw "salamander hills," the burrows of pocket gophers, about a mile above Hosford, "cotton fields near Juniper, and tobacco fields near Hardaway."

He got off the train at Sneads, a railroad depot town west of Chattahoochee in Jackson County, observing, "This is quite a neat place, with eight or ten stores, some of them brick, a bank, hotel, turpentine still." As usual, although it was late afternoon, he took advantage of the last hours of daylight to explore, walking about a mile west of town and back. The countryside between the Apalachicola River and Sneads was "red Lafayette hills" with longleaf the dominant tree. The next morning, he found several log houses in oak-pine barrens, "like in the old agricultural regions of Georgia and Alabama." A train ride from Sneads to River Junction took just twelve minutes, and Harper arrived at the hotel in time for midday Sunday dinner. In the afternoon, he walked north to Chattahoochee on the Florida-Georgia line and found that the town had "twenty or thirty rather neat houses and two or three stores scattered over a high dissected plateau much like that back of Aspalaga, and probably 150 feet or more above the river." Harper walked down a steep bank to an old river landing and then through bottoms and ravines back to River Junction, happily finding "no swamps or briers" but also no stinking cedar. Then he made another thirty-minute walk from the hotel to the landing, where he boarded the southbound steamboat *J. W. Callahan, Jr.* As the boat passed Aspalaga Bluff, he took a photograph of it. Farther downstream, it passed Alum Bluff, "when [there was] just light enough to get a good look at it, but not enough to identify plants on it," Harper noted in his diary. "[It] is a grand sight, equal to all the other bluffs combined. It extends for some distance along [the] river, too." He disembarked for the night at Bristol Landing.

The next morning, Harper found another of Chapman's Aspalaga discoveries, Florida calamint (*Calamintha dentata*), for the first time, in full bloom at the edge of Bristol. "It is common in dry sandy pine-barrens around here, and extends pretty well down into the sandy hammocks, like several other species." It took him two hours to hike from the hotel down to the "second bottoms," a natural terrace about forty feet above the river, and up to a sandy plateau where longleaf pine and turkey oak (*Quercus laevis*) were the dominant trees, before reaching the brow of Alum Bluff. He "clambered over" the bluff for two hours, stepping carefully on the crumbling aluminous clay and coarse sand, taking photographs of plants and the "splendid view." Finding the flora in the ravines less diverse than at Aspalaga, Harper speculated that the soil lacked limestone. There was, however, plenty of stinking cedar and a few specimens of croomia. Harper noted that the Florida yew (*Taxus floridana*), of which there were a few on the bluff, was very similar to the elusive stinking cedar, but with finer, odorless foliage. He made it back to Bristol after ten hours of hiking. Harry Floyd joined Harper there, arriving before dawn the next day and then sleeping for a couple of hours.

The two men left at seven o'clock in a two-horse buggy for Hosford, eleven miles to the southeast, and crossed Mill and Telogia creeks. Harper found White Branch "a beautiful crystal-clear tributary of the Telogia in the Telogia Creek Swamp" with golden club growing at its edges. Between the seventh and ninth mileposts from Bristol, they observed a few specimens of purple pitcher plant, uncommon in the Southeast, growing near a sandy branch swamp in association with titi and sphagnum moss. At the edge of a titi bay, they saw odorless bayberry (*Myrica inodora*), which William Bartram first collected on the Tensaw River in Baldwin County, Alabama, in 1778. About two miles before Hosford, Harper made a stereo photograph of a pitcher plant bog. A mile closer to Hosford, he saw the rare endemic scareweed (*Baptisia simplicifolia*), another of Croom's finds. At midmorning Harper and Floyd reached Hosford, where the stores and houses were new and unpainted. They walked from the depot about two and a half miles down the railroad track and back. The day was sultry, and they stopped to bathe in Telogia Creek. From Hosford, the two men took a train north to Greensboro, where they "made a beeline for the fine new hotel noticed last week." Harper wrote, "It is partly surrounded by fine pine timber which was evidently round up to two or three years ago, and is now turpentined by [the] Herty system." They marveled at the view of longleaf pines from the hotel's upstairs porch. Rather than linger and enjoy the view, however, the men set off on another hike. They first walked a mile through "fine dry pine-barrens" that sloped "gently southeast off [the] plateau" and then through a sandy hammock of the Tallahassee Branch, through the sandy bottoms where Harper noted mountain laurel, beech, Florida anise, and sourwood. After walking another quarter mile to the community of Juniper and then "back east about three-fourths of a mile," they struck a railroad and caught a train back to Greensboro. Harper ended the day's diary entry with "Mosquitoes scarce in Greensboro."

Harper and Floyd left Greensboro at 7:16 a.m. on June 16. (Harper customarily noted the exact time of every arrival and departure.) They walked six or seven miles to Gretna, downhill through groves of southern red oak and level dry pine-barrens. From Gretna, Floyd apparently caught a train back to Apalachicola, while Harper walked west along the railroad track for a mile and back "to investigate a small creek-swamp seen several times from [the] train." At the end of this trek through Apalachicola River country, Harper took a train to Tallahassee and then "went right up to [the] office" to examine the mail. He recorded in his diary that he had received letters from home and from Sargent and Eugene Smith as well as wedding announcements from William Prouty, the geologist he had met on the 1908 Black Warrior River trip, and Marshall Avery Howe, the curator at the New York Botanical Garden.

After completing the field research for the Florida peat study, Harper returned to New York in August 1909. He spent the next few months at his mother's apartment in College Point, where he sorted his "library" of pamphlets, magazines, and railroad timetables in the building's attic; prepared and shipped sets of Florida specimens to the New York and Missouri Botanical Gardens; printed photographs of Florida; and drafted numerous articles, including more "car-window" phytogeographical accounts. He wrote popular accounts of the 1908 Black Warrior trip and other adventures but found no publisher for the manuscripts, and ultimately only had a more scientific version about the river trip published in the *Bulletin*. He sometimes spent a day rambling around New York or in the countryside. Although C. A. Davis, a geologist who was also interested in peat, visited him on October 28 and they discussed Harper's Florida notes on peat, he made little progress on the peat report for the Florida Geological Survey.[10]

In late December 1909 and early January 1910, following George Shull's advice, Harper attended scientific meetings of botanists and geologists in Boston. He met Henry Cowles and added in his diary that on the first day of the conference, he saw "about fifty botanists and fifteen geologists [he] knew, and a good many others who were strangers." He spent some time with Shreve, who was visiting the East Coast from the Desert Laboratory of the Carnegie Institution. He delivered a paper on prairies. At a "smoker," or reception, of the New England Botanical Club, he ran into his old friend and first botany role model, Clarence Knowlton. He showed his photographs of Florida to a geographer, F. G. Clapp, at the final session of the geographers. Harper stayed in Boston two extra days in order to call on Charles Sprague Sargent at Harvard. They discussed a possible Florida expedition for the purpose of finding new trees and new locations of rare plants, including some of Chapman's discoveries.

Harper worked in a more concentrated fashion after the Boston meetings. He wrote in his diary that he "worked some on [a] forestry map of Florida" on January 11, "spent most of the day writing second draft of first chapter on extratropical trees of Florida" on January 13, "typewrote ten pages on extratropical trees of Florida" on January 14, and wrote "five more pages . . . on Florida trees" on January 15. After sending the manuscript on Florida trees to Alfred Akerman on January 19, Harper launched several projects at once. Within two weeks, he began writing the scientific account of the Black Warrior trip, an article about the Everglades swamp, and a "car-window" account of "last summer's northward trip." On February 20, he started creating a map of the Carolinas. During this period, he tended to work on a different project each day. He also spent time every day clipping newspaper articles, mounting the articles on sheets of paper, mailing them to people, and recording to whom he mailed what in his small leather-bound diary. He often printed photographs before supper. One day during this busy period, Roland visited his father's grave in the Flushing cemetery with Bertha.

A few weeks after visiting Sargent at the Arnold Arboretum, Harper mailed him a proposal that Sargent fund a return trip to the area of Florida that Harper had explored in 1909, as well as the more western portion of the panhandle and the Gulf Hammock region. Choctawhatchee National Forest had been established in 1908 by the new United States Department of Agriculture Forest Service under the direction of Gifford Pinchot. Harper told Sargent he suspected that the lower Choctawhatchee River in Walton County had a flora similar to the upper Apalachicola River; perhaps he would find more *Torreya* there. Harper also wanted to follow rumors of *Torreya* at Wakulla Springs, in a region of limestone sinks south of Tallahassee. He warned, "I cannot promise to discover any new trees, for that is a pretty rare event in this day and time; but I generally have pretty good luck in finding rare plants." Sargent wanted Harper to look for Chapman's rhododendron (*Rhododendron minus* Michaux var. chapmanii), which Chapman had described without providing a precise location in 1876. Harper studied the available records at the New York Botanical Garden and speculated that he would find the rhododendron near St. Joseph's Bay in Gulf County or St. Andrew's Bay in Bay County, "for those [were] about the only places on the coast west of Apalachicola that Dr. Chapman [was] known to have visited." He wrote to Sargent, "I will look for it in April, which is said to be its flowering period." Sargent approved a collecting mission and sent Harper an advance of $100 in February 1910. Harper left almost immediately by train for Florida. He stopped in Washington, D.C., on March 2 to visit the National Herbarium and saw a collection of skulls that Theodore Roosevelt, the immediate past president, had sent to the Museum of Natural History from his famous two-year hunting expedition in Africa.[11]

Once in Tallahassee, Harper began a new itinerary of railroad and walking forays through the Florida countryside, first going to Marianna and Ponce de Leon in the central panhandle. By March 23, he had to take a break for a few days to let his blistered feet recover. He spent some time collecting specimens along the Suwannee River in Dixie County and in the adjoining area of lime-sink pine barrens, where most of the original pines had been lumbered and forest lands were being converted to agricultural use. After getting his shoes resoled on April 21, he left Tallahassee for Apalachicola. He spent the first night of this trip at Sopchoppy in southern Wakulla County, after taking a buggy ride "in a car drawn by two white horses," to Panacea, a fishing village originally known as Smith Springs, about seven miles to the southeast on Ochlockonee Bay.

At Panacea he explored the salt marshes and springs, which local real-estate developers promoted for their curative powers. As usual, he made notes of the flora along the road. "I found some specimens of *Cyrilla parvifolia* [littleleaf titi] which are large enough to be called trees. I think it is a distinct species, too, for besides the characters usually mentioned it differs from *C. racemiflora* in its bark. Its range is pretty well defined, too." (George Nash had collected a specimen of titi in Wakulla County in 1895 for the New York Botanical Garden and suggested in the *Bulletin of the Torrey Botanical Club* the following year that it was possibly a new species. However, Sargent did not accept Nash's and Harper's proposed new species of titi, indicating in his *Manual* that *C. racemiflora* is the only species of *Cyrilla* in the Americas.) After half an hour of rambling around Panacea, Harper walked back along the same road. The "intervening country [was] almost uninhabited, but all more or less lumbered and turpentined." It was a "clear cool moonlight night, with west wind"; perhaps a great horned owl called "hooh-hooh-hooh" from the trees. Someone built a fire in a fireplace at the hotel.[12]

A day later, after reaching Apalachicola, Harper struck out along the Apalachicola Northern Railroad through cut-over pine woods in search of Chapman's rhododendron but could not find it, although he noted other Chapman species, including the now endangered endemic, thick-leaf waterwillow (*Justicia crassifolia*), a plant Chapman had collected and named *Dianthera crassifolia* in 1860. He observed that because of lumbering in some places, the coast was visible from Huckleberry Creek. Turning south, he walked through flat pine barrens all the way to the shore of St. Vincent Sound, then along the shore seven or eight miles back to Apalachicola, noting "all gradations between this sea-cliff type of shore line and extensive dry-ish salt marshes, protected from waves by low sandy beaches (no dunes), furnishing grazing range for many cattle." He crossed small creeks with no difficulty, "for some [were] only one or two feet wide at their mouths." He found Chapman's cork-wood in "a small mucky spot" and speculated that he was at the very spot where Chapman had discovered the plant in 1860. Harper saw four snakes, two each of two species, in a big marsh three miles west of town. They could have been Apalachicola king snakes, heavy-bodied reptiles that can grow to be nearly six feet long and have various patterns of blotches, bands, and stripes. Although they are not poisonous, these snakes, which now are rare, would certainly command the attention of a solitary hiker. Or Harper might have stumbled upon a nonvenomous brownchin racer, a subspecies of constrictor that moves quite fast and will bite if provoked.[13]

The following morning, a Sunday, he revisited Chapman's grave and copied the epitaph for John Hendley Barnhart, one of his friends at the New York Botanical Garden. Then he took a train to Beverly, twelve miles to the north, and immediately began walking back to Apalachicola along the railroad track, passing through pine barrens, river swamps, an estuarine swamp, bayous, and open marshes. The railroad trestles over the East and St. Marks rivers were about fifteen feet high, but only about ten feet high in the middle of swamps. He found some "fine dewberries" at a campsite on the bank of the East River. He spotted another patch of corkwood and commented in his diary that it would have been inaccessible before the railroad was built. In the report to Sargent, he told of finding *Fraxinus floridana*, an ash that Sargent described in 1902 as a new species but that is now considered the species Carolina ash (*Fraxinus caroliniana*), acknowledging, "I suppose you have seen it somewhere near there yourself."[14] At 4:45 p.m. he reached the drawbridge over the Apalachicola River and had to wait until six o'clock for the bridge tender to appear and close it. "Rain began just then, and came down pretty hard about 6:30." He chatted with the bridge tender until the rain let up and "got a few interesting points on local geography . . . especially about a big quaking bog traversed by the new railroad about half way between Apalachicola and St. Joseph." Wet, and possibly tired after walking almost twelve miles, he caught a train at a flag station a short distance from town.

He ran into Dr. A. P. Taylor, an acquaintance from Thomasville, Georgia, at the hotel. They strolled around town Monday, and Harper spoke briefly with Harry Floyd on the street. He boarded the steamboat *Ruth No. 2* just after noon for another trip up the Apalachicola River. The sky cleared as they got under way, and Harper rode in the pilothouse, "three stories above the water, most of the time until supper and extracted a lot of information from [the] pilot and captain." He noted that the marshes of the first few miles gave way to estuarine swamps, which in turn yielded to alluvial swamps with larger trees. The boat passed a small settlement with orange groves and small shacks used by lumbermen who were cutting cypress. At one landing where the boat stopped, Harper collected specimens of what he thought was Carolina ash. Steamboats on the Apalachicola were known to serve excellent food—"On the down trips there were 'plenty of hot biscuits, hot cakes, meats, vegetables, pastries and the like'[;] [r]eturning from Apalachicola, plates brimmed with fresh shrimp, oysters, and fish." But Roland cared more for botanical views than for food and was frustrated that he lost a few miles of daylight scenery because supper was served before dark; even after the moon rose at 7:30 p.m., it was still too dark to identify the trees along the way. Harper did not make any new discoveries on the steamboat trip, but he emphasized to Sargent in his report that "[a]lthough Gray, Chapman, and various other botanists ha[d] made that trip before [him], none of them seem[s] to have mentioned the fact that the ranges of [cabbage palm] *Sabal Palmetto* and [American sycamore] *Platanus occidentalis* overlap a little on that river, and probably nowhere else. It was quite a surprise to [him]."[15]

They reached the Blountstown landing on the west side of the river in the middle of the cool and misty night. A local man who was seeing his family off on the steamboat gave Harper a ride into town, where he dropped his baggage at a livery stable and then walked around in the dark. The Marianna and Blountstown Railroad and a single spur to a new sawmill had been completed two months earlier, but there was still no depot, and Harper commented that the citizens of Blountstown seemed "rather primitive." When the train left at 9 a.m., Harper was on it, after not sleeping all night. He made train-window notes of geology and terrain and wondered where local residents quarried the limestone they used for chimneys. He reached Marianna in late morning and checked into a hotel, but began another hike at 1:30 p.m. Harper walked across a bridge over the Chipola River and back, then around the northern edge of town, two miles out through the red hills to the northwest, and back through a new section of Marianna on the west side. He quit for the day at 5:30 p.m.[16]

Intrigued by the limestone chimneys, Harper walked back to the western section of town the next morning, April 27, to make two photographs of them. He mailed postcards to friends, including Clarence Knowlton, before leaving on a train that he noted in his diary was two hours behind schedule. After getting off at Sneads, Harper began another hike to the west and south. He searched for stinking cedar on the western side of the Apalachicola, following "obscure roads through undulating mixed woods, with oaks predominating," where there were "a good many small farms scattered along." He wrote in his diary, "[A]fter going about four miles, [I] met two farmers who were born and raised in this neighborhood, and asked them about Ocheesee Landing, Schurlock's Spring, etc. They said that there was no . . . [stinking] cedar at [the] south end of

[Ocheesee] lake . . . but one of them had seen a few small trees in a sandy hammock" on the west of Ocheesee Lake. Inexplicably, he did not follow this new lead to a locality for stinking cedar.

Harper concluded his mission for Sargent in the last week of April 1910. In a long letter to Sargent a few days later, he admitted he had failed to find Chapman's rhododendron. "I did not find *Rhododendron Chapmanii*, but that is not surprising, and of course it would not do to waste much time looking for a plant whose location is so uncertain. I still think St. Andrew's Bay might be a good place to look for it, but I have not had time to go there this year yet, and there were so many nearer places that demanded attention."[17] It seems odd that Harper found what he believed was the type locality for Chapman's corkwood but did not persist in searching for Chapman's rhododendron—and odder that he would tell Sargent that the very task Sargent had specified, searching for Chapman's rhododendron, was a waste of time. Perhaps seeing four snakes in one day made him hesitate to continue searching creek bottoms and marshes.

After receiving Harper's plant collections, Sargent said that the specimen Harper had identified as Carolina ash was actually *Fraxinus profunda*, adding, "[I]t is interesting to get this fine species from a much more southern station than we knew it before." However, Sargent was disappointed in the number of specimens that Harper had collected for him on the two-month field trip. "There appeared to be forty plants, including several numbers of *Juniperus virginiana* [Eastern red cedar] and several species of *Crataegus* [hawthorn]. These last, of course, are of no value unless the specimens are completed, that is unless we have flowers, fruits and notes." He probably also was disappointed that Harper did not search longer for Chapman's rhododendron. "Perhaps, however, you have only [sent] a part of the specimens you gathered. . . . I hope I shall hear from you again soon."[18]

Although Harper had delivered less than Sargent wanted, he used his notes to prepare another journal article. "The River-bank Vegetation of the Lower Apalachicola, and a New Principle Illustrated Thereby" appeared in the November 1911 issue of *Torreya*. As he often did, he promoted his observations on the river as filling a gap in the findings of explorer-naturalists who had preceded him. He observed that more hardwood trees grew above Owl Creek, about thirty miles upriver from Apalachicola Bay, and more herbs and evergreen trees grew below that point. He hypothesized that fluctuations in water level contributed to development of what he characterized as climax vegetation, reflecting the scientific assumption of the time that vegetative succession was the driving force in ecological change. Harper conceded that observations on a single boat trip could not be considered conclusive, but said he had noted the same phenomena on other rivers. He suggested six possible variables in the ecology of the Apalachicola River vegetation, including cooler temperatures and taller and firmer banks upstream; greater humidity, milder winters, and greater salinity downstream; geological history; and seasonal variations in water volume, and concluded that the last variable, which contributed to greater fluctuations in water level upstream, was the most significant factor influencing the riverbank vegetation. He did not speculate on why water level fluctuation would allow development of hardwood, or climax, vegetation, instead suggesting this was a question that belonged "to ecology rather than phytogeography."[19]

Exploring the Apalachicola River again eight years later, Harper was the first to find stinking cedar in Georgia. He described his discovery in *Torreya*, the journal named, like the cedar itself, for the early botanist John Torrey, admitting that he had only extended the tree's northern range by about a mile, but because the tree was so well known as a Florida endemic, "the new locality being in a different state [would] necessitate a modification of the statements about it in books about North American trees, Georgia plants, etc." In the second edition of his *Manual of the Trees of North America*, published in 1922, Sargent credited Harper for determining that *Torreya*'s range along the Apalachicola River was only on the eastern side, between River Junction and Bristol in Liberty County, and for extending its range into the southwestern corner of Georgia.[20]

Harper's friends were getting married. Despite being interested in one of Harper's sisters in 1907, Forrest Shreve married Edith Coffin Bellamy, a physics instructor at the Woman's College in Baltimore, in 1909 during a return visit to the East Coast from the Carnegie Institution Desert Laboratory. Edith had earned a baccalaureate degree in chemistry and physics from the University of Chicago and taught at Judson College in Alabama before going to Baltimore. She became Forrest's lifelong scientific partner. Prouty, the geologist in Alabama, and Howe, the curator at the New York Botanical Garden, also married in mid-1909. Howe reported the next year that he and his wife had a new daughter, and Harper commented dryly, or perhaps plaintively, to the Pennsylvania ecologist John William Harshberger, "That sort of thing seems to be going on all around me these days." On a visit to Arkansas in 1910, Harper just missed

the Chapel Hill geologist Collier Cobb's wedding in that state. They were
in Arkansas at the same time, and Cobb, having heard that Harper was
in the neighborhood, attempted to invite him to his wedding. He later
wrote Harper: "[I] telephoned around Arkansas trying to get up with you
on my wedding day and have you at my marriage. Mrs. Cobb joins me in
hoping that we may soon have you as a guest in our home."[21]

Although he had met some interesting women in Tallahassee during
his first two stints in Florida, Harper clung to bachelorhood. Nonetheless, it is clear that Harper longed to marry. A. M. Henry of the Florida
Department of Agriculture, one of Roland's rambling, botanizing friends
in Tallahassee, wanted to introduce Harper to a woman he thought would
be a good wife, although he guessed that Roland might be slow to seize
the opportunity. "That girl that I have picked out for you is all-right.
She is between twenty-five and thirty now and I think that she will wait
a while on you. She is good looking, not as tall as you, but weighs about
as much, and has blue eyes, I believe. You had better come and see her."
Charles Rice, who worked in the Office of the President at the University
of Alabama, also had a girl in mind for Roland. He wrote, "Miss Mar-
tin . . . said nice things of you. Really, I think you had better come back
to Old Ala and win you a home with her. Now don't blush, for she likes
you and with a little coaching would come your way. I'm not teasing, so
come back."[22]

Roland had probably confided his wish for a wife and the competing
urge to spend all his time botanizing to his friend H. E. Wheeler. Wheeler
wrote, "Some day your 'princess' will come along, and botany will take a
rest. You will find me rejoicing with you, for a good wife and prudent is
no mean (scientific) equipment. Don't defer the opportunity too long."
Harper seems to have confided an interest in a particular woman. When
Wheeler moved to Arkansas in 1910 to accept a ministerial post and urged
Harper to visit him, he seems to have known that Harper was dreaming
of someone in particular. "I shall be the more delighted if you can bring
with you the young lady whose consent to follow you 'whithersoever' you
go, I shall dream and hope you have obtained. If you deem it expedient
and timely tell this young lady that I already esteem her for your sake.
May a kindly Providence lead you both."[23]

The woman whom Harper mentioned to Wheeler in 1910 may have
been Florence Elsie Blake of Talladega, Alabama. Florence and Roland
were high school classmates in Dalton; afterward, she moved with her
mother and sister to the vicinity of Talladega. Florence visited Roland's

mother in College Point in 1908, and Bertha was thrilled, writing to Roland, "Florence Blake keeps writing very affectionately. . . . She seems to be very fond of you, and has a deep appreciation of your character and knowledge. . . . She is just my ideal of a girl. Has health, beauty, grace, a lot of common sense, independence from much travel, ambition, a good business head, and comes from fine, and long-lived stock. I love her." Florence returned to New York in August 1909 and visited the American Museum of Natural History with Roland and Bertha before departing on a steamship, probably bound for Boston. Florence's mother spent two nights with the Harpers that October while traveling in the Northeast. Harper repaid the visit in 1910, visiting Florence and her mother at their summer home after attending the dedication of Smith Hall at the University of Alabama, and taking the opportunity to ramble over the Pine Mountains of nearby Meriwether County, Georgia. Afterward he boasted to his old friend Clarence Knowlton, "[T]wo girls that I used to go to school with in Dalton about 19 years ago now live in Talladega, Alabama, and they with their mother were spending a few weeks in a summer cottage at the foot of the Blue Ridge, and . . . invited me to come and stay with them awhile while I was up that way." He downplayed his relationship with Florence in a letter to Forrest Shreve, but sent Florence an album of photographs and pressed flowers as a memento of his visit. She was effusive in thanking him for it. They continued to correspond, but Roland also hinted to Florence in November 1910 that there was another woman in Alabama who interested him, and that he wanted nothing more than friendship from Florence.[24]

Eugene Smith encouraged Harper to attend the commencement and dedication of his namesake Smith Hall on the University of Alabama campus. Smith was proud of the new building, which had classrooms, offices for the biology and geology departments and the geological survey, and a stunning lobby and mezzanine with display cases for the collections of the Museum of Natural History. He had helped design the building, which resembled natural history museums in Washington, New York, and Chicago. Joseph Austin Holmes of the United States Geological Survey spoke at the dedication on the morning of May 30. Attending the ceremony was an opportunity for Harper to join a tribute to Smith, his patron and sometime employer. Smith was given a silver loving cup at the university alumni banquet, and Harper wrote, "I guess I was as proud of it as he was." He admired Smith so greatly that earlier in the spring he had challenged a friend, a paleontologist at the Smithsonian Institution, for what Harper perceived to be a scientific slight of Smith. Edward Berry apparently had written about the paleontology or geology of Alabama's coastal plain without acknowledging Smith's research. Berry replied, "My dear Harper, . . . I have a great deal of respect and still more affection for Dr. Smith but I must say that I got absolutely no information from him on this subject."[25]

Harper's solicitousness for Smith seems to have been reciprocated. As Harper completed the Florida peat report in the fall of 1910, with no more work available in Tallahassee and without another collecting commission from Sargent, Smith came through with a new temporary job. Smith did not have money in his budget to give Harper a permanent position, but he offered to hire him temporarily to organize the geological survey's library in its new offices. "I know you took a great deal of interest in that," Smith wrote to him. He also wanted Harper to choose photographs to illustrate a timber report the survey was preparing to publish.[26] And so Harper decamped for Smith Hall.

CHAPTER FIVE

Harper's Heartleaf

For the next two decades, from 1911 to 1931, Roland Harper moved from one temporary job to another, for the most part alternating between the Alabama Geological Survey and the Florida Geological Survey, where Eugene Smith and Elias Sellards each valued his ability to survey the landscape and map vegetative types because this helped them to map soil types. Harper supplemented his income by selling plant specimens to various herbaria and spent one academic year at the University of Georgia. Smith wanted to hire Harper permanently at the Alabama survey—even inviting Harper to become a charter member of the Alabama Natural History Society—but state funding for the survey was inadequate. "I wish I was in position to have you here," Smith wrote to Harper in 1914. "I hope your work in Florida will continue for [some] time anyhow."[1] During this long, nomadic period of his life, Harper formed strong friendships in both states but eventually chose Alabama as his permanent home.

Despite Harper's admiration for William Bartram and his later interest in population genetics, he was apparently unaffected by an encounter with the father of mutation theory, Hugo de Vries, when de Vries came to Alabama to visit the site where William Bartram had collected the largeflower evening primrose (*Oenothera grandiflora*) in 1778. Although Harper wrote a lengthy account of the route he took to meet de Vries' party near "Taensa," he noted almost nothing about the great scientist and in fact spent very little time with him.

On earlier trips to the United States in 1904 and 1906, de Vries had collected specimens of the genus *Oenothera*, and Nathaniel Britton of the New York Botanical Garden suggested to him in 1904 that he visit the type locality for *Oenothera grandiflora*, a species that was similar, or perhaps identical, to the species that de Vries used in his mutation experiments.[2] De Vries belatedly took the advice and traveled through Tuscaloosa and southern Alabama September 21–26, 1912, on his third and last visit to the United States. He was touring the southern states with

H. H. Bartlett of the United States Department of Agriculture, before going to Houston, Texas, to give an honorary lecture at Rice University.[3] DeVries and Bartlett spent one night in Tuscaloosa, where Eugene Smith hosted a reception in Smith Hall and Harper displayed specimens of the largeflower evening primrose that he and a colleague, A. L. Barker, had collected earlier in the day near Riverview on the Black Warrior River.[4]

Smith, Bartlett, and de Vries departed by train the next day for Mobile via Meridian, while Harper remained in Tuscaloosa, preparing to travel more directly to the type locality for Bartram's primrose and meet the de Vries group on the twenty-sixth. He and Barker left by train on September 24; they were joined by a recent university graduate, P. V. Donald, at Marion Junction and continued to Suggsville, where they spent a night in a small hotel that primarily served railroad employees. After taking another train to Jackson the next morning, they set off on foot from the Tombigbee River to the Alabama River. They crossed the Alabama in a skiff at Choctaw Bluff, entering Monroe County. Harper and Barker walked about five miles through "muddy river bottoms" to the confluence of the Alabama and Little rivers, seeing along the way the remarkable five-foot largeflower evening primrose once or twice. Harper "swiped a stalk of sugar-cane and chewed it" before they stopped for the night in open pine barrens, where they made a campfire and slept on pallets of yankeeweed (*Eupatorium compositifolium*), with Barker's raincoat as a roof. As he went to sleep, Harper may have wondered if any rare Florida panthers, the "tygers" Bartram described seeing in the area in 1778, still roamed nearby. Perhaps Harper even heard one's distinctive scream during the night; panthers were considered nearly extinct in 1912, yet one's track was confirmed in adjoining Clarke County in 1961.[5]

The men were wakened by rain at three o'clock and finally arose at 5:30 a.m.; they struggled to rebuild the fire and dry their clothes. They resumed their trek at 7 a.m., walking through more rain and huddling in a small sawmill after crossing the Little River. When the shower stopped, they continued, walking west another three miles "through flattish pine-barrens lumbered and turpentined." They probably carried with them the 1909 soil map of Baldwin County prepared by the United States Department of Agriculture, which showed Dixie Landing on the southern side of the Alabama, just to the west of where the Little River empties into it, inside Baldwin County and slightly west of the community of Little River.

By midmorning, they reached Dixie Landing, believed to be Bartram's type locality for the primrose, where Harper observed "several people fishing . . . with nets, some of them living in tents." Smith, Bartlett, and de Vries arrived at noon on the steamboat *City of Mobile*, having retraced Bartram's voyage up the Mobile Delta, and Harper presented de Vries with some newspaper clippings about his visit to Tuscaloosa. The rain stopped, and Harper took a photograph of the view downriver from the landing, the Alabama broad and smooth, a wide curving sandbar a short distance away on the opposite bank. But he made no record of de Vries' reaction to reaching the type locality for largeflower evening primrose and in fact took little opportunity to observe the great scientist in the field, for he and Barker left in less than an hour on the steamboat. The de Vries party searched unsuccessfully for Lamarck's primrose (at the time considered a separate species from *O. grandiflora* but in 1997 reclassified as a subspecies of it). De Vries observed the cotton fields and weedy areas near the river and commented that the homes of black field workers were not very tidy. Meanwhile, Harper and Barker traveled through the night on the *City of Mobile* and disembarked at Dan Lee's Landing in western Monroe County, where they began another trek.[6]

Harper had at least four opportunities to talk with the famous geneticist: when he and Smith met de Vries and Bartlett at the depot in Tuscaloosa on September 21, at the reception that evening, the next morning when de Vries visited the geological survey office, and finally at Dixie Landing in Baldwin County on September 26. But the only detail Harper preserved in his diary of this momentous encounter was that he "showed mounted Florida pictures to de Vries, and gave him several pamphlets." In contrast, he not only made his usual detailed field notes of changes in elevation, vegetation, and built structures along the way from Jackson to Dixie Landing but also listed the foods he and Barker enjoyed at a picnic they encountered at Rockville on September 25. In his old age, Harper recalled that Dixie Landing was "a very interesting trip."[7] Two months after de Vries' visit, Bradley Moore Davis of the University of Pennsylvania suggested in the *Bulletin of the Torrey Botanical Club* that the plant de Vries used in his experiments was, in fact, the same species that Bartram had introduced in England from Alabama in 1778.[8]

Traveling from Tallahassee to Tuscaloosa in 1924, Harper stopped in Montgomery to see an ornithologist friend, Ernest G. Holt. Holt took Harper to visit his uncle, Lewis S. Golsan, in Autauga County, for the weekend of May 17–19. Shortly after arriving, they explored the woods near Golsan's house. Harper was candid and charmingly informal later in describing how they stumbled across an unknown, endemic species of *Hexastylis*, a relative of wild ginger. "I was walking with Mr. Holt down alongside one of the spring branches about two hundred yards north of the house, and about at the point where the sandy bogs ended and the richer woods began I noticed a few specimens of a heart-leaf (*Hexastylis*), and was about to pass them by as being the common *H. arifolia*, when Mr. Holt stooped down and pulled up a plant, with the remark, 'What's this?' I then saw at once that it had flowers very different from those of *H. arifolia*, or any other species known to me, and I made a note of the time (5:45 p.m., Central Time)." The tubelike flowers emerged from the base of the plant, rather like a cluster of egg cups glazed a vivid maroon on the inside, with white at the bottom of each cup and in rays around the bottom. Holt drew a sketch of the specimen.

The two men went back to the site the next morning, Sunday, and dug up a specimen. On returning to the house, they found that Holt's sister Olivia, who lived in Montgomery, and some other relatives and friends had arrived, bringing a picnic lunch. As the group ate beneath the trees outside the house, Harper probably talked excitedly about the new species with heart-shaped leaves and dramatic maroon flowers. After lunch, he and Ernest rigged a backdrop of white fabric and photographed the plant. Watching them work, Olivia volunteered to have the plant professionally photographed in Montgomery. When she and the others left before dark, she took a sample with her.

Back in Tuscaloosa two days later, Harper sent a postcard to the New York Botanical Garden with carefully drawn side and front views of the flower and this message: "As soon as you report on the plants I sent you from Florida last week I will tell you about a new *Hexastylis* that I found between here and Montgomery a few days ago. Here are two views of the flower, natural size. Did you ever see anything like it?" He subsequently sent a complete pressed specimen, a clear color image of which survives in the digital collection of the New York Botanical Garden, the three heart-shaped leaves and the roots carefully held in place by thin strips of white paper, Harper's handwritten postcard attached in the upper left corner of the sheet, and his typed label, "*Hexastylis*, sandy but moderately rich woods about two miles east of Booth, Autauga Co. R. M. Harper and E. G. Holt, May 18, 1924," and the handwritten annotation "*speciosa*."[9] He also sent a specimen to the United States National Herbarium at the Smithsonian Institution, where it rests in the herbarium's collection of isotypes, the flower's deep red color faded but the dramatic heart shape of the leaves still evident, and the photograph that Harper and Holt made in Golsan's house attached to the specimen sheet.[10]

In a report of the discovery in *Torreya*, Harper thoroughly described the morphology of the plant, declaring it a new species and proposing the name *Hexastylis speciosa* "in allusion to its showy flowers." He ventured, "It seems likely that we have one more to add to the rather long list of very distinct and handsome plants which are more abundant in Alabama than anywhere else, if not confined to the state." Of the photograph Olivia had made at a Montgomery photography studio, Harper wrote that it showed "the appearance of the plant better than words can."[11]

Olivia, forty-two years old and single, was more than a casual friend to Roland. She began wooing him by correspondence in 1919, apparently at Ernest's suggestion. She invited Roland to come to Montgomery to go botanizing with her and some of her friends and repeatedly suggested that Bertha, whom she had never met, visit her in Montgomery. She was strikingly flirtatious, hinting that they should go swimming together and saying that she thought of him "very often." She mentioned in a letter to Roland that she was able to cook for a crowd, and when that did not elicit a response, she emphasized her outdoor skills, at the same time deftly suggesting images of herself in wet clothes and reclining: "I went on a camp, got caught in three rains, walked all night, got back at 3:00 a.m., and went swimming, then slept out with the screech owls in my wet clothes." Describing another botanizing ramble, she created an image of a wanton woman of the woods: "We got lost in a wild jungle and had to crawl through briar patches. Finally we wound up in the swamp and had a wonderful swim in Catoma Creek." She hinted that she thought of him while dressing and undressing: "I always think of you when I go to buy a dress or anything and wonder what you will say about it." Roland did not respond to her hints, advising her that Bear Creek would be too cold for swimming in October and that he was a poor judge of fashion. Still, he corresponded with her and counted her among his "girlfriends," even attending Easter services at a Presbyterian church with her in 1927.[12]

That summer, however, he committed a strategic error, taking Olivia's cousin Clare Shackelford to dinner and a movie, even though he found her silly and shallow in comparison to Olivia. He grew cocky about his standing with Montgomery women, sending a letter to the *Montgomery Advertiser* praising its "many beautiful ladies (of all ages)" and crowing in a letter to his mother that dating in Montgomery was cheap. Harper's indecision over Olivia and Clare must have annoyed the cousins, for afterward they both gave him a cold shoulder.[13] After pursuing Roland for eight years, Olivia seems to have found his courting her cousin Clare too much to tolerate.

Following the dating debacle, Bertha inquired twice about Roland's "Montgomery girl." Perhaps Olivia had stopped responding to Roland's letters for a time, for Bertha commented, "I wonder what happened at Montgomery that you ceased to hear? . . . Well, there are plenty of others." Two months later she probed again: "How about your Montgomery girl? . . . I bet there are just as good at Athens."[14] Roland tried to visit Olivia at her boardinghouse in November 1928, but she declined to see him, claiming to have a cold. He persisted and went to her office the next day, but did not record what transpired between them.

The next month, lonely and on the brink of a life-threatening illness, Harper wrote to Olivia. At the time, in a move that surprised and concerned some of his friends in the basic sciences, Harper was serving a one-year appointment to the faculty of the new Institute for Research in the Social Sciences at the University of Georgia. Alfred Akerman wrote, "Somehow I have felt for several years that you would do better to stick closer to botany; but that is just my notion. Any man should follow his bent, if he has a chance to do so; and since you are not bound by family ties to the same extent that some of the rest of us are, I suppose you are all the more justified." There was an outbreak of influenza on the campus, and by December 19, Harper was seriously ill. For the next five days, he did little but prepare Christmas cards, mailing one to Olivia on December 23. That afternoon, not comprehending how sick he was, Roland took a long solitary walk around the edges of Athens. He worked on some small statistical projects. He spent the morning of Christmas Day inside and put on a new suit to go to dinner at the home of friends. He worked intermittently for the next few days, but on December 28 he called for a doctor and sent word to Otto that he was ill. Two days later, his physician had Harper transported to the Athens hospital by ambulance. Harper wrote in his diary that the doctor told him he had the "flu," but Harper knew it was actually pneumonia, a far more serious condition. He continued to make diary entries until January 2 but was too sick to write again until February 1. During that frightening month, Bertha came from California to stay by Roland's side. Otto also arrived, and Francis sent their brother a special delivery letter, urging him to get better soon.[15]

The family hired a private duty nurse, Evelyn Smith, to attend to Roland, and he became infatuated with her but continued to think of Olivia.

He spent two months in the hospital, undergoing surgery for a lung in-
fection, drawing cartoons of hospital life, and attempting to write various
articles. On Valentine's Day, he wrote to Olivia again. There is no record
that she replied. Still slowly recovering after his release from the hospital
on March 3, Harper visited Otto's home in Harlem, Georgia, accompanied on the train by Otto and Bertha. From there he and his mother
took a train to Augusta, where they visited the nurse, Evelyn Smith. He
presented her a copy of his cartoon of hospital life and as an afterthought
even bought a frame for it. They returned to Harlem on March 14. Roland wrote to Olivia three times that month. When he traveled with Bertha to Montgomery on March 30, he finally was able to see Olivia. They
had dinner together at her home; he also saw her the next day. Perhaps
it was clear to him that there was no prospect of a future with Olivia, for
Roland mailed a souvenir card to Evelyn on the same trip, and even visited
Florence Blake at Talladega that spring.[16]

On a short trip to Warm Springs, Georgia, in May, Harper met Edwin Hicks, the son of a Cornell University botanist whom Harper must
have known. Hicks took Harper to meet Franklin Delano Roosevelt, then
governor of New York, who was at the Warm Springs resort for treatment of polio. They visited with Roosevelt at his cottage for half an hour;
typically, Harper recorded the approximate times of the day's itinerary
but nothing of the substance of his conversation with Roosevelt. Harper
completed his one-year appointment at the University of Georgia, preparing a report of Georgia's natural resources that the university published
in its bulletin, but the long illness prevented him from accomplishing any
major social science projects.[17]

He returned to the type locality for his heartleaf more than once in
the years to follow. In the fall of 1933, Harper found plants that appeared
to be the same species eight miles west of the original location, but since
they were not in bloom he could not be sure. In May 1937, he found *Hexastylis speciosa* in a swamp on Whitewater Creek, about three miles north
of Autaugaville, and again sent a specimen to the United States National
Herbarium. He saw Olivia again in 1939, when he was sixty-one years old
and traveling through Montgomery, but it was a brief encounter.[18]

Living in Tallahassee during his stints at the Florida Geological Survey,
working near the campus of Florida State College for Women, and often
socializing with college faculty members, Harper became friends with
some of the town's socially prominent citizens. He met the Eppes family

of Tallahassee, including Susan Bradford Eppes, the daughter of a Florida planter and physician, Edward Bradford. Her parents had owned Pine Hill, a plantation in the longleaf hills near Tallahassee, until about 1868. Around the end of the Civil War, she had married Confederate Lieutenant Nicholas Ware Eppes, whose father, Francis Eppes, was a grandson of President Thomas Jefferson, an early mayor of Tallahassee, and a founder of Florida State College for Women. A sweet-faced woman with a cloud of white hair, Mrs. Eppes was a popular social and literary figure in Tallahassee and a significant keeper of the flame of southern sentimentality about both the slave system and the lost longleaf forests.[19]

In her memoir, *Through Some Eventful Years* (1926), Mrs. Eppes romanticized life in the prewar South, including trips to springs and the beach. "Oh, for 'the days that are no more,'" she mourned. As Rembert Patrick characterized her work, "She outdid some other partisan Southerners . . . and confirmed the ideas of Floridians who found solace in a delightful never-never land." She rhapsodized about the countryside of longleaf forest north of Tallahassee: "Riding out from Tallahassee on the Thomasville Road, look to your right, where you will see a rather unusual valley with a high hill on either side. . . . In days gone by, these two hills were crowned by lovely woods; [when] the dogwood was in bloom and so numerous were these beautiful trees that the hills seemed covered with a lacy veil. Yellow jasmine gave a touch of gold and the turf beneath was white with the delicate Houstonia." Pine Hill "was situated amid rolling hills and green forests, with little streams here and there, and a clear, quiet stream wending its way to one of the placid lakes, which beautify this fair land. God's Country, its people claim it is." Again she extolled the beauty of the longleaf woods, writing "a solemn silence reigned" over the pine forest on "a bright, beautiful Sunday afternoon in late November. . . . The sun was traveling westward and its slanting rays fell softly on the glistening brown pine-straw, which lay like a thick carpet beneath the trees."[20]

Roland and his mother spent considerable time with the Eppeses during a visit that Bertha made to Tallahassee in 1920, and Bertha must have made a good impression. Mrs. Eppes suggested the next year that Bertha and Wilhelmina move to Tallahassee, indicating they could get jobs at Florida State College for Women. She also hinted at a professorship and two potential brides for Harper if he would settle in Tallahassee permanently. "You know very well it is only your excessive modesty that stands in the way of a Professor-ship for yourself in the Florida State College for

Women. . . . It would be so pleasant to have you living so near; we could have such delightful picnics." She added that "Edward and the daughters," meaning her son and daughters, sent greetings. Bertha apparently became fairly well acquainted with the Eppes family. In a running dispute with Roland over where to store his enormous collection of pamphlets, newspaper clippings, and other papers, Bertha turned Roland's friendship with the Eppeses against him, writing sarcastically that he should tell the Eppes family "what a cruel, heartless Mama you have to tear up the home nest so the fledglings wont [*sic*] know where to go."[21]

Another friend at Florida State College for Women was young Herman Kurz, a junior botanist who became a friend and sometimes accompanied Harper on field treks. On an afternoon in April 1924, they walked from Tallahassee north on the road to Thomasville, Georgia. Harper noted in his diary that they passed by "moderately rich" longleaf woods on a "millionaire's estate." The next month Harper, Kurz, and two "ladies" took a drive or train ride to St. Marks, a town on Apalachee Bay south of the capital. Harper noted that plenty of longleaf was still growing in Wakulla County, although some stands had been turpentined twice. Three years later, while Harper spent another period in Alabama, Kurz wrote to him that he had found a new orchid on the slope of a huge limestone sinkhole near Sopchoppy and a new iris in the flatwoods near Lanark. Kurz essentially retraced Harper's trail on the Apalachicola River in the summer of 1936 to discover if *Torreya* grew on the western bank. He paid homage to Harper in 1938 in a paper on plant associations along the river, acknowledging the foundation Harper lay for ecological study of the Apalachicola River basin in his report on the geography of northern Florida: "Listing one hundred and fifty species he relates them to such habitats as 'bottoms,' 'banks,' 'bluffs,' 'swamps,' 'richwoods,' and so on. Harper's work is also valuable for its references."[22]

Harper roomed in the Tallahassee home of W. L. Marshall and became friends with Marshall and his family, sometimes accepting their invitations to dinner or to accompany them on day or weekend trips to Lanark Village, a resort community on the coast where the Georgia, Florida and Alabama Railroad had built a hotel to lure tourists. On a Sunday outing to Lanark on August 2, 1914, with the Marshalls, Harper got off the train at McIntyre and walked the remaining eight miles along the track. Following the curving track around dense titi bays, he sensed slight changes in elevation where he observed turkey oak and other dry pine-barren plants and exposed banks of yellowish sand, and surmised that the rises were ancient dunes. He noted that except for a few cornfields, the country around McIntyre was "uncultivated and uninhabited." After reaching Lanark, Harper joined the Marshalls and "loafed" until 4 p.m., when, despite the heat, he set out alone to explore the interior, picking his way through "pocosin-like bays" and finding a section of pines that had not been turpentined. Walking back, he crossed more old dunes to rejoin the Marshalls and board the train to Tallahassee, noting that it was a "nice moonlight night." On another Lanark trip in July 1920, he and the Marshalls went swimming in the moonlight two nights in a row.[23]

After Harper returned to College Point for a few weeks in the fall of 1920, young William Marshall wrote to him, "Dear Dr. Harper, I miss you. I want you to come back. When are you coming back? School has started and I don't like it. I don't get time to play any more. . . . Good bye, William Marshall." William's sister Elizabeth also wrote that day. Back in Tuscaloosa in the summer of 1921, Harper sent comics to the Marshall children, and they wrote letters in return. Young Addison wrote that the family had visited an uncle in Apalachicola, staying on St. George Island for a week. "We had turtle, turtle eggs, all sorts of fish and plenty of shrimp. We also had plenty of sand flies, yellow flies and mosquitoes. . . . While in Apalachicola I had a motorboat at my disposal. I sailed (in a sailboat) down the beach about five miles and had lots of fun in some pretty woods."[24]

Friends continued to offer matchmaking help when Roland was in his midforties. Harshberger, at the Brooklyn Institute of Arts and Sciences at the time, found a prospect for Roland in 1921: "If you want a West Philadelphia girl for a wife, I think one might be found with economical tastes, who might be proud to have Roland M. Harper for a husband." However, Mrs. Eppes thought Harper should court a widow named Mrs. Robertson or a woman in Thomasville, Georgia, who had a "lovely, large house" where he could store his books and papers.[25]

On botanizing treks in middle Florida, Roland sometimes stopped over with Fenton and David Alonzo Avant of Mount Pleasant, Florida.[26] Harper had known Fenton Garnett Davis before she married Avant. A student of Latin at Florida State College for Women before her marriage, she enjoyed talking with Roland about the Latin names of native plants. He also helped her in her genealogical research about her family. It was probably Fenton, not her husband, who invited Roland to stay at their home on her family's plantation when he passed through Gadsden County. He accepted this invitation more than once, sometimes showing up unannounced and spending the night on a sleeping porch that Fenton and David had added to the house after they bought it the year they married. Another time, he spent a rainy weekend at the Avants' home, rambling around when the showers stopped and attending Quincy Baptist Church, where David was a deacon, with them. Once he and Fenton took her two boys, eight-year-old David Alonzo Avant II and six-year-old George Avant, on a long trek around the Davis plantation, crossing Plantation Field and going through the bottoms along Mosquito Creek. Another time, the family had planned a picnic with Roland and several teacher friends in Quincy, but rain kept them inside. Harper drew a cartoon for Fenton's little boys that showed the family on an imaginary picnic, including a character George remembered as "the little fool" that was probably Roland's signature cartoon character, the "Maniac." In Avant family legend, Harper was in love with Fenton and regretted not proposing to her. Her husband probably teased her about her friendship with Harper, continuing the ribbing decades later when their grandsons were around to hear the stories. As the story of Roland Harper passed through generations of the Davis-Avant family, the botanist became mythologized as "very smart" but "a weirdo, like a tramp."[27]

Louis S. Moore of nearby Thomasville, Georgia, a wealthy lawyer, railroad buff, and bibliophile, became another good friend of Harper. Somewhat younger than Roland, Moore was a childhood friend of Wilhelmina, Otto, and Francis in Americus and attended the University of Georgia while Harper was at Columbia. Moore and Harper shared the urge to collect books and documents. The lawyer sometimes visited the geologists in Tallahassee; he reported to Roland in January 1921 that Gunter was having the geological survey's property packed for moving into new quarters in the Florida Capitol. He assured Harper that the survey's books were still in order as Harper had arranged them. Moore volunteered to drive Francis to Tallahassee to visit Roland in March 1921. That summer, he described some of his recent book acquisitions to Roland: "I don't know if Pendleton's Okefinokee story is the same as that printed in the Youth's Companion but presume it is. I have another book of his called 'King Tom and the Runaways' whose scene is largely in the swamp. I have also recently found a book of stories by Maurice Thompson called 'Stories of the Cherokee Hills' which I have found quite readable." Moore's library grew to eight thousand volumes, but his loose papers were also striking. A Thomasville newspaper reporter later wrote, "[The] Honorable L. S. Moore has one of the most interesting libraries in the state. It is built up after years of effort and presents a most interesting array of volumes."[28]

When Moore's mother died in 1921, the lawyer became depressed and planned a trip to New York, hoping to see Harper there. The next spring Moore ran for the Georgia Senate, but was self-deprecating about his campaign in a letter to Harper: "My announcement for the State Senate is in the papers this afternoon and I am hoping to be elected without opposition. . . . This doesn't mean that I am getting into politics as you are familiar with the fact that the rotation system makes a senator ineligible for re-election." By 1927, Moore was chairman of the Railroad Committee of the Georgia Senate. On a train trip from Tallahassee to Athens the following year, Harper stopped in Thomasville for noon dinner at Moore's house and a fifteen-mile hike in the countryside. Harper also showed the lawyer some comics and "a few other things" and then called on a local lady friend.[29]

Because of its proximity to Tuscaloosa, Hale County became a favorite field-trip destination for Harper. He returned repeatedly to the prairies and longleaf woods in its southern section, exploring the forests, creek bottoms, and small towns and photographing the built environment as well as the natural landscape. Pieced together, the evidence of his many trips to Hale County reveals his interest in the unfolding history of the place and his sense of himself as a witness to change there.

He apparently first visited the county in January 1906, when he probably walked along the Norfolk Southern Railway from Tuscaloosa to Akron, making a photograph of an "isolated specimen" of sweet gum near the track.[30] He passed through Hale County a second time in 1908 on the houseboat trip with Smith, Wheeler, and the other geologists. On the eastern bluff above the river were the remaining mounds of a Mississippian community. The rolling terrain of Hale County's prairies, directly south of Tuscaloosa, was the southern edge of the Fall Line hills, themselves the base of the Appalachian Plateau and the Piedmont. Here the earth rolled gently up and down, and the wide valleys were like shallow green bowls beneath the vast sky.

In May 1911, Harper photographed valleys and hills in the northeastern part of the county, where longleaf still covered the land. He photographed a pasture and the valley of a small creek four miles southeast of the county seat of Greensboro in March 1919. In the fall of that year, he captured a "Black Belt upland scene about nine miles south of Greensboro, showing

[a] big barn, silos, and pastures," where live oaks hugged the meandering creeks and streams. Walking along Highway 61 on the eastern edge of the county on September 2, 1922, he passed cattle fields and pecan groves and crossed Dry and Big Prairie creeks, taking a picture of "three wagons gathering alfalfa in [the] bottoms of Dry Creek." Later the same day, he passed Newbern, a community with several brick and clapboard commercial buildings, at least one of them two-story, and photographed a grove of loblolly pine northwest of town.[31]

He returned to the eastern part of the county three weeks later. Referring to the times he noted for his photographs, the United States Geological Survey's topographical map of the county, and a 1931 soil survey map by the United States Department of Agriculture, one can deduce that he walked or rode from Moundville down Highway 69 through Havana, stopping around 11 a.m. to make three photographs of the shady ravine along a branch of Gile Creek. Heading for Greensboro, he continued southwest on Highway 69 for a short distance, came to the Southern Railway, and turned down it to the southeast. At 3:30 that afternoon, he photographed a stock pond in a pasture. Climbing to a hilltop northwest of the tiny community of Rosemary at 4:10 p.m., he photographed the "undulating prairies," which had "a good deal of original prairie vegetation on dry chalky uplands, though damaged by grazing."[32]

Harper went back to the prairies south of Greensboro the next spring and photographed a "grove or thicket" above Cedarville, probably along Highway 69, and that afternoon made pictures of rolling prairie and cotton and cornfields southwest of the town. At Prairieville, he photographed a substantial old two-story house with a central corridor and balcony and the lovely Gothic-style St. Andrew's Episcopal Church and adjacent cemetery, noting that all the trees in the graveyard were cedars.[33]

Harper and Tomlinson Fort, a member of the university's Department of Mathematics who was eight years Harper's junior, took a drive on June 7, 1924, from Tuscaloosa to Demopolis in Marengo County. They detoured down eastern Hale County through Havana, where they visited the grave of Julia Strudwick Tutwiler, a famous college administrator and prison reformer who had died eight years earlier. They stopped in Greensboro for a midday dinner, and Harper made a picture of mule-drawn wagons of hay and the view east down Greensboro's main street.[34] After heading south on Highway 25, they took a rutted road east toward Rosemary, where Harper again photographed the prairie, composing views with Boykin's milkwort (*Polygala boykinii*) in the foreground. Returning to Highway 25, they drove south through the communities of Whitsitt, Sledge, and Laneville. Immediately south of Laneville, they passed a pair of matching stone gateposts with "Bell" chiseled on the left post's cap and "Hill" chiseled on the right, marking the entrance to Bell Hill on the west side of the road. Pecan trees lined both sides of a drive leading to the base of a hill that resembled a Mississippian mound. Turning west on Highway 25, Harper and Fort crossed Cottonwood Creek and passed through Prairieville before reaching Demopolis at 5:15 p.m. That evening they visited Hudson Strode, a professor in the Department of English, and Strode's parents, and also called on the father of two former students at the university.[35]

The next surviving photographs of Hale County by Harper indicate that he returned to the vicinity of Prairieville on March 23, 1932, two days after tornadoes struck the Deep South, killing 268 people, most of them in Alabama. He noted overturned and broken cedars in a pasture. In May 1933, he examined the Black Warrior River bottoms in the county, collecting several specimens of moss. He took more landscape photographs from the high hills near Rosemary on May 2, 1934. He also made a close-up picture of lance-leaved bluets (*Houstonia lanceolata*) in the prairie there and collected a specimen of eastern whiteflower beard-tongue (*Penstemon tenuiflorus*) that he sent to the New York Botanical Garden. The following day, he photographed a grove of loblolly pine and, after returning to Greensboro in the afternoon, the "back side of [an] old house with Ionic columns" in the center of town and a view of large water oaks along College Avenue. Still in Greensboro on May 4, he photographed the "old wooden office building . . . opposite [the] court house, and [an] old hotel next to it." He went back to Havana in March 1937, explored a fern glen in the area, and made six photographs of it; he returned to Cedarville in April 1938 for more pictures of the prairie and a creek gorge.[36]

Harper attended a ceremony of the Hale County Historical Society at Five Mile Church, between Greensboro and Akron in the northwestern part of the county, on May 26, 1938, and made photographs of Miss J. Nicholene Bishop reading to the assemblage in front of the church and of a local history authority, William E. W. Yerby, standing beside a monument that the society apparently dedicated that day. Afterward, he went to Miss Bishop's home, Tanglewood. He returned in the fall of that year for another Hale County Historical Society event, this one at Newbern Baptist Church, and photographed an old house built of cedar in 1830. Three

years after that, in May 1941, he visited the site of an antebellum Greek
Revival–style home on a bluff overlooking the Black Warrior at Arcola. He
took two photographs to create a stereoscopic picture of the brick house,
noting that the builder, Alfred Hatch, lived from 1799 to 1879. While he
was there, Harper also made habitat and close-up photographs of a jujube
shrub (*Ziziphus zizyphus*) growing in the yard. Standing fifty feet above
the water at the edge of the bluff, he took an excellent photograph of the
river. By late afternoon, he was close to Cedarville and photographed a
wetlands aster, prairie Indian plantain (*Arnoglossum plantagineum*) in a
"weedy prairie." He went to Rosemary again to take more views of the
prairies on October 18, 1941, and that afternoon photographed a historic
African American home in Greensboro that he noted was "said to have
been [the] first public school in Hale County." He returned to the Arcola
escarpment on the Black Warrior on June 24, 1944. The last photograph
from Hale County in the Hoole collection is one Harper made at the
site of Greene Springs School at Havana, an academy established by Julia
Tutwiler's father, which he visited with his wife, Mary Sue Wigley Harper,
and some of her relatives in 1951.[37]

Without an automobile of his own, Harper found that his world shrank
as he aged, so it is not surprising that he returned to Hale County so
many times. However, the county was more than a convenient, next-door
field for his phytogeographical research. He went to the higher elevation
at Rosemary at least four times over a period of nineteen years, documenting changes in the surrounding landscape. Here was a microcosm
of the intriguing Fall Line hills—a borderland between the uplands and
the Gulf Coastal Plain that blocked the migration of some species while
allowing others to pass—and of the vanishing longleaf pine forests. Here
was the essence of death and change and resurrection that is revealed in a
landscape to those who look closely.

Eugene Smith died on September 7, 1927, twenty years after Roland's
father had died, and another of Roland's patrons and mentors was gone.
When he heard that Smith was seriously ill, Harper rushed from Montgomery to Tuscaloosa and stayed there through the funeral, canceling
other travel plans. He mourned his "good old friend" and recruited others to join him in writing eulogies to Smith for scientific journals. Perhaps thinking of Harper, Walter B. Jones wrote that Smith's memory was
"deeply engraved . . . in the hearts of the few pioneers who survive[d]
him."[38]

Jones became acting director of the Alabama Geological Survey some months before Smith's death. He had known Harper since the younger man was a freshman at the university in 1914. Although Harper was not yet a full-time employee of the survey, Jones decided to assign the map room in Smith Hall to him as a permanent office. Harper's old friend H. E. Wheeler, by then curator of the natural history collections in Smith Hall, wrote, "Dr. Jones has assigned to your use the old shop or map room with agreement that such shelving and equipment as necessary be provided, and we hope that it will be a comfortable work room for you." Jones gave Harper a permanent appointment with the survey in 1931, and Smith Hall became Roland's home for good.[39]

CHAPTER SIX

A Struggle for Synthesis

Harper's body of phytogeographic work consisted of papers and monographs of three general types. The first type was descriptions of botanical
discoveries. The second was geographic analyses of geology and vegetation. During the productive period between 1910 and 1930, Harper prepared detailed analyses of vegetation and its relationship to soil types for
the Alabama and Florida surveys as well as commissioned reports on natural resources in Georgia and other states. The Alabama agency published
his "Economic Botany of Alabama, Part I," in 1913. The Florida survey
published his massive report on the northern part of the state as part of
its annual report in 1914 and another lengthy analysis of Florida vegetation types in its next annual report in 1915. Harper prepared a 236-page
analysis of central Florida geography for the Florida survey's 1921 annual
report. He completed his report on the state with a third installment,
about southern Florida, in the Florida Geological Survey's eighteenth annual report in 1927.[1]

Harper based the 1927 report on southern Florida on fieldwork he had
conducted in 1909, 1924, and 1925, boasting that he had traveled "on
nearly all the railroads," had made "several short trips by boat, on both
fresh and salt water," had "traversed some country remote from railroads
by automobile," and had covered more than three hundred miles on foot,
taking notes "on nearly every mile, whether riding or walking." Harper
described the geology and mineral resources, topography, soils, climate,
vegetation, floristics, and fauna and explained his division of southern
Florida into regions. He explained in the introduction that he used statistics extensively to describe "artificial or human features" of southern
Florida such as "density and composition of population, acreage and yield
of crops, kind and value of manufactures, etc., etc." He commented that
statistical treatment of physical geography was less challenging than that
of human geography: "Physical geography is indeed also capable of some
statistical treatment, in the way of soil analyses, weather records, stand of

timber, etc., but such statistics are usually much simpler than those used in human geography." Harper allowed his sense of humor a few appearances in the report while taking a slight dig at "booster" literature: "In this report, in conformity with the established policy of this department (and practically all other state geological surveys) we have tried to present the important truths impartially, not overlooking the fact that some of the soils are below the average in fertility, some of the water is hard, the weather is not always perfect, some of the trees are crooked or otherwise of little use, mosquitoes are occasionally seen, etc." He acknowledged Francis, who was then with the Boston Society of Natural History, Marshall Howe of the New York Botanical Garden, and other friends and acquaintances who had helped with the bibliography.

In the 1927 report, Harper criticized "developers" for "trying to destroy the vegetation as fast as possible, to make room for cities and farms," bemoaning that some plant species he had studied in southern Florida in 1909 and 1910 were "gone forever." He turned to Charles Torrey Simpson for help in dramatizing the loss of biodiversity that real estate and agricultural development caused, quoting him extensively in a footnote, including these lines: " 'We advertise the beauties and attractions of Florida. . . . Then we destroy every vestige of its natural beauty, we cut down the hammocks, drain the lakes and mutilate the rivers. We clear out the mangrove borders which nature created to guard our shores from the destruction by the sea during hurricanes and in their places build hideous sea walls. . . . What natural beauty will we have left for another generation?"[2] Harper decried destruction of virgin longleaf stands by "turpentine and lumber men," providing a photograph of a clear-cut longleaf area four miles east of Arcadia in DeSoto County, Florida. "Thousands of square miles in Florida have been devastated like this in the last decade or two," he observed. In a caption for a photograph of longleaf flatwoods three miles south of Fort Drum in Okeechobee County, Florida, Harper warned, "[T]his is one of the few remaining virgin stands of long-leaf pine, and it may not remain long, on account of its accessibility." He discussed the introduction of nonnative plants, such as agricultural and ornamental plants that escape to the wild, explaining that he did not "believe in going to the extreme that some botanists do, of counting as a wild plant any cultivated species that persists for a few years after the field in which it was cultivated is abandoned, or the house around which it was planted burns down, just to claim as many species as possible for the flora. For many such alleged escapes, like the banana, pineapple, date and watermelon, cannot perpetuate themselves very long without human assistance in planting the seeds or keeping wilder plants from choking them out."[3]

The Society of American Foresters published a presentation he had made, apparently at a conference in 1915 or 1916, about his forest census of Alabama. He used his findings about soil types in Alabama and western Florida in an article for the journal *Soil Science* in 1917. In 1914 he described the pocosin in Pike County, Alabama, countering observations by Charles Mohr and E. Q. Thornton in the nineteenth century that the vegetation was swampy, and suggested that luxuriant evergreen pocosin vegetation was the climax plant community for the sand hills, and that this vegetation had climbed from creek valleys "up the ravines to their heads, and then across the sand, making more humus all the time, and crowding out the intolerant sand-hill plants, as in normal succession the world over."[4]

Although Harper focused on the southern coastal plain, he did not waste any opportunity to contribute observations about the phytogeography of other regions. In 1913 he wrote an article about the Appalachian valley for *Torreya*. When he occasionally returned to College Point, he visited coastal plains and peninsulas of the Northeast and published "The Hempstead Plains: A natural prairie on Long Island" in the *Bulletin of the American Geographical Society* in 1911. He went to Provincetown on Cape Cod in Massachusetts in October 1920 with Clarence Knowlton and described the Cape's vegetation in *Torreya* the following year. He provided a statistical analysis of changes in forest cover in New England in the seventeenth, eighteenth, and nineteenth centuries in the *Journal of Forestry*, demonstrating graphically the increase in forest cover since 1850. He recommended that the United States Census begin noting the relative proportions of different trees in each locality: "One person even in a few weeks of travel by rail and on foot should be able to get results accurate enough to show beyond a doubt what is the most abundant tree in a given state, county, or natural region, and what species are more abundant in a given area. . . . The quantitative data thus gathered would also assist materially in mapping the ranges of species and determining their soil preferences—matters that we do not yet know as much as we should." In an article in the journal *Torreya* in 1918, Harper also suggested a systematic geographical classification of tree species and criticized the Massachusetts state forester for calculating percentages of Worcester County, Massachusetts, that were forested, tilled, open pasture, and so on, but not classifying timber by species. The forester's report "would have been more useful, not only to manufacturers who might desire a particular kind of timber for a special purpose, but also to botanists and other scientists."[5]

The third type of scientific paper addressed Harper's survey and mapping techniques. He used his train-window notes as a basis for analyses of coastal plain vegetation in Florida, Georgia, and South Carolina, and of northern Mississippi, Louisiana, and Arkansas. His friends in New York usually published his car-window observations in the bulletin of the Torrey Botanical Club or, less frequently, in *Torreya*, but Forrest Shreve published the articles about Arkansas in *Plant World*, a journal he began editing in 1911. Harper also explained his train-window technique in the annual report of the Florida Geological Survey: "Taking notes from the car-window and on hurried journeys on foot tends to show relative frequency rather than relative abundance; for if I saw ten specimens of a certain tree in every mile for ten miles and a thousand specimens of another in one mile and no more for ten miles the former would figure more largely in the returns. But such extreme cases are unusual and likely to counterbalance each other." In another report, he acknowledged the drawbacks to car-window botanizing, writing "in rapid reconnaissance work it is not possible to take specimens of all unfamiliar plants for subsequent identification."[6]

It must have been gratifying to Harper when George Shull, who earlier had questioned the value of articles based on car-window notes, retracted his criticism, acknowledging that Harper often went back on foot to survey areas he had first viewed from moving trains. "I take no exception to the general accuracy of your car-window observations and the conclusions you draw from them, especially in view of the fact that you have had so many excellent opportunities to actually compare those results with what you find in going over considerable parts of the same area more slowly on foot." Another friend reported in 1920 that traveling with three small children was hindering his own car-window note taking, adding, "Why should I do such work when you do it so much more effectively?"[7]

Harper occasionally lent his voice to advocacy for conservation. Pleading eloquently for preservation of untouched natural areas in an article for the magazine *Natural History* in 1919, Harper vividly described the destruction of the landscape: "[P]rimeval forests are cut down to make room for farms and settlements, or are used up faster than they grow for fuel and building material, or in some localities are killed by fire, smoke, or smelter fumes. . . . [W]aterfalls and rapids are dammed up for power or navigation, or both. As progress is the prevailing ideal, the conversion of irreplaceable natural resources into wealth is almost universally looked upon as not only inevitable but highly commendable, especially by those who do not look very far ahead." He recommended that 1 percent of the land in every county and 5 percent in every state be "left intact for the benefit of all who may wish to enjoy it now or hereafter. There is perhaps no purer pleasure than that derived from the contemplation of nature's masterpieces, and a world in which some of them are within easy reach of every one ought to be a happier world than one wholly dominated by commercialistic motives." He provided photographs of Little River Falls on Lookout Mountain in Alabama, taken on August 30, 1911, and two views of Cahaba lily blooming at Squaw Shoals on the Black Warrior River, one showing construction of a lock in 1913. Concerning another of his favorite types of wetland habitat, Harper wrote, "[O]n any stream the most picturesque places are usually its falls and rapids, and it is just these which suffer most from the encroachments of civilization, for every water-power development, or dam for slack-water navigation, disfigures or obliterates one of them."[8]

He railed against the destruction of Squaw Shoals on the Black Warrior, calling it "a beautiful place, and . . . one of the few known localities for the rare spider lily, *Hymenocallis coronaria*," *Harperella fluviatilis*, and other rare plants, and describing in detail how Squaw Shoals was destroyed. He also described Lookout Mountain and Mussel "(commonly misspelled Muscle)" Shoals in Alabama. Mussel Shoals had "recently been selected as the site of the proposed government nitrate plant, which [would] mean a large water-power development there, to which local 'boosters' [would] doubtless point with pride."[9]

Turning to Florida's threatened natural areas, Harper included photographs taken March 28 and 29, 1909, in the Everglades, of a man with a hat, leggings, and a rifle, presumably his guide, standing in sawgrass, and of Royal Palm Hammock. He warned that the soil of the Everglades was not as fertile as many supposed, and thus draining it to create agricultural land "would not only destroy a scenic feature that [had] no counterpart anywhere else in the world, but would also nearly exterminate countless birds and other interesting creatures, as well as the Seminole Indians, a formerly warlike but now very peaceful tribe." He concluded this overview of imperiled and destroyed southern scenic wonders at a rock outcrop, Stone Mountain, Georgia, a "huge dome of granite rising about seven hundred feet above a comparatively level country, and covering about two square miles." He objected to the plan to create a massive sculpture on the northern face. "Although the Georgians (of whom the writer was one during the best years of his youth) are to be commended for cherishing the memory of the Lost Cause, in this case they are taking a very extravagant way of showing it."[10]

Harper proffered a second rationale, in addition to providing sanctuaries from commercial life, for conserving natural areas: so that field scientists could study them. "Every interference with nature diminishes the opportunities for studying the workings of the laws of nature; and without a knowledge of such laws we do not get as much out of life as we should. . . . [I]t behooves those who have the rare gift of making correct generalizations from observed facts to embrace every possible opportunity to learn nature's ways." He ranked forests above rivers and rock formations like Stone Mountain in a hierarchy of ecological areas that should be preserved. "Forests are among the most easily destroyed of natural features, and their loss is most disastrous to science, for many types that occupied our most fertile soils have disappeared entirely, and can never be restored exactly by letting the land grow up in trees again, or even by re-planting the same species." He recommended that plant ecologists study forests by selecting "a number of tracts of virgin forest and [studying] them without interference for several or many years in succession, counting and measuring all the trees every year or so, and calculating the percentage and rate of growth of each species." He acknowledged several conservation organizations: the American Scenic and Historic Preservation Society; the Wildflower Preservation Society, organized at the New York Botanical Garden; and the Ecological Society of America, which he said had "the right point of view, and [was then] gathering data about places of ecological interest in the United States and Canada that ought to be preserved for scientific study." The Ecological Society of America included a description of Alabama by Harper in its *Naturalists' Guide to the Americas* in 1926.[11]

As he struggled to synthesize botanical and geological data, Harper was not always successful. Barrington Moore, who followed Forrest Shreve as editor of *Plant World*, renamed *Ecology*, published Harper's article about limestone prairies in Wilcox County, Alabama, but rejected a manuscript called "Some Interesting Relations between Soil, Vegetation, Precipitation, and Mineral Deposits," saying he did not have enough space for it, even though Harper's work was "of the greatest value in bringing about a proper appreciation of the importance of soil in studies of plant distribution, a factor which [had] been too often overlooked." The editors of the *Annals of the Association of American Geographers* and *Economic Geology* were less diplomatic. Richard E. Dodge of the geography association told Harper his manuscript was too general and would not make "a real contribution to the cause of geography." Alan M. Bateman of Yale said that although he and other reviewers felt Harper's idea had some merit, they thought that he had not considered all possible factors in a discussion of sulfur and coal. Even an article about pitcher plants met with rejection, when Herbert F. Schwarz, editor of *Natural History*, said it was too technical for the magazine's general audience.[12]

Despite Shull's praise for his prolific writing, Harper may have tried to write too many analytical articles at a time. He also may have damaged his own prospects with editors by criticizing their work, as when he complained that his entry in the Ecological Society's guide was "marred by numerous editorial and typographical errors." In another instance, he wrote to the editor of the *Journal of Heredity* in 1928 to offer unsolicited criticism of graphic clinical information in the journal. Robert C. Cook replied, with evident sarcasm, "Am sorry to learn that the *Journal* nauseates, but I am not quite clear as to how it is possible to study heredity without studying diseases and abnormalities. In view of what can be seen and heard in the way of abnormalities and perversions in dozens of magazines with circulations in the hundreds of thousands and millions, and in thousands of theatres and movies, I can't see how women and even children can be seriously upset by the small amount of clinical information in a few of the *Journal* articles." The president of the National Geographic Society, Gilbert Grosvenor, was more tolerant when Harper criticized the magazine *National Geographic* in 1922, thanking Harper for his comments while saying he could not agree with them, and insisting that Harper keep some mementoes that the society had given him. "I shall always be glad to hear from you," Grosvenor added in a postscript.[13]

Harper's production of self-published analyses of demographics was steady: In 1920, "The Regional Geography of South Carolina Illustrated by Census Statistics" and "Some Relations between Soil, Climate and Civilization in the Southern Red Hills of Alabama"; in 1922, "Distribution of Illiteracy in Alabama in 1920"; in 1923, "Urban Culture in the North and South and Rural Standards of Living in the South"; in 1924, "Tuscaloosa's Advantages over Larger Cities: Quality Versus Quantity" and "Per Capita Wealth in the United States." He employed census data to trace the development of agriculture in Georgia from 1850 to 1880 in two articles for the *Georgia Historical Quarterly* in 1922. He worked on the Florida state census in 1925 and analyzed agricultural conditions in Florida for the journal *Economic Geography* in 1927.[14]

"My dear Rambling Botanist," Harper's friend J. Russell Smith at Columbia wrote in 1921, "are you getting to be so much interested in economic things that you think you are not a botanist?" A temporary job with the United States Department of Agriculture in Washington, D.C., in 1917–18 had stimulated Harper's interest in economic changes in the coastal plain, and he wrote *Resources of Southern Alabama: A Statistical Guide for Investors and Settlers, with an Exposition of the General Principles of Economic Geography* for the Alabama survey in 1920. *Economic Botany of Alabama. Part 2* appeared in 1928.[15]

Harper was interested in the relationship of demographic change to phytogeographical change as early as 1904, when he wrote to a friend that he was confining his dissertation to the Altamaha Grit region in part because the area had experienced a dramatic increase in population. When he worked in Washington, helping prepare a regional map for the United States Department of Agriculture, he found the department's collection of statistical information fascinating. "I had more ready access to census reports than ever before, and I became much interested in demographic problems, which I had dabbled with a little before."[16]

Working outside a university faculty, Harper frequently used letters to newspaper editors as an alternative to the working papers that scientists in academia often exchange for discussion. In Tuscaloosa in 1919, he commented on a series of articles about south Alabama counties in the *Montgomery Advertiser*, praising the newspaper in a letter to the editor for recognizing the "high state of civilization" among white residents of southern Alabama. He suggested that a good indicator of "civilization" was the value of farm buildings and described how he had derived the relative value of farm buildings owned by white and black farmers in every county of Alabama and in several counties with high proportions of black residents in other states, using the 1910 United States Census report. Not surprisingly, his calculations revealed that white farmers owned more valuable real property than black farmers. Also not surprisingly, for Harper was in no way prescient about race relations, but rather was a staunch defender of the southern status quo, he interpreted those statistics as meaning that the presence of a large majority of black workers could be an economic boon for whites.

These statistics agree very well with what well-informed people like your-self doubtless already realized in a general way, namely, that in rural dis-tricts (not necessarily in cities, for they present a different set of conditions) where Negroes are most numerous the whites are most prosperous and cultured. It is also a matter of common observation, thought it may not be possible to show it statistically, that in just such communities the Negroes are generally more contented and peaceable than where the numbers of the two races are more nearly equal; and they are far from being a downtrod-den class like the serfs and peasants of Europe and the peons of Mexico and South America.

(He acknowledged Booker T. Washington's book *The Man Farthest Down* as his source on the relative status of peasants in Europe and the southern United States.) Harper was blind to the economic injustice in southern Alabama's plantation economy. "It should not be assumed that the whites in the black belt are dishonestly enriching themselves at the expense of the Negroes, who therefore ought to be educated and 'uplifted' by out-side interference; nor on the other hand that we can have more prosperity and culture by getting more Negroes. The ratio between the races, like many other social conditions, is determined largely by soil and climate, which we cannot change materially."[17]

A few colleagues and friends encouraged Harper to pursue his interdis-ciplinary explorations of geographic and cultural phenomena. A social scientist at the University of North Carolina praised Harper's 1920 bul-letin on the resources of southern Alabama: "I wonder if you realize how unique it is. The geological geographer who pushes his thinking into eco-nomics and sociology is developing a new type of student and a new field of learning." A statistician with Metropolitan Life Insurance Company suggested in 1924 that Harper collaborate with Alabama's state health officer to make presentations at the upcoming Southern Medical Associa-tion meeting in New Orleans "with respect to closer cooperation between the departments of economics, sociology and geology in Southern uni-versities and the state health departments." Others urged him to compile his phytogeographical research of two decades in a book. The botanist William L. Bray of Syracuse University, an authority on longleaf pine, suggested, "[T]he flora of the pine-barrens . . . should be both taxonomi-cally and ecologically worked up. That was a job I especially wanted to get at but never did. I had in publications called attention to the grass-land

make-up of the forest floor, and its relation to the periodic burning of
pasturage. . . . I wish that I had as intimate a knowledge of the vegetation
east of Texas in the south as you have." The Pennsylvania ecologist John
Harshberger thought Harper could write a fascinating travelogue of his
explorations, although he seemed to intuit that Harper might be slow
to undertake or complete such a project. "Someday you ought to bring
together in a single book the results of your trips by canoe and on foot
and by railroad through the southern states. You ought to adopt the more
modern aeroplane and get photographic transactions of various parts of
our country from a phytogeographic standpoint."[18]

The University of Chicago Press tentatively invited Harper to write a
regional geography, but in 1921 cancelled its plan for a series of such books.
He continued to plan such a book nonetheless, and in 1922 Huntington
at Yale encouraged Harper to make it a book about the natural history
of the South that would appeal to tourists. Five years went by, however,
and Harper seemed to meet with increasing editorial rejection. In 1927 he
asked Huntington for advice, much as he had sought George Shull's help
in 1908. Huntington urged him to use less raw data and a more enjoyable narrative style. "You are too high-brow, if I may put it that way; that
is, you insist on giving great masses of figures which the ordinary person
cannot digest. You do not seem to try very hard to make them interesting.
Even I, who am always interested in your work, often find it hard reading. If that is so in the case of a person as interested and sympathetic as
myself, what must it be in the case of the busy, nervous editors who are
not much interested?" Like his brother Francis, Roland Harper thought
that "popularizing" scientific or sociological research amounted to "sugar
coating" the facts. Huntington disagreed. "I think you are wrong about
the sugar coating. Such coating is bad if it means that you conceal or dis-
tort the facts. It is good if you make the facts interesting." Huntington
urged Harper not to give up. "I am going to keep talking to you about [a
book] until you publish it." Huntington may have had second thoughts
about Harper's publishing prospects after Harper wrote to him in 1928
to argue with Huntington's analysis of the relationship of family size to
neighborhood property values. In responding, Huntington suggested
that Harper's grasp of socioeconomic issues was not as strong as his grasp
of phytogeography. "I want to assent most heartily to one thing that you
say. You certainly have done a well-finished and well-rounded piece of
work on your botanical studies and on your physiographic regions of the
South. There I take off my hat to you and accept your conclusions unless

some new fact comes up. In these other studies the same will doubtless be true when you get around to working them up in final form."[19]

Harper sometimes suspected that there was no place—in academia or government—where he really fit. He wrote a lengthy essay called "Optimism versus Science: Georgia's Problem," in which he attempted to analyze the relative dearth of scientists in that state. The University of Georgia's alumni magazine, the *Georgia Alumni Record*, published the piece in March 1930, and Harper had it reprinted, making corrections and additions as he often did. He was again living in Tallahassee, and the tone of the piece suggests that he wished the University of Georgia had extended his appointment, but he believed his type of social science research was not welcome. He argued that university professors were not entirely free to conduct research and publish ideas—"Many college professors in various parts of the country in the last twenty-five or thirty years have lost their positions for expressing unpopular views." Harper pointed out that he had been criticized for arguing in an article that family size was related to the rise and fall of civilization, but defended his premise: "If I had depended solely on that measure it might well have been questioned, for there are many individual exceptions; but in the aggregate it correlates so nicely with other measures that it cannot well be disputed." The problem of scholarly freedom extended beyond the academy, in Harper's mind. Bureaucrats and administrators also could oppress scientists at museums and in government agencies. He recalled a budget cut for the Alabama Geological Survey twenty years earlier, when Eugene A. Smith, whom he described as "a very lovable man" and "a scientist of high rank," temporarily lost some of his state funding after supporting the loser in a gubernatorial race. Perhaps Harper was blocked or discouraged from doing some kind of quasi-demographic research during his appointment at the University of Georgia, for he wrote that in Georgia, "some subjects are more or less tabooed, and restrictions in one line of research in an institution or community tend to put a damper on all."[20]

While Harper was sometimes lost in a thicket of half-formed theories and research methods, many of his friends and colleagues, his sisters, and even his mother found paths to publishing success. Forrest Shreve's first book, *Plant Life of Maryland*, appeared in 1910, a mere three years after he had completed his dissertation on pitcher plants. He completed a monograph on the Jamaican rain forest, which the Carnegie Institution of Washington published, in 1914, and just a year later another, *The Vegetation of a Desert Mountain Range as Conditioned by Climatic Factors*, for the same institution. Then in 1921 the Carnegie Institution released a massive work, *The Distribution of Vegetation in the United States, As Related to Climatic Conditions*, by Shreve and Burton E. Livingston, who was the permanent secretary of the American Association for the Advancement of Science. As early as 1912, R. J. H. DeLoach, one of Harper's classmates at the University of Georgia, had had two books published, one a collection of sentimental essays in tribute to the nature writer John Burroughs, the other an agriculture textbook. The prestigious scholarly career of another of Harper's classmates, Ulrich B. Phillips, was well under way that year, with the release of his third book, *American Negro Slavery*. The prolific writer and naturalist Charles Torrey Simpson, the former Smithsonian scientist who had retired to Miami, had a commercial success with *In Lower Florida Wilds* in 1920, thanks in part to photographs and help that Harper provided. "I have sold quite a good many and they are for sale at Miami, Fort Myers, Palm Beach, Tampa, etc.," he wrote to Harper in 1921. Simpson's and Harper's mutual friend, John Kunkel Small of the New York Botanical Garden, completed the second edition of his *Flora of the Southeastern United States* in 1913 and a third edition in 1933, with some help from Harper. The Science Press published Small's *From Eden to Sahara: Florida's Tragedy* in 1929. Hermina had a book of poems published in 1911, and Wilhelmina published a retelling of the folk tale "Gunniwolf" in 1918, beginning a long career as an editor and compiler of children's literature. With Wilhelmina as her agent, even Bertha wrote a memoir, *When I Was a Girl in Bavaria*, which was published in 1932.[21]

Harper's friends and colleagues roamed far and wide on adventures scientific and otherwise. The Brittons, Nathaniel and Elizabeth, made annual trips to the Caribbean beginning in 1902, and he published monographs on the flora of Bermuda and the Bahamas with a coauthor, Charles F. Millspaugh. After searching the Blue Mountains of Jamaica on horseback for new plants, Shreve turned to desert ecology. According to his biographer, Janice Emily Bowers, Shreve treasured the memory of his first ride into the Santa Catalina Mountains in 1908, so he may have told Harper about it. "He recalled, 'It was taken for granted that I knew how to tighten my own cinches and was accustomed to an entire day in the saddle, both of which happened to be the case.' He found the trip from the base to the top of the mountains 'impressive and unforgettable.'" Shreve became director of the Desert Laboratory, a research station of the Carnegie Institution of Washington, in 1928. Ernest Holt explored the "unknown interior of Central Brazil" in 1920 and British Honduras in 1926. Henry Rusby embarked on a final grand expedition in 1921, at the age of sixty-five, when he directed the Mulford Biological Exploration of the Amazon Basin. His memoir of his adventures, *Jungle Memories*, was published in 1933. The mathematician Tomlinson Fort left the University of Alabama for Hunter College around the time of his and Harper's automobile jaunt around Hale County, and six years later, in 1930, drove north across Africa from Johannesburg to Cairo, stopping along the way to climb Mount Kilimanjaro.[22]

Roland's younger brother Francis was part of several scientific exploration teams. After working in New York for six years to support their mother, Francis finally returned to Cornell University, where scientists on the faculty were beginning to investigate wildlife in Okefenokee Swamp. He made the first of many trips to Okefenokee in 1912, a decade after Roland canoed into the swamp, and spent seventeen days studying the birds there. He returned to the South in 1913; he used a camera to document wildlife such as Banks ponies on Carrot Island off the coast of North Carolina and sent some of his photographs to Roland, who found them "fine." A year later, Francis received an appointment as part of a team that explored the region of Great Slave Lake in Canada for the Victoria Memorial Museum of Ottawa. Francis also went to war, enlisting in the United States Army in September 1917.[23]

Harper had his own opportunity to blaze a trail to fame and possible wealth. In 1927, Thomas Alva Edison invited him to survey Florida for new plant sources of rubber. The automobile and tire magnates Henry Ford and Harvey Firestone had challenged Edison to find a rubber source closer to their factories, and the search became the last venture of Edison's long career. Edison heard of Harper's talent as a field botanist from Marshall Howe at the New York Botanical Garden, and possibly from Harper's Georgia classmate, R. J. H. DeLoach, who was a camping friend of Edison, Ford, Firestone, and John Burroughs.[24] Edison offered Harper a job and even a car if he would search Florida for new sources of rubber. "I am thinking of using a field man in this connection [and] have thought of hiring a Ford roadster for the man who undertakes this search." But Harper turned Edison down—perhaps because he did not want to drive a car—declining an opportunity to work in association with Edison, Ford, and Firestone, and perhaps to make a botanical breakthrough even more significant than Rusby's discovery of a new method for processing coca for cocaine production. John Kunkel Small subsequently took up Edison's quest, searching in Florida and conducting hybridization experiments in the laboratory at the New York Botanical Garden until 1931, when Edison died.[25]

The southern coastal plain, and particularly its wetlands and longleaf forests, was where Harper chose to take his stand, returning to the sites of his earlier discoveries again and again and delving into industrial, agricultural, and socioeconomic data in hopes of forming a comprehensive, ecological understanding of the region. Each time he revisited a familiar place in the landscape of Georgia, Florida, and Alabama, he found something new. His friend Herman Kurz described a typical day of discovery for Harper after he and Harper found "a new and remarkable habitat" for the Florida stinking cedar.

> On February 12, 1927, Dr. R. M. Harper and the writer were guided about [a] half-mile into the fastness of Johnson's Juniper Swamp by Mr. L. R. Carson of Bristol. This swamp, already described and located as eight miles south of Bristol by Harper is totally unlike the Flat Creek habitat [of the Florida yew]. The waterlogged, peaty substratum is highly acid. . . . Fallen logs in all stages of decay criss-cross so that exploration becomes very arduous. The luxuriant mats of a number of species of Hepaticae and Musci attest to the very humid atmosphere of this hydrophytic forest. . . . To our amazement in this contrasting habitat and among such strange associates, we found the supposedly very "selective" *Taxus Floridana*.[26]

"Reading the Funnies Every Night at No. 329," November 1932.
W. S. Hoole Special Collections Library, University of Alabama, Tuscaloosa.

The Harpers at their College Point, New York, home.
Courtesy of David B. Harper.

Roland Harper (center), probably at Aspalaga Bluff, Florida, with
Elias Howard Sellards and Herman Gunter on March 5, 1909.
Courtesy of the Florida Department of Environment's Florida Geological Survey.

Pine barren, Franklin County, Florida, June 11, 1909.
W. S. Hoole Special Collections Library, University of Alabama, Tuscaloosa.

Road in Leon County, Florida, October 16, 1910. W. S. Hoole Special Collections Library, University of Alabama, Tuscaloosa.

Close-up of Cahaba lily (*Hymenocallis coronaria*), Squaw Shoal, Black Warrior River, Alabama, June 4, 1913. W. S. Hoole Special Collections Library, University of Alabama, Tuscaloosa.

Bertha Harper in the woods near Wakulla Spring, Florida, April 14, 1920. W. S. Hoole Special Collections Library, University of Alabama, Tuscaloosa.

Canoe trip on the Black Warrior River, Alabama, May 26, 1921. W. S. Hoole Special Collections Library, University of Alabama, Tuscaloosa.

View of Waheenah, Jefferson County, Florida, May 10, 1925. W. S. Hoole Special Collections Library, University of Alabama, Tuscaloosa.

Roland McMillan Harper,
September 19, 1932,
portrait made in
College Point. Courtesy
of David B. Harper.

Roland and Mary on
their wedding day,
June 23, 1943,
Sand Mountain, Alabama.
W. S. Hoole Special
Collections Library,
University of Alabama,
Tuscaloosa.

Anne and Lyman Findley with the pasteboard houses.
Courtesy of the author.

Roland Harper, Anne Findley, and Herbert Lyman Findley on the
front porch, 329 University Avenue. Courtesy of the author.

Chalk gorge south of Demopolis, Marengo County, Alabama, November 12, 1932.
W. S. Hoole Special Collections Library, University of Alabama, Tuscaloosa.

Cemetery, Bryce Hospital, Tuscaloosa, Alabama, April 3, 1940.
W. S. Hoole Special Collections Library, University of Alabama, Tuscaloosa.

Sand Mountain family,
DeKalb County, Alabama,
November 27, 1943.
W. S. Hoole Special
Collections Library, University
of Alabama, Tuscaloosa.

Harper with Wigley children,
DeKalb County, Alabama,
November 29, 1943.
W. S. Hoole Special Collections
Library, University of Alabama,
Tuscaloosa.

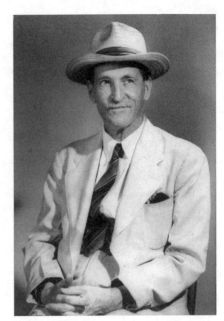

Roland McMillan Harper,
May 24, 1948.
Courtesy of David B. Harper.

Harper with
Herman Coolidge
and Clermont Lee,
Upper Lotts Creek,
Georgia,
September 2, 1961.
Courtesy of
Clermont Lee.

Roland and Mary Harper in the Findley rose garden, April 23, 1954.
Courtesy of the author.

Roland Harper at the base of a pine. Courtesy of Hazel R. Delcourt.

CHAPTER SEVEN

A Devotee of Swamps

The entire southern coastal plain beckoned Harper as unexplored territory, but the vast, mysterious Okefenokee Swamp in southeastern Georgia
was particularly alluring. When Harper did his graduate fieldwork at the
turn of the century, much of the enormous freshwater wetland, with a
surface of unstable peat deposits up to fifteen feet thick, was still untouched by logging because its quaking ground made hauling timber so
difficult. The first corporate effort to harvest cypress timber in the swamp
failed, and a second effort was not yet under way when Harper sent a
proposal to the botanist F. V. Coville of the United States Department
of Agriculture in 1902, suggesting there should be a thorough botanical
survey of the swamp, and that time was short. Loggers would soon find
a way to destroy the swamp for its cypress timber; soon the Okefenokee's
natural history would be lost to science forever. Still in graduate school,
he hinted that Coville could hire him to accompany a more senior botanist into the swamp. One of Coville's colleagues, Percy L. Ricker, liked
the idea and wanted to go. Ricker persuaded Coville to contract with
Harper for the month of August 1902 and arranged to meet Harper in
Georgia on August 1.[1]

Waiting for Ricker's train to arrive at Waycross, Harper hiked along the
Satilla River through longleaf woods that were "considerably tampered
with by the operations of turpentine, lumber, agriculture, etc." Ricker
arrived late in the afternoon, and they spent the evening planning their
swamp expedition, with Harper somewhat worried about the dangers they
faced. The next morning they walked eleven miles to Glenmore, following a railroad track through boggy longleaf woods that to Harper seemed
"not very remarkable," and rode the train back to Waycross. Harper
watched out for snakes but saw none on their hike. After another two days
of preparation, Harper and Ricker took a train to Folkston, at the edge
of the Okefenokee, on August 4; Harper made car-window notes during
the trip. Talking to local people about the swamp, he found reassurance

that the Okefenokee was not a distinctly dangerous place. "No one is known to have ever perished in there from snake-bite or any other cause," he wrote.[2] This was a relief; despite his intrepid hikes through woods and over mountains, the young scientist feared snakes.

After a six-mile hike up the railroad beside the St. Marys River and back the next day, the two men bought a supply of crackers and canned food as the final step of their preparations. They left in the early morning of August 6 by wagon and passed through heavily lumbered and second-growth longleaf woods to reach Camp Cornelia on the East Fork of the Suwanee Canal. There, Harper and Ricker hired a local man, Sam Mizell, with a small boat to take them into the swamp, and Harper got someone on the bank to take their photograph as they embarked in midafternoon. Passing abandoned steamboats and dredges, Harper observed peat burning on the canal's banks and again was relieved to see only one snake. So many cypresses had been cut that he had a clear view of the surrounding bog.[3] Perhaps a Carolina wren buzzed at the men as Mizell's paddle made a rhythmic splash. They may have heard a prothonotary warbler singing, "Sweet, sweet, sweet," and then spotted the vivid yellow bird darting between cypress knees.

They reached Bugaboo Landing, seven miles into the swamp, in three hours and fifteen minutes and pitched a camp there for the night. Mosquitoes infiltrated their tent and made sleeping difficult. Lying awake, Harper could have heard a barred owl hooting from a branch nearby and another one answering from a distant tree. He rose before dawn to explore the small area of elevated ground, collecting two plant specimens, including one of sphagnum moss (*Sphagnum portoricense*) that he later sent to the New York Botanical Garden.[4] The three men set out on foot for Bugaboo Island just before 7 a.m., with Harper wearing a suit, high-collared shirt, and felt hat. The swamp's name is derived from a Native American word meaning "quivering earth"; the boggy ground was so soft that Harper often sank almost to the top of his knee-high boots. He found enormous specimens of hooded pitcher plant (*S. minor*) with leaves nearly four feet long, or more than three times as tall as the same species in the pine barrens. After four hours of hiking, the men returned to their campsite and departed soon by boat to travel another five miles along the southern edge of Chase Prairie, an interior marsh. They probably saw Florida sandhill cranes stalking through shallow water, hunting for fish. When Mizell pointed out a vine that grew up cypress trunks by inserting itself beneath the bark, Harper urged him to paddle closer to the bank and found it was a climbing form of heath (*Pieris phillyreifolia*) that grew twenty to thirty feet up the tree.[5]

They spent the second night in an abandoned shack, where, somewhat protected from the mosquitoes, Harper was able to sleep. Rising again at 4:30 a.m., he collected two more specimens and made notes in his field diary before they began the return trip to Camp Cornelia at six o'clock. Although L. H. Dewey, the acting botanist for the Bureau of Plant Industry, had instructed Harper to collect "as complete a set of plants as possible" from the Okefenokee "during the time [he was] engaged," the water was so low in August that the men could not navigate outside the canal, so most of the great swamp was inaccessible.[6]

Harper spent only two days in the swamp itself and, according to his own journal, collected almost no plants, yet the Okefenokee intrigued him. The day after returning to Camp Cornelia, he hiked two or three miles through heavy rain into the pine barren on the rim of the swamp, collecting several specimens while carrying an umbrella. Then he set out alone on foot for Folkston, leaving Ricker to bring the baggage and plant driers by train. On August 11, after Ricker departed for St. Augustine, Florida, Harper hiked for several hours along the bluffs and bottoms of the St. Marys River. The following day, he covered another ten miles on foot, following a defunct railroad through sand hills to the Satilla River, and found the swampy area "particularly interesting." Crossing the swamp on a path that was "nearly choked up with weeds and briers," he emerged from the swamp shortly after noon and saw a house and cultivated field for the first time in several hours. After another twenty-minute walk, he reached a house whose owner, a black farmer, gave him some water, telling Harper that his well was inexhaustible because of a fissure caused by the Charleston, South Carolina, earthquake of 1886. After walking for another hour, Harper reached Bull Head Bluff and then walked back to Folkston by the same route.[7]

He prepared a lengthy, detailed report of his fieldwork for Coville, with a companion list of plants. His initial account of his two days in the Okefenokee seems inconsequential—a description of a well-populated area, with no new plant discoveries except the oversized hooded pitcher plant and the oddity of the climbing heath, and no hypotheses or conclusions. Although Harper characterized himself on the handwritten cover of his plant list as an "expert . . . in botanical investigations and experiments," he was young and inexperienced. His mentors at Columbia, Britton and Rusby, were as much explorers as scientists, mentors who had not challenged him to synthesize and interpret his findings. Coville was disappointed in Harper's report. "The data you have brought together are too fragmentary to warrant us publishing it." However, the young botanist succeeded in having two brief reports of his expedition published in the journal *Torreya*. The first was an excerpt of a letter he wrote to John Kunkel Small at the New York Botanical Garden, which had both a sense of breaking news for the journal's readers and the intimacy of a letter to friends. "I suppose you received my card from Folkston?" Harper wrote. He told Small that the plant life of the swamp was rebounding from the damage of logging operations. "The big game in the swamp was conspicuously absent. We saw one snake and one alligator (killed the former), but nothing bigger. The one thing that bothered us was mosquitoes, and those only at night. I had naturally expected the swamp to be a dark gloomy place, but it is nothing of the kind. . . . A great deal of the swamp . . . is open prairie." He reported the unusual pitcher plant with leaves two to almost four feet in length and described "acres of [Virginia chain fern] *Woodwardia virginica* with ninety-nine per cent of the fronds facing east." The other article was a two-page report of the climbing heath. He acknowledged that Chapman had described the plant from Florida in 1840 but pointed out that Chapman omitted it from his 1860 flora.[8]

Harper also wrote a lengthy and provocative article, "Some Neglected Aspects of the Campaign against Swamps," which appeared in the magazine *Southern Woodlands* in 1908. In it, he criticized the drainage of wetlands as economically unviable. He provided a classification system of swamps as freshwater or saltwater, wooded or treeless, flowing or stagnant, alluvial or nonalluvial, and as pocosins (shrubby, swampy peat bogs), pine barren ponds, savannas, Florida prairies, or other formations, and discussed each. He critiqued the notion that swamps were "a menace to health," first thought to be the source of "miasmas" and then of malaria, refuting the premise that swamps were sources of disease and using the healthy people of Okefenokee Swamp as evidence. Finally, presaging his plea in *Natural History* in 1919, he called for preservation of swamps. In a draft of the article, he wrote,

> [W]ith the passing of the swamps the opportunity for discovering certain of Nature's laws will be forever lost, for the swamps present innumerable biological and geographical problems which are not encountered

elsewhere. . . . Last (and perhaps least in this age of commercialism), the swamps should be preserved for their beauty, though this may strike some people as absurd. It has been stated somewhere that there is no evidence in literature that the beauty of natural scenery, even of mountains, was fully appreciated anywhere up to a century or two ago. Even yet few people can see beauty in a swamp, and many regard them with aversion, but they will probably be appreciated more hereafter than they are now. Nature undefiled is always beautiful.[9]

Harper received some welcome compliments for the piece. A friend who was apparently in the New York Assembly wrote,

You are making yourself famous. The *Literary Digest* quoted in its issue of several weeks ago, Prof. Roland M. Harper's article on Swamps extensively. I think however it is a pretty muddy proposition to handle at best, but certainly an engrossed set of resolutions should be presented to you by "The Committee of Misquitoes [*sic*], representing a numerous body of the Insect Department of Animal Life" for your most laudable defense of the institution on which their very existence seems to be founded. On the whole, Roland, I believe however that you are correct and I hope that your views will be justified to the public and endorsed by some of your contemporaries.[10]

Howe of the Torrey Botanical Club wrote, "I suppose you noticed that Professor Bessey said some rather nice things about you in *Science* a few weeks back. Perhaps he can help you to a good position somewhere." Gifford Pinchot, one of the country's first professional foresters and chairman of the National Conservation Commission, acknowledged Harper for sending a copy of the *Southern Woodlands* article. A zoologist at Ohio State University agreed completely with Harper that swamps should not be drained and suggested that Harper present papers on the issue at the next conference of the American Association for the Advancement of Science in Baltimore. "You evidently have had extensive experience and acquaintance with some of these problems, and could speak with an authority that would have great weight, perhaps especially in connection with those tracts in which timber might be said to be the permanent resource."[11]

During his 1909 peat assignment in Florida, Harper spent a few days camping in another coastal plain swamp visited by few botanists, Florida's

Everglades. Before beginning this swamp adventure, he read *Across the Everglades: A Canoe Journey of Exploration*, by Hugh L. Willoughby, a former lieutenant commanding the Rhode Island Naval Reserve. Willoughby's story of an 1897 canoe trip, complete with encounters with American Indians, alligators, and snakes, such as a moccasin that attempted "to crawl up [the] left shoulder" of a person in the canoe party, caused Harper no little trepidation. He still recalled his anxiety eighteen years later: "One who had no information on the subject might imagine that in the almost tropical climate of South Florida reptiles would be very abundant, if not dangerous." Willoughby wrote, "When camps were made at night many moccasins were killed. Indian signs were again encountered, their poles sticking up at landing-places on the small islands, and the ground well strewn with the shells of the Everglade terrapin which they had eaten." Willoughby retained a guide who he believed was "just the man to face with [him] whatever dangers there might be in store in [his] attempt to cross the Everglades." Harper read of how the guide showed Willoughby the bones of a rattlesnake he had killed two years earlier. Willoughby and the guide reconstructed the skeleton and concluded that the snake was eight feet long. Concerning alligators, Willoughby described coming upon a giant one, perhaps thirteen feet in length, which eluded his shot. "With a gentle slide, and without splash, this splendid fellow sank and was seen no more. Every inch of that beast and of his huge crawl is photographed on my memory." Harper read how Willoughby's party ran out of food and had a difficult time returning to Miami, sometimes having to wade in water up to their armpits. Fortunately, according to Willoughby, the Seminoles were "happy" and "stalwart," no threat despite the theft of their property by white settlers and developers, which Willoughby deplored.[12]

In Miami, Harper visited Charles Torrey Simpson, a malacologist retired from the Smithsonian Institution, who oriented Harper to the south Florida trees and advised him on the logistics of reaching the Everglades. Torrey and his wife often entertained visiting scientists at their home, known as The Sentinels, on Biscayne Bay. Harper was envious of their house and their lifestyle: "He picked out the prettiest spot he could find, bought it, and built a house on it with his own hands. . . . He has a fine library and a large collection of shells, and he amuses himself with them and with cultivating all kinds of tropical fruits and ornamental plants. I don't quite understand how he does it with the savings of only 13 years, but his expenses must be very small, as he raises most of his provisions himself. He takes a good many magazines, also the *Atlanta Semi-Weekly Journal.*"[13]

Harper hired a local hunter to accompany him and help him carry camping gear and plant presses. They set out in a hired wagon, drawn by a blind mule, over a rutted road from Homestead, Florida, to a spot where surveyors sometimes camped. "Our driver estimated that only fifteen or twenty different men had visited Camp Jackson in the whole history of the place. Of this number probably about half a dozen were botanists, and the rest surveyors, drivers, guides, etc." Harper and his guide made several walking trips into the swamp. Before leaving their camp, Harper tied a palmetto leaf to a pine at the edge of the woods, to help him find his way back. "We crossed a narrow but very rough strip of pine land, and Long Key was then in plain sight, two or three miles away, [a]nd to my relief there was no water in the Everglades as far as we could see." He "didn't see as many birds as [he] expected," he wrote later. "Those that I remember are Buzzards, jackdaws, ibises, fork-tailed kites, and Everglade kites"—the last birds easy to recognize because of their habit of plucking apple snails from the marshes while hovering above the water. He may have prepared this list from memory in anticipation of writing an article for the magazine *Florida Review*, expecting its readers to be interested in wildlife of all kinds. He collected about one hundred pounds of plant specimens for Sargent during his four-day exploration of Long Key and vicinity and packed them by moonlight for shipment to the Arnold Arboretum. Writing to his mother a few weeks later, Harper said he hoped that if he made another trip to the Everglades, Booie could go with him and recommended that his brother read Willoughby's book in preparation. "The dangers and difficulties seem rather exaggerated in this book, but it is quite interesting, and pretty well illustrated."[14]

The *Florida Review* published Harper's two-part article in 1910. Harper did not describe any botanical discoveries in the Everglades, but he did extol the beauty of a hammock known as Paradise Key, on which grew "about a hundred magnificent specimens of the royal palm (*Roystonea regia*), towering above all the other trees and visible for miles in every direction. There [was] no other place like it in the vicinity, and as long as an explorer [could] keep these palms in sight he [had] no need for a compass." Harper predicted that with more road and railroad construction, timber companies would reach the hammock soon "and its doom [would] probably be sealed."[15]

Writing for a general audience, Harper made some uncharacteristic observations about the fauna of the Everglades. He warned that the alligator could be extirpated by hunting since the Florida legislature had repealed a law protecting it. "It will probably not be many years before the alligator is as nearly exterminated as the buffalo was a generation ago." Harper included some amusing wildlife anecdotes in the article for the *Review,* including one of a water moccasin that he and his guide encountered in open prairie, which "assumed a defiant attitude, coiling up and opening its mouth as wide as possible," until Harper beat it to death with a stick. He told another story, which did not survive the editing of the article, with a dry, self-effacing wit. Awakened in their tent "by some small animal rattling the pots and pans near [his] feet," Harper woke his guide "to get his opinion on it. After listening a few moments he decided that it was nothing but a rat. . . . In the morning the only evidence [they] could find of [their] nocturnal visitor was the marks of its teeth on a cake of soap . . . a strange taste for a wild animal, surely."[16]

He called the article "Tramping and Camping on the Southern Rim of the Everglades." Striving, as usual, to make the case that his foray was pioneering, Harper characterized his brief Everglades expedition as different from those of earlier botanists because he reached Long Key, actually an island within an interior marsh or prairie, on foot during a relatively dry season, whereas previous naturalists who explored the swamp by boat were unable to get to the key. However, Harper acknowledged the explorers and botanists who preceded him. He described how the geologist L. S. Griswold tried and failed twice to reach Long Key in 1896, first by boat from Miami and then on foot, "walking across the jagged rocks of the pine land for a distance of eighteen miles." Harper acknowledged Willoughby, who only managed to get within sight of Long Key. He also recognized that John Kunkel Small and Percy Wilson of the New York Botanical Garden had preceded him, managing to wade to the island from the east "under great difficulties" in May 1904.[17]

The editor of *Florida Review* omitted an important section of this article in which Harper specifically addressed the ecological role of fire. Harper noted that pines in the southern Florida uplands

> cover at least ninety percent of the area, are rather slender, and grow far enough apart so that one can always see about a quarter of a mile through them in any direction. A dense undergrowth of saw-palmetto about two feet tall is everywhere present in the pine woods, which, like those of northern Florida and neighboring states, are burned over about once a

year, sometimes purposely, sometimes by accident, and perhaps sometimes from natural causes. The pines have been accustomed to fire since long before the dawn of history and do not mind it much, and the palmetto when its leaves are burned off soon puts out a new crop.

Harper also described hardwood hammocks, with tropical species, "some of them rejoicing in such curious names as mastic, gumbo-limbo, iron-wood, poison-wood, satin-leaf, stopper, fiddlewood, wild rubber, para-dise-tree, pigeon plum, and Jamaica dogwood. These grow so close together and make such a dense shade that there is little chance for shrubs and herbs to develop in the rich leaf-mold which covers the ground in such places, and is damp enough to be almost immune from fire." Wrapping up his account of the Everglades camping trip in the manuscript for the *Florida Review*, Harper commented that if the wagon driver had not returned to Camp Jackson to pick up Harper and his guide, his "plans would have been seriously deranged." He probably meant "derailed," but the slip escaped the *Review* editor's notice and appeared in the published version.[18]

After almost seven years of rejections, Harper finally found a publisher for an account of his other important swamp expedition, the Okefenokee Swamp trip in 1902. Using the example of his friend Forrest Shreve, who had an article about carnivorous plants in the magazine *Popular Science Monthly* in 1904, Harper submitted an article about the Okefenokee to the same magazine. The earliest comprehensive description of the Okefe-nokee, the piece appeared in June 1909, while Harper was in Florida. In it, Harper made one of his first published observations about the relation-ship of fire to forest ground cover, noting the rarity of grass on Bugaboo Island and attributing it to the thick understory, which he speculated flourished because of the island's protection from lightning-caused fires. In the final paragraph, Harper called for preservation of Okefenokee "as a forest and game preserve for all future generations." To ensure that the right people received the message, he paid for two hundred reprints and mailed them from Tallahassee to many friends, colleagues, acquaintances, and opinion leaders, including Percy Ricker, the economic botanist from the United States Department of Agriculture who had accompanied him into the Okefenokee; Hoke Smith, a recent governor of Georgia; Clark Howell, the managing editor of the *Atlanta Constitution* and a political opponent of Hoke Smith; and Eugene Smith in Tuscaloosa.[19]

Francis followed in Roland's steps to Okefenokee Swamp in 1912 and discovered the locale that would become his greatest passion. For the rest of his life, Francis went to Okefenokee whenever he could, writing often to Roland about his observations there, sociological as well as biological. For example, after spending two weeks in the swamp with a Cornell University research team led by Albert Hazen Wright in 1921, when he lived with two swamp families whom he called "mighty nice people," he wrote to Roland, "We found . . . two frogs not previously recorded from the swamp—the Gopher Frog (*Rana aesopus*) and the Carpenter Frog (*Rana virgatifes*), the latter being new to the state." In his love for Okefenokee, Francis found a voice that was far more eloquent than Roland's:

> The dense cypress bays are places of deep shade and almost oppressive gloom, and yet have a certain somber beauty. Their atmosphere is typically expressed in the deep, uncanny notes of the Florida Barred Owl. This is the haunt of bats; the refuge of Bear and Wildcat when pursued by hounds and men; the home of the Parula Warbler, nesting in the vast drapery of Spanish moss; or the Prothonotary Warbler, a radiant form in the dim light; of the Cottonmouth Moccasin, lurking in the bushes; of chorusing Cricket Frogs and Green Tree-frogs; of wasps, with their paper nests; of Ivory-billed and Pileated Woodpeckers, and a multitude of other creatures. Here also the hunters of Otters and Raccoons tend their trap-lines during the winter months, and as they push their boats along the homeward trail, make the dim recesses of the bays resound for miles with their yodeling.[20]

Francis and his wife, Jean Sherwood Harper, became two of the nation's leading advocates for establishment of the swamp as a national wildlife refuge. Seconding Roland's 1909 recommendation in the *Popular Science Monthly* article, Francis penned a dramatic appeal for preservation of the swamp for the *Brooklyn Museum Quarterly* in 1915: "No devotee of virgin nature, in looking upon such a scene for the first time, could fail to be moved by its grandeur and utter wildness." Jean made personal appeals to President Franklin Delano Roosevelt and Eleanor Roosevelt, whom she knew. Francis reported to Roland in May 1934 that the president had "personally reassured Jean" the previous Christmas that he supported preservation of the swamp, and Eleanor Roosevelt invited Jean to the White House before and after the president established the Okefenokee National Wildlife Refuge in 1937.[21]

CHAPTER EIGHT

On the Bartram Trail with Francis

Before Francis and the Wrights, even before Roland, another naturalist had ventured into the somber, mysterious Okefenokee Swamp. William Bartram, a Quaker from Pennsylvania, first explored the American South with his father, John Bartram, in 1765 and made a more extensive survey of the Deep South during the years 1773 to 1777. A memoir of his adventures was a bestseller of the time. Bartram only briefly described Okefenokee, focusing on American Indian legends about the swamp, but in the introduction to one of his first published articles about the Okefenokee, Francis quoted a passage in which Bartram used strikingly erotic language to tell a legend of a "peculiar race of Indians" whose women were "incomparably beautiful" and whose "young warriors were enflamed with an irresistible desire to invade, and make a conquest of, so charming a country."[1]

While Roland often crossed Bartram's path in his surveys of the coastal plain, it was Francis who wanted to make a definitive study of the naturalist's route through the South in collaboration with his friend and colleague at the Academy of Natural Sciences, the Quaker and self-taught botanist Arthur Newlin Leeds. He and Leeds made trips to Georgia in 1934 and 1936 to find Bartram's trail and explicated some of Bartram's unpublished notes about his most beautiful botanical discovery, *Frankliana alatamaha*, which the two Bartrams found in 1765 on the Altamaha River in Georgia. In a 1938 article in *Bartonia*, the proceedings of the Philadelphia Botanical Club, Francis and Leeds acknowledged Roland first, basing their conclusion about *Frankliana*'s ecological niche on Roland's categories of habitats in the Altamaha Grit region. Leeds, unfortunately, was in declining health. In April 1938 Francis wrote to Roland, "[Leeds] had his gall-bladder removed last fall, and is now getting treated for internal ulcers. He is just beginning to get around to the Academy again." Leeds died in January 1939. Grieving for the man who, he wrote, "occupied a unique place in the minds and hearts of those who were privileged to know him well," Francis sought Roland's help and company in following William Bartram's route through lower Alabama and the Florida panhandle.[2]

Throughout their lives, Roland had encouraged his younger brother's interest in science and nature and taken field trips with him whenever he could. In 1909, for example, while Roland was in College Point between stints in Florida, they spent a night in a trapper's cabin on a tributary of the Forge River and explored the estuary at Moriches Bay. Despite his forced interlude away from college for lack of funds, Francis was becoming a serious naturalist at that time and was named secretary of the Linnaean Society of New York at the American Museum of Natural History in 1910. He continued to share his finds with his older brother, whom he still sometimes called "Wowo," a nickname leftover from babyhood. He wrote to Roland from College Point in 1910, "Dear Wowo: While traveling down the southern slope of High Hill . . . I noticed an old crow's nest in a pine. Something about the tree reminded me of some Jersey pines I had seen near Matawan, New Jersey. . . . On closer examination I saw that it was unmistakably *[Pinus] virginiana.*" Roland was so proud of Francis's find that he wrote immediately to Charles Sargent at Harvard's Arnold Arboretum: "I have just heard from home that my brother has found *Pinus virginiana* on Long Island." The brothers may have discussed Roland's emerging interest in the role of fire in pine forests, for Francis added, "I found an almost unquestionably native white pine in an out-of-the-way nook of the Half Hollows. It was a grand old fire-scarred tree."[3]

Roland could be critical of Francis's efforts. At the age of twelve, after receiving Roland's response to some plant specimens Francis had sent to him, the younger brother wrote, "It is quite true, as you say, that my experience . . . is limited, and I thought you understood that before. I have only been botanizing only about three and a half years, and have distributed not more than 350 specimens. But none of the specimens I have collected in the past three years have ever been found fault with before. I have given a number of specimens to the University of Georgia and to Harvard . . . and they were appreciated at both places." As Francis became confident of his own expertise, he sometimes challenged Roland's interpretations of wildlife biology. Taking issue with a report on Florida that Roland was drafting in 1921, Francis wrote, "I don't see where you can get your estimate of only ten or twelve percent of water birds for the entire world. You better omit this." He persisted in trying to correct Roland, writing again ten days later: "There is a great big chance of error in your method of estimating percentages of land birds and water birds."[4]

Outside the family, however, Francis paid considerable homage to his older brother. In his first major work about Okefenokee, a 1927 monograph about the mammals of the swamp, Francis categorized the swamp's flora in habitat groups similar to those Roland had defined for the Altamaha Grit region, and he acknowledged Roland's influence: "In preparing the phytogeographic part of this report, I have found certain papers by R. M. Harper (1906, 1914, and 1915) highly useful, the one on the near-by Altamaha Grit region of Georgia being practically indispensable. A considerable number of habitats in the last-mentioned region correspond quite closely to some in the Okefinokee region." Discussing the importance of fire in the survival of pine barrens, he cited Roland: "Here, as elsewhere in the longleaf pine regions of the South, ground fires occur every few years on nearly every square mile, being often set purposely to improve the grazing for cattle. So far from causing any great permanent damage to the plant life, fires actually serve, by keeping out the oaks, etc., to perpetuate the pine barrens (cf. R. M. Harper, 1913, p. 26; 1915, p. 147–165, 170)." He also noted receiving from Roland "a great deal of valuable advice and criticism in the preparation of the notes on vegetation" in the swamp. Francis sometimes worried about Roland; in 1934, he wrote, "I was disturbed at the news received through [Francis W.] Pennell about your having had pneumonia. I wish I could believe that you would always take sufficient care of yourself in such simple matters as rubbers, overcoat, and food. Are you all well again by this time?"[5]

In planning his expedition along Bartram's historic route in 1939, Francis knew that Roland could help him because of his familiarity with historic maps of Alabama and access to many maps at the Alabama Geological Survey. He also needed his brother to identify and collect specimens of the plants that Bartram had described. He promised to pay for Roland's expenses with the funds from a grant he had received from the Penrose Fund of the American Philosophical Society. He wanted Roland to meet him in Athens, Georgia, and travel with him to southern Alabama, Florida, and back up the eastern seaboard to Swarthmore, where Francis and Jean lived, and New York. Roland wanted to accompany Francis along Bartram's entire route but could not take enough time from his job in Tuscaloosa. Eager to help, however, he wrote to acquaintances along the route Francis was to retrace, for example, notifying the director of the journalism school at the University of Georgia, who replied that the university would try to publicize Francis's stop in Athens. He sent a letter to Peter A. Brannon, a Bartram scholar with the Alabama Department of Archives and History, on March 30. Brannon replied, recommending eighteenth-century resources. Confident that he could help define Bartram's route through Alabama, Brannon offered to show Roland and Francis the maps in the state archive.[6]

Francis left Swarthmore on May 15, 1939, and took a month to explore Bartram territory in the Carolinas and Georgia, collecting plant specimens that he shipped from Athens to Philadelphia, probably to the Academy of Natural Sciences of Philadelphia, and writing to his brother several times along the way. He visited their childhood friend Charles Cotton Harrold, in Macon, Georgia, on June 10; Harrold showed Francis his own copy of a 1772 map by the British surveyor David Taitt. Two days later, Francis sent a telegram from Columbus to Roland's rooming house on Hackberry Lane: "Will look for you in Montgomery Wednesday afternoon [June 14]. Francis."[7]

Roland went to Montgomery by train the next day, where he ran into Olivia and Ernest Holt's older brother, Frank Sanders Holt, on the street. He called at Olivia Holt's home but missed her. He saw Page Bunker of the Alabama Forestry Commission and his longtime friend Walter Jones, director of Moundville Archeological Park, while at a restaurant for breakfast the following day. Roland called on Brannon and Frank Holt at their offices and finally found Olivia but as usual did not record in his diary what they said to each other. He joined Holt and the editors of the *Montgomery Journal* and the *Birmingham Post* for lunch at a cafeteria. Francis arrived, his car loaded with camping equipment and maps, in midafternoon. Although Francis was reluctant to spend any time on a social call, Roland took him to Lewis Golsan's home in Autauga County and to the home of Olivia's cousins, the Shackelfords.[8] (He did not note in his diary whether he saw Clare Shackelford, but he mailed a postcard to her from Montgomery before he and Francis left two days later.)

The next morning, Roland took Francis to Brannon's office. Francis carried a copy of Bartram's *Travels*, perhaps the 1928 edition edited by Mark Van Doren, and the three men referred to Bartram's description of traveling to the vicinity of Montgomery. Brannon pointed out that the Old Federal Road followed earlier American Indian paths along ridges above swampy areas. The three men examined copies of the Taitt map and one by another eighteenth-century explorer, Joseph Purcell. Brannon suggested that Bartram probably passed the present Fort Mitchell through Uchee to Tallassee; traveled thence along the south side of the Tallapoosa River to Coolome, ten miles east of Montgomery; thence southwesterly by way of Snowdoun and Fort Deposit, crossing Catoma, Pintlalla, and

Pinchony Creeks; and finally along the divide between the Alabama and the Escambia river basins to the vicinity of Stockton on the Mobile Delta. Brannon pointed out American Indian sites and examined the map in Roland's 1913 monograph on Alabama and maps in a 1921 biological survey of Alabama by Arthur H. Howell. Together, the men pinpointed locations Bartram had passed between the Chattahoochee River on the Alabama-Georgia line and westward to the Tallapoosa River. Brannon wrote in his Sunday column for the *Montgomery Advertiser* the next week that he had enjoyed the visit by Roland, "Alabama's distinguished botanist," and Francis, "a distinguished zoologist."[9]

In the afternoon, a local archaeologist, R. P. Burke, drove the Harpers to Coolome, an American Indian mound site east of Montgomery. Francis and Roland each made notes and probably referred to Bartram's text: "The Tallapoosa river is here three hundred yards over, and about fifteen or twenty feet water, which is very clear, agreeable to the taste, esteemed salubrious, and runs with a steady active current." A little beyond Cook's Station, they parked and walked through fields to the mound. While Francis took two photographs, Roland found yellow bractspike (*Yeatesia viridiflora*), on the southern bank of the river. They explored a meadow south of the Western Railway track, where Roland found a large patch of the native perennial golden colicroot (*Aletris aurea*) in bloom, as well as many sedges. In their hotel room that evening, Roland marked newspapers to clip later and pressed the specimens he had collected.[10]

Bartram had departed the village on the Tallapoosa in July 1775, following the Indian trading path through "a magnificent forest, just without or skirting the Indian plantations frequently having a view of their distant towns over plains or old fields." After covering about eighteen miles, the Bartram party stopped for the night and made camp "under shelter of a grove of venerable spreading Oaks, on the verge of the great plains; their enormous limbs loaded with *Tillandsia ulneadscites*, waving the winds." Although Arthur Howell had placed Bartram's campsite on the Tallapoosa, Francis speculated that it was near the present town of Snowdoun. He drove south from Montgomery on Woodley Road, through Pinedale, a small community east of Barachias, and through the bottoms of Catoma Creek. Roland observed that no original vegetation survived along their route. Turning west a little south of the creek on Snowdoun-Chambers Road, he and Francis drove on to Snowdoun.[11]

From there, Francis turned onto a remnant of the Old Federal Road that ran east-west, passed through the community of Colquitt, and crossed Pinchony Creek, where he and Roland stopped to explore. They referred to a 1926 soil map of Montgomery County and compared the roadside scenery to Bartram's description of a "sylvan landscape of primitive, uncultivated nature" and of creeks whose banks were "ornamented" by crab, plum, and dogwood trees and strawberry vines running through plains "clad with tall grass, intermixed with a variety of herbiage; the most conspicuous, both for beauty and novelty, a tall species of *Silphium*." Roland speculated that the beautiful plant was kidneyleaf rosinweed (*S. terebinthinaceum*), explaining that the nineteenth-century naturalist Stephen Elliott had reported the species in Alabama's prairies but that it was no longer found there. He pointed out to Francis that the topsoil Bartram called "black, soapy and rich" was the characteristic soil of the Black Belt and the substrate was Selma Chalk. Roland further explained that Bartram's course from Snowdoun to the Alabama River took him through several distinct geological regions: the Blue Marl Region, the Southern Red Hills, the Lime Hills, and the Southwestern Pine Hills. While Roland made notes, Francis concentrated on determining Bartram's exact route and correcting errors in other scholars' interpretations of Bartram's account. Whereas Bartram had estimated that the Federal Road ran within two or three miles of the Alabama River, Francis observed that he was "quite mistaken." The old road turned sharply to the southwest but became impassable near the Lowndes County line, so the brothers backtracked to Colquitt and turned south on Highway 31, which was paved. Roland made car-window notes on the transition from the Black Belt to the Southern Red Hills. They passed through Fort Deposit at about six p.m. and stopped for the night in Greenville a half-hour later. After they checked into an old hotel, Roland clipped articles from some month-old newspapers he had brought along.[12]

The next morning Francis and Roland found another remnant of the Old Federal Road a few miles west of Greenville and took it to the southwest, passing the community of Shacklesville and crossing into Monroe County. Roland observed that most houses were small and unpainted, some made of logs, many with rock chimneys. Recent rain had made the red clay of the old road slippery, and Francis had trouble rolling forward. They detoured across fields in Monroe County, where the farms appeared a little more prosperous, and then south on Highway 47 to Midway, "a small settlement with a new filling station." From there they drove down Highway 83, past farms with painted houses, some with windmills, through Skinnerton and China to Evergreen. Francis hoped to find a dogwood forest that Bartram had described as "a very remarkable grove of Dogwood trees." The expanse of dogwood forest was nine or ten miles across, according to Bartram, with "here and there a towering *Magnolia grandiflora* . . . [the dogwoods] about twelve feet high, spreading horizontally; their limbs meeting and interlocking with each other, [forming] one vast, shady, cool grove, so dense and humid as to exclude the sun-beams and prevent the intrusion of almost every other vegetable." Bartram had camped that night "on the banks of a glittering rivulet amidst a spicy grove of the *Illicium Floridanum* [Florida anise]." When the brothers did not find the dogwood grove, Francis speculated that it had been south of Midway but had been cut over, the wood "now converted largely into shuttles and the like"—a sardonic comment, considering that Roland had surveyed parts of Georgia and Alabama in 1911 for the shuttle industry.[13]

Three-and-a-half years after their trip along Bartram's route, while scanning newspaper articles, Roland came across a reference to "Dogwood Flats" at the location of Fort Bibb near Butler Spring in Butler County. This triggered a memory of a book in the collection of the Alabama Geological Survey, a history of Butler County by John B. Little published in 1885. Roland found the volume and was thrilled that it contained a folded map indicating Fort Bibb in relation to local roads. He wrote excitedly to Clare Shackelford that Dogwood Flats must be Bartram's dogwood forest, concluding that he and Francis had turned southwest too soon from Highway 10 after leaving Greenville. They had missed it by "two or three miles." Roland reported his discovery to Francis, too, and Francis incorporated his brother's conclusion into the annotated edition of Bartram's *Travels* that he eventually completed, quoting Little: "The level portion of low, flat land between Reddock and Pine Barren Creeks, was originally covered with a pine forest and a dense undergrowth of dogwood."[14]

After their unsuccessful hunt for the dogwood grove, Roland and Francis stopped only ten minutes in Evergreen before continuing south on U.S. Highway 31, through pine barrens dominated by slash pine, to Brewton. Roland noted that the Louisville and Nashville Railroad was not visible from the highway on this southward leg, but at Brewton they found a tourist home near the train station and spent the night there. Precursors of motels, tourist homes were private homes where the owner-residents rented one or more bedrooms, with bathroom privileges, often only in summer tourist seasons.

The drive west on Highway 31 from Brewton to the county line took two and a half hours the next morning. They crossed Little Escambia Creek and Big Escambia Creek, and Roland noted that the water was "mostly coffee-colored, some swift and shallow, with gravelly beds, *Chamaecyparis thyoides* [Atlantic white cedar] on most of the creeks and rivers." They were in longleaf country, Roland's favorite ecosystem. Bartram had described it as "not much unlike the low countries of Carolina . . . one vast flat grassy savanna and Cane meadows, intersected or variously scrolled over with narrow forests and groves, on the banks of creeks and rivulets, or hommocks and swamps at their sources; with long leaved Pines, scatteringly planted amongst the grass, and on the high sandy knolls and swelling ridges, *Quercus nigra*" and other oaks. Creeks ran swift and shallow "over gravelly beds, and their banks [were] adorned with *Illicium* [Florida anise, or *Illicium floridanum*] groves, *Magnolias, Azaleas, Halesia* [*Halesia diptera*, or two-wing silverbell] *Andromedas,* etc." Bartram found that "the highest hills near large creeks afford[ed] high forests with abundance of Chestnut trees," but Roland told his brother that chestnuts no longer grew in south Alabama.[15]

Noting that the longleaf they passed was all second growth, perhaps Roland reread Bartram's description of clear-cutting of longleaf in Carolina: "The slaves comparatively of a gigantic stature, fat and muscular, mounted on the massive timber logs, the regular heavy strokes of their gleaming axes re-echo in the deep forests, at the same time contented and joyful the sooty sons of Afric forgetting their bondage, in chorus sing the virtues and beneficence of their master in songs of their own composition." If Roland continued reading Bartram's passage on longleaf clear-cutting in South Carolina, he found another of the explorer's lapses into erotica, an envious encounter with young newlyweds: the son of the plantation owner who was cutting the forest and "his lovely bride arrayed in native innocence and becoming modesty, with an air and smile of grace and benignity, meets and salutes us: what a Venus! what an Adonis! Said I in silent transport."[16]

Francis and Roland passed the town of Flomaton to the south and then the communities of Canoe, Malta, Atmore, and Nokomis, following the highway paralleling the Louisville and Nashville Railroad through more cutover longleaf woods. Just across the line into Baldwin County, Francis took a county road to the northwest to reach Perdido, turning then onto a dirt road that wound west across the county, at times along the route of the historic Old Federal Road. Again following Bartram's path, he descended Gopher Hill, a ridge known for the gopher tortoises that were once common there, although Francis saw few signs of them. Roland noted painted farmhouses, sheep grazing in the woods, and turpentine stills. He spotted a plant with tubular, drooping flowers that he thought was perhaps a species of *Macranthera*, but not the rare and beautiful flameflower (*M. flammea*) that the Harpers' friend Francis W. Pennell believed was the plant Bartram described as *Gerardea*.[17]

The Harpers found the home of Professor I. P. Mason at Stockton, where the dirt road ended at a north-south road, Highway 59, and called on him in midafternoon. They examined a 1912 soil map of Baldwin County with Mason before one of Mason's sons drove Roland and Francis north to Melton's Landing, a point near the mouth of Hall's Creek. This was the location that Bartram called "Taensa," south of the stretch of river where he had discovered the largeflower evening primrose and where Roland rendezvoused with Hugo de Vries in 1912. Bartram had written, "[A] few miles above Taensa, I was struck with surprise at the appearance of a blooming plant, gilded with the richest golden yellow. Stepping on shore, I discovered it to be a new species of the *Oenothera* (*Oenothera grandiflora*) . . . perhaps the most pompous and brilliant herbaeceous plant yet known to exist. . . . The flowers begin to open in the evening, are fully expanded during the night, and are in their beauty next morning."[18]

Roland observed that the plantations Bartram described had "reverted to forest" and the primroses were gone, and fishermen were working on boats on the muddy channel. He and Francis briefly explored the area above and below Melton's Landing, gazing across a wide, still section of the river channel that runs east-west and surveying the trees on a fifty-foot bluff just north of the landing. Roland described the area later as "a labyrinth of smaller channels" where the Alabama and Tombigbee rivers lose their identity and the two principal navigable channels become known as the Mobile River, on the west, and the Tensaw River on the east. If he noticed the prehistoric American Indian mounds that Walter Jones had told him and Francis were in the vicinity, Roland made no note of them. He saw spruce pine; a species of laurel, perhaps hairy wicky (*Kalmia hirsuta*), which is found in pine savannas, or mountain laurel, which is found on the bluffs of streams and creeks; and common sweetleaf (*Symplocos tinctoria*), the northernmost species of a genus that extends to Puerto Rico and the Virgin Islands. He was surprised to find, in a location so far south, the now rare pyramid magnolia (*Magnolia pyramidata*), a small tree with fantastically beautiful flowers that Bartram had ecstatically described from his type locality at a point ten miles or so miles farther up the Alabama River: "I recline on the verdant bank, and view the beauties of the groves." Roland collected specimens of the magnolia, later sending one to the New York Botanical Garden, and photographed the still channel and the dense forest of cypress on the other side.[19]

Glad that pavement began just a few yards from Mason's house, Francis and Roland headed south on Highway 59. They drove through vast areas of second-growth longleaf and free-range cattle and sheep, passing Bay Minette a half-hour later. Cotton fields gave way to corn, vegetables, and flowers as they continued on the same road, east of the pioneer town of Blakeley and the Confederate Fort Blakely, where a Civil War battle occurred the same day as General Robert E. Lee's surrender, and on past Stapleton. The sun set as they passed through Loxley. At Robertsdale, they veered southeast on U.S. Highway 90, a scenic highway built within the previous decade that lured tourists to the Gulf Coast's stunning beaches. The highway crossed Blackwater Creek and then Perdido River, the border between Alabama and Florida. They passed several "tourist camps," stopovers for travelers pulling campers, but continued to Pensacola and checked into a tourist home at the intersection of the highway and Palafox Street. It was too dark to see the Gulf of Mexico from the bluffs at Pensacola, but Francis probably imagined Bartram, who had also arrived in the evening, sailing around the point and docking near the Government House.[20]

Roland strolled about downtown in the morning, shopping at a dime store and mailing some postcards. He and Francis visited Julien Chandler Yonge, the editor of the *Florida Historical Quarterly*, in the late morning, probably to examine maps or other items in Yonge's personal library of Floridiana. The brothers spent the afternoon in the car, going to Fort Barrancas on the city's peninsula, in order for Roland to determine that hooded pitcher plants did not grow in the vicinity of Pensacola despite Bartram's reference to them there. (The Harpers' friend Edgar T. Wherry had suggested in 1935 that the species did not extend to western Florida. Wherry shared Francis's and Roland's interest in Bartram and had written an article on *Franklinia alatamaha* for the journal of the Washington Academy of Sciences in 1929.) Roland confirmed the absence of hooded pitcher plants and collected a few specimens. He told Francis that a scarlet-flowered plant Bartram had seen there might have been scarlet calamint (known in 1939 as *Clinopodium coccineum*).[21]

Bartram had stayed at Pensacola only two nights before returning to

Mobile, and Francis gave the area little more than a page in his commentary on Bartram's trip. Before leaving the colonial port town, however, he took Roland along on a visit to the ornithologist Francis Marion Weston. Since discovering the previous fall that many migrating birds crashed into the three-mile bridge over Pensacola Bay connecting the city to Santa Rosa Island and then fell dead on the roadway, Weston had been collecting information about bird casualties on the bridge. A one-dollar toll made frequent bay crossings prohibitive, but Weston drove over the bridge whenever he could, collecting dead birds and identifying as many as possible. He also asked friends to stop and pick up birds, so he probably asked Francis to collect carcasses and write to him about any he identified.[22] While he and Francis talked, Roland took note that Weston smoked cigarettes and had a much younger wife with bobbed hair.

The brothers concluded their visit at Weston's house just before 6 p.m. and drove down Palafox Street to the toll bridge over the bay. After reaching Santa Rosa Island, they turned east on U.S. Highway 98, and Roland made more car-window notes: stunted longleaf, dry savannas, sand hills, a few cottages, cows grazing in the woods, a dead hog in the road. They stopped for Roland to explore a dry savanna, where he collected a specimen of a beaksedge. They returned to the mainland for the night and camped for the first time on this trip, choosing "a neat tourist camp" with white frame cottages and parking pads for cars and campers, where a paved road from Milton met U.S. Highway 98 at Camp Navarre. Roland changed his plant driers and at about eleven at night bathed in the sound. The water glimmered with the phosphorescence of swarms of single-celled algae. Had Roland read the literary scholar John Livingston Lowes's 1927 book, *The Road to Xanadu*, an analysis of the influence of William Bartram's and other explorer narratives' on the poet Samuel Taylor Coleridge? If so, perhaps he thought, as he bobbed in the phosphorescent glow, of Coleridge's "elfish light," of his "flash of golden fire." Or perhaps Roland thought of Olivia, the Montgomery siren who had tried to lure him into the creeks of Autauga County.

Francis and Roland lingered at Navarre until ten the next morning and then headed east on 98; Francis stopped frequently for Roland to make photographs and collect specimens. When they reached Fort Walton at 11:20 a.m., Francis again crossed the sound by bridge to Santa Rosa Island, so that they could explore the dunes. The pine trees were very stunted, only knee-high when mature enough to produce cones. Beach plants were half-buried by windblown sand drifts. Roland noted yaupon

(*Ilex vomitoria*), pinewoods milkweed (*Asclepias humistrata*), earleaf greenbrier (*Smilax auriculata*), Maryland goldenaster (*Chrysopsis mariana*), and peelbark St. John's wort. The sun was directly overhead when they turned back to Fort Walton and headed northeast on a fairly new road through the longleaf woods of Choctawhatchee National Forest.[23] Roland and Francis stopped for lunch at crystal-clear Juniper Creek between Valparaiso and Niceville, where Roland noting jointed spikerush (*Eleocharis equisetoides*), Atlantic white cedar, and goldenclub growing at the edges of the water. Mats of weird watershield (*Brasenia shreberi*), each plant a single oval platter, floated on the surface. The area was so beautiful and the plant diversity so rich, Roland prevailed on Francis to stop at two more small creeks and a steephead. They turned east on U.S. Highway 90 north of the national forest, but Roland was disappointed to see that a fifty-foot swath on the north side of the road had been cleared. They went through the town of De Funiak Springs around five o'clock and into Holmes County, which Roland thought was economically poorer because most of the houses along the highway were unpainted. They reached western Marianna on the Chipola River, checked into another tourist home, and ate supper at a downtown restaurant. Back in their room, Roland put the specimens he had collected that day into his press and wrote a note to Louis Moore's brother Henry in Thomasville, Georgia.

The next morning was hot. Before exploring the area, the brothers wanted to visit the grave of N. M. Hentz. Their friend Collier Cobb, the geologist at the University of North Carolina, had written about Hentz in the journal of the Elisha Mitchell Scientific Society a few years earlier. An interesting figure in scientific history, Hentz was born in Versailles, France, in 1797, and died in relative obscurity in Marianna in 1856. A mentally unstable physician, educator, naturalist, and illustrator, he had moved often from job to job—not unlike Roland and Francis's father—apparently driven by a paranoid jealousy of his wife, Caroline Lee Whiting Hentz, a popular and prolific novelist, playwright, and poet whose literary accomplishments vastly overshadowed his own.[24] The Harpers found Hentz's gravestone, and Francis made a photograph of it before he and Roland went on to investigate Spring Creek east of town. They passed black field workers using oxen to pull wagons and plows and then traveled north into Georgia. They stopped for a half-hour for Roland to examine the vegetation on the Georgia side of the Chattahoochee River. He made notes about the geology of the banks; he undoubtedly also searched for stinking cedar since they were quite near the Flint River locality in Georgia where he had found the elusive tree in 1918, but he did not record seeing any.

After detouring to visit friends in Donalsonville, Georgia, Roland and Francis headed southeast for Thomasville. Francis was finished for the time being with tracing Bartram's route, and they wanted to visit Louis Moore's brother, Henry, even though Louis was away. On June 22, Henry accompanied Roland and Francis to a local nursery belonging to P. J. Hjort to see specimens of *Franklinia alatamaha*. Hjort had solved part of a *Frankliana* mystery in 1935 when he reported that the shrub bloomed in the summer, as collectors of cultivated specimens knew, *and* in April and May, so that Bartram's record of seeing it in bloom in the spring could have been correct. Later in the day, Roland and Francis paid a call on Herbert L. Stoddard Sr., a forester who was primarily interested in longleaf. Stoddard was away, but Roland and Francis chatted for a couple of hours with his wife and the forester Roy Komarek before driving on to Tallahassee. They checked into another tourist home and then went to the offices of the Florida Geological Survey. Herman Gunter, Roland's geologist friend, also was away, but they spent a while talking with J. Clarence Simpson, another survey employee. Simpson showed Francis locations on a map of points Bartram visited on the Suwannee River. After Roland checked the post office for mail, he and Francis spent the evening with Mark F. Boyd of the Rockefeller Foundation, talking of Bartram and looking at Boyd's collection of books and maps related to Florida history. When they returned to the geological survey office, they found Herman Kurz, but Francis had little time to chat. He departed by four o'clock and headed for the Suwannee River to resume tracing Bartram's trail in eastern Florida. In all, Francis's 1939 expedition along Bartram's trail would cover five thousand miles and lasted two months.[25]

Roland spent one more busy day in Tallahassee, visiting Susan Bradford Eppes and other old friends, going with Addison Marshall and his family by car to their house in northeast Tallahassee, spending the afternoon with the psychologist Paul Finner, and having dinner with Simpson and his family at their home. Simpson drove Roland back to his hotel around ten o'clock, but Roland was restless and wrote a card to "S.C." (perhaps this was Clare Shackelford, with the initials accidentally reversed in his diary) and walked to the post office to mail it.

Up early the next morning, Roland had breakfast, packed, and stopped by the geological survey one more time. He found Gunter there even though it was a Sunday and talked with him for an hour before catching a bus to Montgomery. Riding northwest across the coastal plain, Roland again observed that slash pine had largely supplanted longleaf. In Montgomery, he left a note for Brannon at the post office and then took a train to Tuscaloosa, where he went by taxi to his rooming house. Slipping back into his routine, he rose early the next morning and hurried to his office to change the plant driers and put some of the specimens he had collected in Florida in a press. He noted in his diary that he also "worked on vital statistics of Thorndike's fifteen 'best' and 'worst' cities, and found that the former have more deaths from heart disease and cancer (as expected) but less from other causes." He read some recent newspapers, marking articles to be clipped and filed.

A week later, Roland received a scathing letter from Merritt Fernald at Harvard concerning a manuscript Roland had sent him just before departing on the Bartram expedition. The manuscript probably was a submission to the journal *Rhodora*, which Fernald still edited. In it, Roland discussed conifers in Virginia, probably relying on car-window notes he had made on a trip to Richmond, Virginia, the previous December. Fernald wrote, "Many of your statements of apparent fact are so far from actuality to those who seriously botanize and explore in southeastern Virginia!"

This was not Fernald's first challenge to Harper. Roland had made the trip to Richmond to attend a meeting of the American Association for the Advancement of Science. Possibly in informal conversation, possibly in an open session in the Monticello Room of the Jefferson Hotel, where several of Harper's friends and acquaintances, including Forrest Shreve and Edgar Wherry, could have been present, Fernald disputed Harper on the question of whether longleaf pine grew in Virginia.[26] Harper reported that he had seen it from a train, probably on the trip he had just made to Richmond; Fernald scoffed. It was a rude challenge by the northerner to the reserved southern scientist.

Fernald was an expert on the flora of southeastern Virginia, having made numerous botanizing trips to the area, particularly the section south of the James River from the coast to Brunswick County. On the other hand, Harper had been intrigued for years by the upper limits of longleaf's range, observing in 1907 that longleaf had not been recorded in Virginia since the turn of the century—"I know of no one who has seen it in that state in the last decade or two"—and wondering again in a letter to Alfred Akerman in 1923 about whether there was longleaf in

Virginia.[27] Considering that range extensions above and below the Fall Line, in general, and the species *Pinus palustris*, in particular, were topics of special interest to Harper, it was highly unlikely that he would err in declaring that longleaf did exist in Virginia.

In fact, he did not err. After Harper left the American Association for the Advancement of Science conference, Fernald prevailed upon some people with a car to drive him to Harper's "supposed location" in a pine barren, near the town of Zuni, which Fernald had explored several times. He described the incident with wry self-effacement later that year: "Slowing down at our old parking-spot in the pine barrens south of Zuni, we were startled and grieved to hear Mrs. Correll announce: 'Why, there's longleaf pine right there!' And there it was! . . . We had half-a-dozen times brushed by the great columnar young pines without their 'registering.' Not only young columns were there; plenty of old fruiting trees . . . we have not yet got over our chagrin."[28]

While Fernald made a joke publicly of his mistake in challenging Harper, the episode apparently still rankled when he received Harper's paper on Virginia conifers the following summer. He grudgingly allowed in his response that Harper had extended the range of longleaf into Brunswick County, Virginia, but said, "that record could, if [one] wished, be made in a single paragraph or two." Furthermore, he warned Harper, "If the paper is published in its present form it would be necessary for me to make a great many contradictions of your statements, which would not be particularly pleasant; but it is not the policy of the editors to write the papers for contributors, but to allow them to say whatever they wish under their own names. I could not, therefore, modify your paper except as to improbable lapses in English, but I should be obliged to put in many footnotes signed by myself to the effect that the implications of your statements are contrary to facts as shown by actual collected specimens." Fernald went on to refute Harper regarding fourteen species.[29] Harper probably withdrew the manuscript submission. Fernald's animosity must have been discouraging to him. Although he had worked in phytogeography for thirty years, he seemed always to be on the margins, never fully accepted, by Fernald, at least, into the highest circle of botanists.

CHAPTER NINE

A Prophet for Fire

Riding a bus through Walker County, Alabama, in July 1942, Harper passed a virgin longleaf pine forest he had investigated in 1906 and was "agreeably surprised" to see plenty of longleaf still standing. That summer he was gathering final photographs and information for his second major report on Alabama forests, and he made a note of the surviving longleaf stand in the manuscript. Harper also prepared a long section on fire for the report, reiterating a point he had been making for decades, that the longleaf ecosystem is highly dependent on fire, and arguing that complete fire suppression, the official policy of the United States Forest Service, was "as short-sighted a policy as moving the Eskimos to a warmer climate to make them more comfortable."[1]

Fire, he wrote, is "necessary for the perpetuation of longleaf pine, for several reasons. Its seeds germinate best on bare sandy soil, exposed to the sun, so that if they were prevented from reaching the ground by thick grass, or dead leaves, they might die before germinating. . . . Hardwood trees in the neighborhood would be detrimental to the pine, for they would contribute more leaf-litter . . . and they also produce shade, which the pine seedlings do not want. Fire also helps keep in check the 'brown-spot,' a fungus disease that attacks the leaves of longleaf pine seedlings close to the ground." He went even further, saying that fire was *good* for longleaf forests because it released mineral matter from leaves, making the minerals available as plant food.[2]

Around the time that he was polishing his manuscript on Alabama forests, Harper received a letter from H. H. Chapman at Yale University. Chapman enclosed his own newest contribution to the literature on fire ecology, a bulletin that recommended periodic controlled burning in loblolly forests. "As you were one of, and may have been the first[,] of the scientists who concluded that fire had an indispensable place in the ecology and silviculture of southern pines you may be interested in this bulletin," Chapman wrote to Harper.[3] Harper hurried to add Chapman's new work to a bibliography about fire that he had compiled for his mono-graph. The gesture reflected his meticulous attention to bibliographic lists but also a reciprocal scientific chivalry that was typical of Harper's quiet, yet pioneering role in fire ecology.

Since 1908, Chapman and Harper had been speaking up to counter the dominant forest management idea of the time, that all forest fires were bad and should be prevented and suppressed at all costs. Longleaf forests were significantly reduced across the southern coastal plain by a combina-tion of lumbering, turpentining, and the unintended consequences of for-est fire suppression. Hardwood species had spread through an estimated 39 percent of longleaf forests in South Carolina, for example. As early as 1906, in his dissertation concerning the Altamaha Grit region, Harper had listed fire as an ecological factor that affects vegetative diversity. After going to Coosa and Clay Counties in Alabama with other forestry stu-dents at Yale University in 1908, Chapman suggested in an unpublished senior paper that burning forest ground could facilitate seed germina-tion. Harper continued thinking about fire's role in pine forests. He com-mented in a letter to J. H. Foster in August 1909, "The pine woods must have been burned ever since prehistoric times. (There is plenty of evidence to support this.)"[4]

During his early research along the Fall Line of Georgia, the bluffs of the Black Warrior River, and in Florida, Harper was particularly in-terested in hammocks, pocosins, and other wetland ecotones, the tran-sition zones between wetlands and uplands. He pondered the fact that the coastal plain was swept by frequent fires—fires that were ignited by lightning as well as by the grazing and hunting practices of American Indians and Celtic settlers. He specifically referred to pine's resistance to fire and to the protection from fire that wetlands provided to hardwood hammocks in his 1909 manuscript about the Everglades for the magazine *Florida Review*, although the editor deleted that passage from the pub-lished version.[5] In 1910 or 1911, Harper wrote, "All of the longleaf pine forests of which I have any knowledge (and I have seen them in seven of the nine states and about 200 out of some 300 counties in which *Pinus palustris* is found), even the more or less isolated ones in the mountains of Georgia and Alabama, bear the marks of frequent fires. . . . Although fires may not be started by lightning on any one square mile oftener than once in several decades, a fire once started in the grassy carpet of an unbroken pine forest might easily spread over several square miles, so that every acre of such forest if not protected in some way would be likely to be burned over every few years." How, then, did hammocks and other lush pockets of broad-leaved trees, shrubs, and vines, such as Aspalaga Bluff, escape the conflagrations? The answer was clear to him: bodies of water, such as streams or the seasonal lakes that surround hammocks, and sand hills that supported little combustible vegetation, were natural firebreaks. Only the areas protected from fire reached climax conditions. Harper published his theory of climax vegetation in the *Bulletin of the Torrey Botanical Club* in 1911.[6]

A corollary of his theory was that the coastal plain's dominant ecosystem, the longleaf-wiregrass forest—all the terrain not protected by water or sand hills—not only survived but *flourished* in conditions of frequent fire. This was a profound insight, and while it was initially obscured by Harper's interpretation in terms of ecological succession, it challenged the prevailing view of scientists as eminent as Harper's sponsor at Harvard, Charles Sargent. In a report for the United States Census in 1884, Sargent declared that, contrary to the beliefs and practices of farmers, controlled fires in longleaf forests "often caused serious destruction of timber" and "less valuable species now occupy the ground once covered with forests of the long-leaved pine, through which annual fires have been allowed to run to improve the scanty pasturage they afford. Stockmen have been benefited at the expense of the permanency of the forest."[7] Directly contradicting this conventional wisdom, Harper's idea would bedevil the nation's foresters for decades.

Chapman seconded Harper in the journal *American Forestry* in 1912, arguing that there was "a striking difference between southern and northern pine in their resistance to fire. White pine is killed easily by fires even when mature. But the three southern pines are all remarkably fire resistant and the longleaf pine has adapted its whole structure and growth as a seedling to the primary object of surviving ground fires." He conceded that careless and deliberate burns for the purpose of improving grazing conditions could damage longleaf forests but argued that complete fire suppression was inappropriate in southern woods. "The proper *use* of fire and not complete fire prevention is the only solution . . . in the South." He recommended fire suppression at some stages and use of controlled burning at others. "A promiscuous enforcement of forest fire laws, borrowed whole from Northern States, and utterly unsuited to the South, will never result in anything but dissatisfaction and contempt on the part of practical men for forestry."[8]

By 1913, state and federal fire prevention policies were intensely controversial. When Harper observed, in a report on forests for the Alabama

Geological Survey that year, that the longleaf's seeds could not germinate except on recently burned ground, reaction was mixed. C. D. Howe, the forester whose position Harper had considered filling at Biltmore in 1908, was editor of the *Journal of Forestry*. He mocked Harper's statements about fire. However, the editor of *American Forestry* (later renamed *American Forests*) invited Harper to elaborate on his ideas in an article for that journal, which he did, and his article appeared in October 1913. The *Literary Digest* also published a one-page excerpt from Harper's monograph, with the title "A Defense of Forest Fires" that year, noting that Harper's view of fire's importance to longleaf was "quite at variance with current traditions and teachings." In an article about conifers of eastern North America in *Popular Science Monthly* in October 1914, Harper noted each species' relationship to fire. In his report "Geography and Vegetation of Northern Florida," for the Florida Geological Survey, he asserted, "[I]t is reasonably certain that if fire were kept out of a longleaf pine forest long enough hardwood trees of various kinds would come in and choke out the pine (which does not thrive in shade), and thus convert the pine forest into a hammock. Most of our hammocks are in situations protected from fire by the topography, as on slopes down which fire would not travel readily, or in places partly surrounded by water." In the western Florida lime-sink region, "the prevailing type of vegetation is open forests of longleaf pine, so open that wagons can be driven through them almost anywhere (and consequently the minor roads are ill-defined and changeable). The scarcity of underbrush seems to be due primarily to the fires, set originally by lightning, and now mostly by man, either purposely or accidentally. The fires burn over every part of the pine woods nearly every year, usually in the latter part of the dry season (early spring), with little injury to the pines."[9]

Harper never claimed to be the first to realize fire's importance to longleaf pine. He acknowledged G. Frederick Schwarz in the 1911 article for suggesting in 1907 that longleaf, once it was four or five years old, was more resistant to fire than any other southern tree. Harper also gave credit to Ellen Call Long of Tallahassee, who he thought "must have been a very brilliant woman, [for sounding] one of the first discordant notes in the chorus of denunciation of fire." Although he was not familiar with her work when he wrote the 1911 article or the 1913 report, once he learned of it, he noted that an address she delivered in 1889 to the American Forestry Congress "was so heretical that little attention seems to have been paid to it at the time." The daughter of Governor Richard Keith Call, Long was, like Susan Bradford Eppes, a prominent figure in Tallahassee society. Also like Eppes, Long wrote a memoir, *Florida Breezes, or, Florida New and Old*, with romantic images of Florida's past, such as picnics at St. Marks, "where [they] danced by moonlight, (to old Fred's fiddle) on top of the fort, over what were once dungeons, and while caressed by gulf zephyrs," and longleaf forests where "the whistle of the Partridge, shriek of the Jay, the clear clarionette note of the Wren, and varied song of the Mocking-bird, made the woods resound, while the baying of dogs pursuing timid rabbits and fleeing squirrels, made a bass to nature's orchestra that accompanied [them] on all sides." (Unlike Susan Eppes, however, Ellen Long was a liberal on racial matters.)[10]

Harper also acknowledged George V. Nash of the New York Botanical Garden, who observed in 1895 that frequent fires in Florida pine forests did not seem to damage the trees or ground cover because the plants tended to have "thick roots well below the surface." Another botanist, E. F. Andrews, described her observations of fire and longleaf in the vicinity of Rome, Georgia, for the *Botanical Gazette* in 1917, and Harper called her "a talented lady" who "made some experiments which [he] could not have done because [he] never stayed in one place long enough."[11]

Harper continued to argue in the 1920s that fire was a natural part of ecosystems, speculating in his 1927 report on southern Florida that during prehistoric times lightning had caused fires that burned across many miles as frequently as every two years, on average, in any particular location. Fire suppression was an entrenched public policy during this period, however. The United States Forest Service issued a bulletin for farmers, "Making Woodlands Profitable in the Southern States," which recommended complete fire exclusion in longleaf stands, and reissued it in 1922, 1924, and 1932. Harper found few who accepted the idea that fire suppression would gradually destroy longleaf-wiregrass communities. When he worked briefly for the Alabama Forestry Commission in Montgomery in 1927, the state forester, Page Bunker, a New Englander whom Harper considered a "fire fundamentalist," did not agree. As Harper told the story years later, "When [Bunker] discovered that I intended to tell what I took to be the truth about fire (under longleaf pine, etc.) he withdrew his support, and I went back to Tuscaloosa." Harper complained that in a commission newsletter the following year, Bunker characterized Chapman's view on fire as naive, without even acknowledging Harper's own contributions to the scientific literature on fire. Opposition also came from old friends. John Kunkel Small argued that all fires were destructive to southern forests in his 1929 book, *From Eden to Sahara*.[12]

Another scientific discipline lent support to Harper's position. Two wildlife biologists, one working in Georgia and the other in Mississippi, reached the same counterintuitive conclusion that fire could be good for forests. Herbert L. Stoddard Sr. studied the declining population of northern bobwhite quail in southern Georgia for about six years and determined that fire suppression had altered the natural longleaf-wiregrass environment so drastically that it had become uninhabitable for quail. When he went to a conference of the American Forestry Association in Jacksonville, Florida, in 1929, Stoddard found that some foresters were already aware of his conclusion. One might suppose Harper's suspicion that the Alabama state forester, Page Bunker, deliberately ignored Harper's work on fire was somewhat paranoid, but Stoddard had a similar experience at the conference. "I have never attended a meeting with a more pervasively hostile atmosphere," Stoddard remembered. "The chairman, who obviously feared that I might contaminate my hearers, actually cautioned them not to take too seriously what I might say. I fear I took a perverse pleasure in reading the chapter to them, though I had a feeling of futility at the solid wall of opposition with which it was received," Stoddard wrote in his memoir. Stoddard released his report two years after that conference, in 1931, recommending controlled burning to foster growth of leguminous plants that were important food sources for quail.[13]

S. W. Greene was perhaps the only sympathetic listener at the Jacksonville conference. At the time that Stoddard first presented his ideas about fire and longleaf forests, Greene was conducting an experimental study of controlled burning on grazing lands and in longleaf forests in Mississippi. Greene also made a presentation at the meeting, demonstrating that cattle gained more weight when they grazed on lands that were burned annually, because the fires encouraged tender new growth. Greene described fire's relationship to longleaf in an article, "The Forest That Fire Made," that appeared in *American Forests* in the same year that Stoddard's book was published. Greene did not cite Harper's earlier article on fire in the same journal.[14] Harper wrote to Greene to give him a capsule review of the historic literature on fire, a summary that warrants lengthy quotation here because it demonstrates the care Harper took to acknowledge his predecessors:

The earliest reference that I know anything about is on page 69 [of] the second volume of Sir Charles Lyell's 'Second Visit to the United States,'

published in New York and London in 1849. He was visiting Tuscaloosa
in February 1846, and went out into the hills northeast of here. He says—
'These hills were covered with long-leaved pines, and the large proportion
they bear to the hard wood is said to have been increased by the Indian
practice of burning the grass; the bark of the oak and other kinds of hard
wood being more combustible, and more easily injured by fire, than that of
the fir tribe. Every where the young seedlings of the long-leaved pine were
coming up in such numbers that one might have supposed the ground to
have been sown with them; and I was reminded how rarely we see similar
self-sown firs in English plantations." You see he had the right idea, and
he did remarkably well to give so much detail the first time, and in a book
devoted primarily to geology.[15]

Harper also was determined that Ellen Call Long would receive proper
credit. He told Greene about her papers of forty years earlier, in which she
suggested that if fire were kept out of longleaf forest long enough, the forest would convert to hammock. A few months later, he wrote to Greene
again, enclosing a copy of one of Long's articles. He told Greene that
she had originally read the article at a meeting of the American Forestry
Congress in Atlanta in December 1889, and that it was published in full
in the proceedings of that meeting.[16]

     Harper, Chapman, Stoddard, and Greene became part of a small but
persistent movement to overturn fire suppression policy. Edward V. Komarek Sr. later dubbed the group the "Dixie Pioneers," in contrast to the
"Dixie Crusaders" of the Forest Service, who traveled the South, urging
landowners to stop annual controlled burns. The debate over fire suppression continued for years. Harper had a brief commentary, "Fire and
Forest," published in the *American Botanist* in 1940. He cited Greene's
and Stoddard's work, concluding that it was "folly" to apply the same
fire-management practices in different ecosystems. By the time Harper's
monograph on Alabama forests appeared in 1943, the Forest Service was
reeling from disastrous wildfires, including one in Osceola National Forest in Florida that burned 70,000 or more acres, and was finally recon-
sidering its anti-fire stance. Chapman spoke out again in 1944, asking in
an essay in *American Forests*, "Why has it taken so long for us to realize
that longleaf pine, which will not begin to grow in height until its stem
and bud at the ground line is an inch thick and comparatively fireproof,
cannot survive even in the shade of a sweet-fern bush but must grow in
full sunlight?"[17]

Nonetheless, Alabama's state forester snubbed Harper in 1948 by delivering a paper, "The Present Condition of Alabama's Forest Resources," at the annual meeting of the Alabama Academy of Science that included historical information but no reference to Harper's two reports on Alabama forests (1913 and 1943), although, Harper said, "he could not possibly have been unaware of them, as [Harper] was in the same office with him in 1927." This was quite an insult to Harper, a faithful member of the academy. Harper speculated, "The reason for his omission was presumably that if his hearers were informed about my work they might get some ideas about fire that the foresters preferred to keep covered up."[18]

Harper's major phytogeographical work was behind him after completion of the 1943 monograph on Alabama forests, and he was no longer on the forefront of fire ecology, but he continued to think about the future of longleaf pine in the South. On a car trip across Georgia in the summer of 1953, Harper observed that second-growth slash pine forests tended to have a thick understory of saw palmetto (*Serenoa repens*), wax myrtle, and gallberry (*Ilex glabra*). He wrote to Herbert Stoddard, who, after directing the privately funded Cooperative Quail Study Association from 1931 to 1943, had become a private forest management consultant. "In my Altamaha Grit flora, 1906, I had only two records for the myrtle . . . now it is in sight most of the way from Jesup to Tifton, and I guess the gallberry has increased in about the same proportion. I am inclined to attribute most of that change to the anti-fire propaganda of the foresters." Harper criticized "greedy lumbermen" who cut trees faster than their forests could regenerate for not caring about "what became of the land afterward." He worried that it would be impossible to restore longleaf forests even if fire-suppression policy could be overturned, because the understory of wax myrtle and gallberry would be so difficult to eradicate. "In the old days the seeds of the various bushes must have been dropped by birds all over the pine woods, as now, but fire came often enough to nip them in the bud and keep them from getting started." He asked Stoddard, "What do you think about all this?"[19]

Stoddard deeply admired Harper for his expertise as a field botanist, for his wide knowledge of the southern coastal plain, and for his determination, calling him "probably our greatest living Southeastern botanist and a pioneer student of the ecology of the country, especially as such is [molded] and shaped by fire." When Harper proposed a visit to Thomasville or Tallahassee in 1955, as he recovered from another serious case of pneumonia, Stoddard replied promptly, asking Harper to call him to arrange a meeting. Sensitive to Harper's financial situation, he urged him to make the call collect. He wrote, "[I will] meet you in Tallahassee or anywhere and if possible would enjoy nothing more than showing you over any country you want to visit nearby and having a good talk after all these years."[20]

Stoddard and Henry L. Beadel, along with Edward V. Komarek, founded Tall Timbers Research Station, a privately funded experiment station with a strong emphasis on the longleaf-wiregrass community and fire ecology. At the time, controlled burning for forest management was still very controversial. Komarek organized the first Tall Timbers Fire Ecology Conference, which they held at Florida State College for Women, by then renamed Florida State University, in Tallahassee in 1962. Stoddard, Beadel, and Komarek wanted the conference to establish the early history of the science of fire ecology. Chapman was gone. Harper, however, still lived in Tuscaloosa, walking from his house to his office in Smith Hall each morning and back at lunch, making the trip a second time each afternoon (although he would soon cut back to one round trip per day and eat a sack lunch at his desk). Stoddard and Komarek invited Harper to speak at the conference and arranged for his transportation and lodging in Tallahassee.[21]

Harper's appearance at the conference was a dramatic moment for those who knew the early history of fire ecology. Somewhat frail, formal in an old-fashioned suit with a stiff shirt collar and a narrow tie, Harper was a living legend.[22] He was reunited with his old friend from Aspalaga Bluff, Herman Gunter, by then retired from the Florida Geological Survey, and with Herman Kurz, the botanist at Florida State University who had explored areas of the Florida panhandle and the Apalachicola River Basin with Harper as early as the 1920s.[23] Once again, Harper paid homage to Lyell and Long as the first naturalists to see how fire enlivened the longleaf-wiregrass woods. He told the ecologists at the conference that he first noticed that fire was frequent in longleaf forests while doing his doctoral research in Georgia in 1900–1904, but confessed, "I did not give it much thought. In the spring of 1904 I even took a picture of fire burning in some pine tops lying on the ground after logging in Emanuel County, and I published it in 1906 in my study of the Altamaha Grit region. In that I discussed fire a little, and treated it as one of the effects of civilization, but did not realize its significance, as I would have if I had been aware of the work of Mr. Lyell and Mrs. Long." He said he "began to wonder" if fire was "universal" in longleaf stands in 1905. When he described his realization that fire suppression contributed to climax vegetation in a note in the *Bulletin of the Torrey Botanical Club* in 1911, he recalled, "[S]ome of my 'fire fundamentalist' friends were pretty skeptical." He remembered walking through "large areas of longleaf pine forest" in Citrus County, Florida, in March 1914. The land "had been burned over quite recently, leaving the ground pretty bare. Pine seedlings, a few inches high, were scattered over the area at a rate of three or four to the square foot, or about 100,000,000 per square mile. If all had survived, they would have made such a dense growth of trees in a few years that it would have been impossible for anything much larger than an ant to get through." In closing, Harper noted dryly that "if nobody worried about fire any more, many foresters, rangers, etc., who [spent] much of their time fighting it, might soon be out of jobs."[24]

Harper attended a barbecue at Greenwood Plantation northwest of Thomasville, where he observed a patch of hybrid corn, perhaps thinking of his old friend George Shull. Addison Marshall, the boy who wrote to Harper in 1921 about his family's vacation to St. George Island, now middle-aged but still fond of Harper, stopped by Harper's motel the night before the old man left Tallahassee, bringing him a copy of the local newspaper and showing him a stamp album that Harper had made for him in 1915. Harper noted in his diary without comment that on his way home from the fire-ecology conference, while waiting in Montgomery for a bus to Tuscaloosa, he ran into the widow of Page Bunker, his one-time nemesis at the Alabama Forestry Commission who had ignored Harper's early insights about fire ecology—leaving the irony for anyone who would later read his diary to recognize.[25]

The same year as the Tall Timbers conference, Harvard University Press published a history of fire ecology by Ashley L. Schiff. Schiff retraced the same history that Harper had in his 1931 letter to Greene, citing Charles Lyell's observations in 1849 of longleaf stands near Tuscaloosa and Ellen Long's declaration in 1889 that annual burns were "the prime cause and preserver of the grand forests of *Pinus palustris*." Schiff identified Harper and Chapman as the first scientists to recognize fire's role in longleaf forests and the value of controlled burns, saying that Harper "plagued the [U.S. Forest] Service with a series of articles, appearing from 1911 to 1914," but that the Forest Service had been "indifferent" to both men. He wrote, without attribution, that Harper was dismissed as a "car-window botanist," a characterization of other professional foresters' reaction to

Harper that probably came from Chapman. In his own memoir, Stoddard paid homage to Harper's pioneering recognition of fire's role, writing that Harper, "the most experienced of all southeastern botanists, . . . [began] calling attention to the important, even vital, role of fire in the southeastern pinelands in his writings several years before [Stoddard] became involved in the controversy."[26]

CHAPTER TEN

A Kindred Spirit

Immediately after the death of his beloved mentor Eugene Smith in 1927, Roland formed a new friendship with Brother Wolfgang Wolf, a Catholic monk who was a self-taught botanist. Wolf was a member of St. Bernard Abbey, which Benedictine monks had built in the early 1890s on Eight Mile Creek east of the small community of Cullman; they had chosen the site because of its proximity to the Louisville and Nashville Railroad and had established a preparatory school for boys there. Soon after joining the community in 1897, Wolf had begun botanizing. In 1918 he found a hybrid oak, which he named for St. Bernard, and in 1920 he described a new species of fameflower and named it *Talinum mengesii* for one of the first abbots of St. Bernard. He and Harper had corresponded for several years and finally met when Harper visited Wolf two weeks after Smith died. Unique among Harper's relatives, friends, and colleagues, Brother Wolfgang offered him unfailing encouragement *and* a knowledgeable interest in phytogeography.

Harper was apprehensive about visiting a Catholic monastery, writing to Bertha, "I didn't like the idea of making my first visit to a Catholic institution after dark, when the gates might be closed, and everybody busy counting beads, or something of the kind," but he overcame his suspicions and went to Cullman, where he stayed in a hotel and called on Brother Wolfgang.[1] Both men were born in the 1870s, of German descent, and both were bachelors. Harper found a new kindred spirit in the balding man with the white goatee and a kind, steady gaze. Despite his limited finances and the gasoline rationing in the war years, Harper visited Brother Wolfgang at St. Bernard Abbey thirteen times over the next twelve years.

In the 1930s, when Wolf began a study of the genus *Erythronium*, he and Harper repeatedly explored the ravines of Eight Mile Creek and Brindley Creek near the monastery, an area of stone outcrops, some with a layer of boggy vegetation, deep, shady sandstone gorges, many creeks, and "luxuriant hardwood forest." Wolf recommended Harper as a collector for the herbarium of Notre Dame University, which could have provided valuable extra income to Harper. They both gave presentations at the annual meeting of the Alabama Academy of Science in Mobile in 1934, Harper on the Tennessee Valley in Alabama and Wolf on pawpaw trees.[2]

When Wolf's health began to fail and he was no longer able to hike up and down the steep gorges of Cullman County, he encouraged Harper to write to him about his own botanizing adventures. Harper responded with many letters about trips near and far, taking care to include details that Wolf would find interesting. For example, he referred to his diary or field notes in April 1932 to give Wolf an account of the walking tour he made on March 22 of an area of the Black Belt where tornadoes had killed ten to twenty people: "It was a cloudy day with wind from the south all day, and a little rain in the afternoon, but not enough to cause me to seek shelter until after four o'clock. . . . When I got to the hotel . . . the clerk said a cyclone a few hours before had struck the edge of town." As he told Wolf, he spent the next day in Demopolis, photographing tornado damage, and the day after "went on to Uniontown, walking about half the distance, and crossing the tracks of two more branches of the same storm, at Allenville and Faunsdale." He noted, "At Prairieville I saw a grave being dug for a young man who had been killed by the storm at Faunsdale."[3]

In the same letter, he told Wolf about a reconnaissance trip to one of his favorite localities, the ravines on the Black Warrior River. He was anticipating a visit by H. E. Wheeler to hunt for croomia on the Warrior. Harper recounted, "[I] found the spring flora at its best, with an abundance of *Viola Canadensis, Dodecatheon* [shooting star], *Trillium decumbens* [trailing wakerobin], *Isopyrum* [false rue anemone], and other comparatively rare things. *Neviusia* was also in bloom, and I saw a magnolia with yellow flowers, perhaps the elusive *M. cordata*. I was looking especially for croomia, which I found in one of those ravines ten years ago, but failed to find it."[4]

He told Wolf about accompanying an entomology expedition to north Alabama in 1932. The group included Walter Jones and "two entomologists from Mobile, and a chauffeur, cook, etc.," their primary mission to collect beetles. He met the group in Huntsville a week after it had set out. "They were camping then on the north side of Monte Sano, a beautiful spot on a shady limestone slope, near the coldest spring in the state. I had part of an afternoon and morning there, and found some very interesting plants" including some that Charles Mohr did not record from that area. "The next day we went up the valley of Paint Rock River in Jackson County, about eighteen miles from the railroad. That is a limestone valley between outliers of the sandstone plateau. I was surprised to find *Acer saccharinum* (*dasycarpum*) [silver maple] extending up the river as far as we went, for it is not usually on such small streams."[5]

When Harper made a six-week trip to California in 1934 to attend the annual meeting of the American Association for the Advancement of Science, he told Wolf all about it in a letter. "On the way out I went as far north as Cheyenne, Wyoming, which was one state I had never been in before. I tried to take notes all the way, but of course could only guess at some of the plants. I saw a few unfamiliar plants before I got out of Arkansas, and the number increased westward. Even in California, where I have been twice before, and could look at the plants closely, there were many that puzzled me, for I did not get hold of a flora until I had been in the state about two weeks." After attending the meeting in Berkeley and visiting Bertha and Wilhelmina in Palo Alto, he traveled back through Arizona (perhaps visiting Forrest and Edith Shreve), Texas, and Louisiana. He wrote, "In Texas I spent one day in Fredericksburg, north of San Antonio and west of Austin, where nearly everybody speaks German. . . . The people do not look much like Germans now, but they have kept their mother tongue. In the city cemetery nearly all the names and about nine-tenths of the inscriptions are German. About half the people are Catholics, and one-fourth Lutherans." Stopping in Lafayette, Louisiana, he found that "most of the people [spoke] French, and about nine-tenths of them [were] Catholics." He added, "[A] lady who studied botany with me here last year teaches there, and I was a guest at her home."[6]

Upon returning to the area of his doctoral research, the Altamaha Grit in Georgia, in 1939, Harper found a "sad sight" and described it to Brother Wolfgang. The virgin longleaf forest he had explored at the turn of the twentieth century was "reduced to one-tenth or less." Harper lamented, "Some of the several new plants I described from there might be hard to find now, or even completely extinct." He added, "[P]erhaps it does not make much difference, as civilization may go all to pieces in a few more years anyway."[7]

Harper sometimes sent or took traveling botanists to meet Wolf and see the botanical wonders in Cullman County. In 1928, he directed Edgar Wherry, the mineralogist with the University of Pennsylvania and the Academy of Natural Sciences who shared Roland's and Francis's interest in Bartram, to St. Bernard. Wherry was traveling by car with Ralph Curtis Benedict, who, like Harper, was a botany graduate of Columbia and the New York Botanical Garden program. They were hunting for species of phlox. Harper gave Wherry directions to Wolf in Cullman but wrote Wolf to warn him: "I wouldn't advise you to show him anything very rare, though, for he has a mania for grabbing everything he can get, both for herbarium specimens and for transplanting to his back yard in Washington." A Duke University botanist, Donovan S. Correll (who with his wife would drive Fernald to the Zuni longleaf site in Virginia two years later), visited the Mohr Herbarium at the University of Alabama in 1937, and Harper suggested that he go to Cullman to see Wolf's herbarium. In 1938, Harper guided Allan F. Archer, a malacologist visiting from the University of Michigan, around north Alabama and took him to St. Bernard to meet Brother Wolfgang. Afterward, Harper took Archer to "an abandoned limestone quarry south of Bangor in Blount County." He wrote to Wolf later that the wooded slopes above the quarry "looked like a good place for flowers and snails. Much of the slope had been burned over some time this year, but a hundred yards or so north of the quarry face [he] found some un-burned woods, with *Trillium decumbens* [trailing wakerobin] so abundant that [he] could hardly keep from stepping on it."[8]

He sent another Michigan scientist to see Wolf in 1940. "Dr. J. T. Baldwin, of the University of Michigan, who had written to you about *Talinum*, etc., is here for a few days, and wants to see you pretty soon, on his way back. I have been out in the woods with him twice, and shown him *Croton, Neviusia, Croomia, Sedum Nevii* [Nevius' stonecrop], and other rare things, though there are not many flowers in the woods at this season, and *Erythronium* [dogtooth violet] and most of the *Trilliums* are of course entirely invisible now. He is young and enthusiastic, and I believe you will enjoy talking with him, if you feel well enough." Baldwin later recalled meeting Harper on the Alabama trip. He had heard of Harper from H. H. Bartlett, whom Harper met in 1912 when Bartlett accompanied Hugo de Vries to the state. "Professor H. H. Bartlett had told me that I would find Doctor Harper to be a strong individualist: I am glad to say that I was not disappointed. Then and later he proved to be marked in kindness, unselfishness, forthrightness, enthusiasm, and in recollection of events and people and plants and places of former years. I greatly respected him as a person and as a botanist. He was for the rest of his life a loyal friend."[9]

Harper sometimes seemed jealous of other botanists who received St. Bernard hospitality. He was "distressed" in 1931 when Wolf entertained William Willard Ashe, a prominent southern forester and botanical collector from North Carolina. Ashe had become an enthusiastic naturalist at an earlier age than Harper, exploring the woods and fields around his family's estate in North Carolina; before dying at the age of fifty, he described 510 plants new to science, including the beautiful and endangered Ashe's magnolia (*Magnolia ashei*), which Ashe described from Okaloosa County, Florida, in 1925, and which was reclassified as a variety of bigleaf magnolia (*Magnolia macrophylla*) in 1989. After learning of Ashe's visit to Cullman in a letter from Wolf, Harper replied from Tallahassee: "[Ashe is] a rather irresponsible person who does not care how much trouble he makes, and many of his attempts to split species seem to have done more harm than good. Of course there may be other botanists who make as fine distinctions as he does, but they do not do it in such a careless way, without investigating what has been done before. This month's *Torreya* (which you may have seen) contains an article by him which ought never to have been published, for he tries to mix up some of the magnolias and oaks, and makes some inexcusable errors in citing localities for them." Back in Tuscaloosa that fall and expecting a visit by Ashe, Harper wrote, "I have Ashe's paper on *Polycodium*, but I do not know any more about the genus now than I did before I read it. It looks as if he has just mixed them up a little more, as he usually does with everything he handles."[10] Harper wrote to Wolf more frequently after Wolf met Ashe, who died the following year.

In May 1937, Brother Wolfgang became seriously ill. Roland urged him to rally and continue studying fameflowers, particularly some in Chilton County, Alabama, that were unusual in having five stamens. "As the *Talinums* bloom more or less through the summer, perhaps there is no particular hurry. But whoever goes after it should try to get there in the morning, for I believe the flowers close up in the afternoon." Encouraged, Wolf did visit the Chilton County fameflower site that summer and reported to Harper in a letter on August 30. Harper replied, "I was interested to learn that you had been able to confirm my hasty observation on the *Talinum* with five stamens in Chilton County. Very likely it should be considered an undescribed species, as you have based your *T. mengesii* on number of stamens almost entirely. Of course much depends on whether or not intermediate forms can be found. At present I suppose none are known." Harper visited the monastery three times in the spring of 1938 and again that summer. On the summer trip he rode to Cullman County with H. K. Svenson of the Brooklyn Botanic Garden. Since Wolf could not accompany Harper and Svenson up and down the creeks east of Cullman, Harper described their outing to him in a letter later. "In the rocky gorges we found one plant which I believe I had not seen for thirty-five years, namely, *Hexalectris* [probably *H. spicata*, the now endangered spiked crested coralroot]. There were only three specimens in sight, and I persuaded Dr. Svenson not to take any of them."

Harper caught Wolf's interest in the Alabama species in the genus *Erythronium*, the dogtooth violet, the fawn lily, and trout lilies, and began his own field research on the genus. Twice in the spring of 1939, he and A. V. Beatty, a botanist at the University of Alabama, examined colonies of *Erythronium* in the ravines of the Black Warrior near Holt, and Harper wrote a detailed report to Wolf, enclosing specimens. "We found some facts that may not be in the books. Many or most of the one-leaved plants had long white runners extending out from the base of the bulb, and some of them were a little thickened at the end, as if a new bulb was going to develop there; but in no case did we find two plants connected." He also climbed a bluff on the Buttahatchie River near Hamilton in Marion County to examine *Erythroniums* there. In Atlanta in April, he went to a granite outcrop with a botanist at Emory University, where he was surprised to find *Erythronium* growing in sunny spots and thin patches of topsoil. Harper even wrote to at least two old friends, Clarence Knowlton in Massachusetts and Charles Deam in Indiana, to ask them to collect specimens of their local *Erythronium* and send them to Wolf at St. Bernard. Knowlton promptly complied, collecting specimens of dogtooth violet (*E. americanum*) in a thicket near the sea at Hingham, packing them in a tin box, and mailing them to the monk, with the note, "If these do not reach you in fair condition please let me know at once and I will make some pressed specimens for you to study."[11]

In March 1940, Roland went back the ravines on the Black Warrior River to hunt for *Erythronium* specimens, which he shipped to one of Wolf's colleagues, Father Lambert, telling him, "I would be glad if you would put them in pots immediately, and show them to Brother Wolfgang a little later, if he is able to look at them." Roland wanted to visit Wolfgang and told the priest, "If Brother Wolfgang does not get worse, I may bring some of those plants from here next week . . . to him myself." He made it to St. Bernard later the same month, probably riding with a friend, and again in April.[12]

Harper continued to press Wolf, collecting *Erythronium* specimens for him in Franklin County in April, sometimes hunting for them with other St. Bernard faculty members. Knowlton sent another batch of specimens to the monk in May, probably at Harper's suggestion, and added, "Let me thank you rather belatedly for your good paper on *Talinum*." Harper wrote the same month to tell Wolf of seeing "an *Erythronium*, with fruit nearly ripe," on the Little River in North Carolina, which he explored with the Chicago-trained botanist H. L. Blomquist of Duke University, and more on a small branch in Loudoun County, Virginia, a few days later. He also went to the National Herbarium to check its collection for *Erythronium* information. Harper worked on his own manuscript about *Erythronium* at the same time that he encouraged Wolf to report his findings, but as usual he was often diverted by the temptations of demographic research. "I must try to get a preliminary account of [*Erythronium*] published before next spring, so that people can be on the lookout for them all over the country," he wrote to Brother Wolfgang. "I had hoped to send off the manuscript before this, but have been interrupted by many other things. I may bring it up and show it to you in its unfinished state about the middle of next week, and stay around Cullman a couple of days to get some more statistics from the cemetery and court-house."[13]

Roland's encouragement and assistance worked. Brother Wolfgang rallied and completed a manuscript about *Erythronium*, declaring that the beautiful yellow flower Harper found on the Buttahatchie River was a new species and naming it for his friend. *Castanea* published the articles by Harper and Wolf in back-to-back issues in 1941. Inspired by his new namesake, Harper wrote to Brother Wolfgang that spring, "I would like nothing better than to start in northern Florida, about the first of next March, and take about two months to follow the *Erythroniums* as they bloom, all the way to Maine, with some zigzag trips westward toward the Mississippi River. If we had only known what we do now, about twenty years ago, you might have made such a trip with me, and perhaps turned up a dozen new ones."[14]

As they became close friends, Harper sometimes confided in the monk about the trouble he had managing his time. He did not specifically mention his newspaper clipping and hoarding habits or his time-consuming "statistics" work, but he confessed, "I am always trying to do about a dozen things at once, and many things have to be postponed." He closed that letter affectionately, "Take care of yourself, and I will try to do likewise."[15]

CHAPTER ELEVEN

The Maniac

Although Harper's role in instigating the science of fire ecology is a demonstrable legacy, many of his discoveries of new genera and species of plants in the southern coastal plain are hidden in botany's continually changing nomenclature. He was prodigious in his fieldwork and his production of scientific articles, and yet he provided no major theories of coastal plain ecology beyond his insights about the importance of swamps and about fire's relationship to longleaf pine. He prepared no geography or flora of the region. The reason he did not prepare a phytogeography of the southern coastal plain can be found in the humorous persona he projected to close friends and family, the alter ego he called "Maniac."

Harper felt an uncontrollable urge to go back to his room at the end of each day, pick up his shears, turn to the omnipresent stack of neatly folded newspapers, and cut out articles that pertained to his many interests. He dated the clippings; sorted them by subject; sent some to friends, colleagues, acquaintances, and strangers; sometimes typed copies to keep; and saved thousands in notebooks, envelopes, and boxes. After clipping, he turned to his small leather-bound diary, where he made a careful record of his day, beginning with the weather, listing persons he saw and his travel itinerary, including exact departure and arrival times, summarizing car-window notes and other observations from his field notebook, and itemizing letters and other mail sent and received. If work or travel upset Roland's schedule so that he could not clip newspapers and write in his diary each evening, he caught up as soon as he could, referring to the raw information in his field notebooks to update his diaries and saving the newspapers until there was time to clip them.

In the absence of family, a permanent residence, or a steady job, his drive to sort and preserve the information he gleaned from newspapers and from his days lent structure to Harper's life. He believed that the manual activity of clipping, labeling, sorting, and filing articles enabled him to remember the information they contained. "I don't like to read a paper that doesn't belong to me, for I can't hope to remember things that I don't cut out, so it is just a waste of time reading them."[1] He knew the newspaper-clipping habit was odd, and he also realized that it absorbed more and more of his time, time he could have spent in field research or in compiling a synthesis of his years of fieldwork across the coastal plain. But the urges to clip and save or distribute newspaper articles and to constantly create lists were even stronger than his powerful longing to explore the woods and bogs. All in all, he felt comfortable with the way he organized his life and the products of his work, and as the scrapbooks and folders of clippings accumulated, and the field notebooks and diaries multiplied, he deposited them when he could in his mother's attic in College Point and carried more with him from one temporary home to another. When his young cousin Anna Tower nicknamed him the "Maniac" and teased him in childish cartoons, he was not bothered.

Hints of Harper's intermittent depression, beginning in Southbridge in 1898; the arguably manic nature of his many simultaneous writing projects; and his all-day hikes, even through extreme heat and storms, as well as the actions of others in his family, could indicate that Roland had bipolar disorder, a condition with a clear genetic basis that involves swings between severe depression and mania and can lead to hallucinations. Hermina may have experienced mania at the age of twenty-eight, when she wrote an entire book during a summer break from teaching and talked about marrying someone if only she could raise some money.[2] Bertha's brother John Tower alternated between "cackling," nonstop talk and hostility. Otto Harper married impulsively in 1910 and was deeply troubled by a fear of germs and difficulty keeping a job. Even Wilhelmina had a "breakdown" and was unable to sleep in 1939. These behaviors all could be interpreted as signs of bipolar disorder. If so, the Harper siblings may have inherited this disease through the Tauber line. However, with no evidence that Roland experienced psychosis, his eccentric characteristics, and most of the eccentricities of his relatives, also resemble the constellation of traits that psychiatrists categorize as an "obsessive-compulsive spectrum disorder."

In the prevailing psychiatric view, obsessive-compulsive personality disorder is part of a spectrum of disorders that also includes Tourette's syndrome, eating disorders, extreme impulsivity, and the distinct obsessive-compulsive disorder. Obsessive-compulsive personality disorder is defined as "a pervasive pattern of preoccupation with orderliness, perfectionism, and mental and interpersonal control, at the expense of flexibility, openness, and efficiency, beginning by early adulthood." The current psychiatric view is that persons with obsessive-compulsive personality disorder do not believe they are ill, and in fact may be proud of their perfectionism, inflexible moral standards, or other traits. Obsessive-compulsive disorder is characterized by more debilitating obsessions and compulsions, such as extreme fears of contamination, injury, or disaster, and patients typically believe that they are ill and would like to be cured. Obsessive-compulsive spectrum disorders are believed to have a genetic basis and thus to run in families.[3]

Psychiatrists diagnose patients with obsessive-compulsive personality disorder if they exhibit at least four of these traits: (1) preoccupation with "details, rules, lists, order, organization, or schedules"; (2) "perfectionism that interferes with task completion"; (3) excessive devotion to work; (4) being "over-conscientious, scrupulous, and inflexible about matters of morality, ethics, or values (not accounted for by cultural or religious identification)"; (5) an inability "to discard worn-out or worthless objects even when they have no sentimental value"; (6) reluctance "to delegate tasks or to work with others unless they submit to exactly his or her way of doing things"; (7) "a miserly spending style toward both self and others; money is viewed as something to be hoarded for future catastrophes"; and (8) rigidity and stubbornness. Most compellingly, the urge to hoard objects with little or no value, except in the mind of the hoarder, is considered a trait of obsessive-compulsive personality but not a symptom of bipolar disorder.[4]

Roland Harper's eccentricities fit fairly neatly into the diagnostic criteria for obsessive-compulsive personality. His perfectionism, or "long reflecting over any subject," indeed interfered with task completion. In 1910 he wrote to his friend Florence Blake that he had been working on a report about Florida peat for several months, but noted, "[T]he more I write the more I think of to put in it." His car-window notes and daily diary, two of his most prominent habits, were essential techniques of the field naturalist, yet were also forms of counting and list making. His plant lists were important as records of his field observations and as analytical tools in his scientific articles, although some editors, including his old friend Alfred Akerman, balked at including long lists in published articles. His lifelong commitment to collecting railroad timetables, which he had undertaken by the time he was twelve years old and living in Dalton, and his constant recording of the precise times of his activities were literally a preoccupation with schedules. Harper's curious unwillingness to ride a horse or drive a car and his apparent significant fear of snakes can be seen as risk avoidance, another typical trait of obsessive-compulsive individuals.[5] He botanized in the places he could reach by train or bus, on foot, or by rides in friends' cars—thus he never could systematically cover the coastal plain.

His staunch objection to women with "bobbed hair," probably one of the stands that his mother was thinking of when she praised his "great integrity and high ideals," is an example of inflexibility "about matters of morality, ethics, or values." So was his steadfast belief that smoking prevented one from having male children, despite plenty of evidence to the contrary, an attitude that struck a University of Alabama student as an "obsession."[6]

Harper didn't hesitate to criticize the work of good friends. As he emphasized the unique ecology of southern Florida, Harper made a gratuitous stab at an old friend, criticizing a report by John Harshberger as "the most pretentious paper" on the subject yet one that lacked "adequate indication of relative abundance, which [was] very important. Furthermore, that paper [did] not cover the Keys, and [did] not always identify the species correctly or distinguish between native plants and weeds." He also scolded John Kunkel Small for not acknowledging Harper's report of a particular plant in a 1924 publication, since Harper had sent specimens to him. When *The Distribution of Vegetation in the United States, as Related to Climatic Conditions,* by Forrest Shreve and Burton E. Livingston, appeared in 1921, Harper wrote to Livingston at Johns Hopkins University to criticize the new book. Livingston responded patiently, "We didn't try to make a review of the literature. The book represents tests of several possible methods of studying distribution and climate. I don't regard it as any more than that." He tried to counsel Harper: "Don't find fault with any publication because it doesn't cite your own papers, no matter how important the latter may be; it doesn't do any good and may do harm."[7]

These occasional attacks on old friends and other scientists are mystifying unless one interprets them as examples of being "over-conscientious, scrupulous, and inflexible" and "excessively devoted to work and productivity to the exclusion of leisure activities and friendships"—in which case they are not at all surprising. Harper wrote to M. L. Fernald to question his writing style and repetition of a certain fact in a journal article.[8] It seems a very odd point on which to challenge one of the country's most influential botanists, until one considers Harper's compulsion to prepare manuscripts in painstaking order and detail. He undoubtedly combed other scientists' writings with the same meticulous attention to detail— and lacked the social skills to realize that it could be unwise to criticize friends and other scientists on every minor discrepancy he uncovered in their work. If Fernald resented Harper's temerity in criticizing his article, this incident could have ignited the antagonism that simmered between the two men for decades.

Harper's diaries reveal that, throughout his life, newspaper clipping was a very important part of his daily routine. On a June evening in 1913, he noted that he "cut out clippings after supper, as usual." He did not want to skip clipping articles when his mother visited him in Tallahassee in April 1920. After supper on the first evening she was there, he clipped articles he had marked in the previous month's newspapers. In November 1928, he noted in his diary that he had crated two boxes of clippings from January and February of that year. When he attended an economics conference in Atlanta that month, Harper had dinner with acquaintances in a nearby cafeteria but then went back to his hotel room to cut out some articles before catching a train for Birmingham. Attending a huge May Day party in Tallahassee in 1930, he left after just an hour to return to his room and clip some recent newspapers plus a three-year-old issue.[9]

His habit of clipping articles and pasting them in notebooks or sending them to friends and relatives was strikingly compulsive, considering that so many of the recipients could not hide their bemusement or lack of interest in the clippings. An economist at the United States Department of Agriculture wondered how Harper completed so many articles and monographs, considering, as he remarked in a letter to Harper, "all the clippings that you send to your friends." Francis ridiculed the habit, saying Roland's letters to him were nothing but "a few bunches of clippings that [weren't] worth looking at before throwing them into the fire." Francis's criticism of Roland's newspaper clipping may have stung, but it did not stop Roland from sending his brother more packets of articles just two weeks later. Francis's daughter, Molly Harper, remembered sixty years later how the family laughed about boxes of newspaper clippings that Uncle Roland sent to them. Even while visiting Bertha and Wilhelmina in Palo Alto on a rare trip to California in 1934, when he attended the summer conference of the American Association for the Advancement of Science—and gave a paper, "Some Phenomena of Succession in Human Society," at a concurrent meeting of the Ecological Society of America—Roland spent much of his time clipping newspapers. His mother complained, "[Y]ou were busy with your clippings every minute." She called the clipping routine a "mania" and speculated, "[T]his mania has no doubt kept you from finding the place in the world which you ought to have occupied long ago and which would have enabled you to go to all those important meetings, make your worth be felt, and have your old age provided for. You must admit yourself [wasting] the time you spent all these years in reading every available paper, every insignificant item, so that you might do good in the world and benefit your friends with piles of clippings which were hardly ever read (I know this for a fact)."[10]

Although Harper gave away many clippings, he hoarded many as well. He also hoarded other print material. He began writing away to request copies of pamphlets and saving them as his "library" as early as 1899, while working at the optical factory in Southbridge. He told his friend Clarence about it, and Clarence commented politely, "Your botanical library must be decidedly interesting. I suppose I could collect one if I had time to send for things." Eugene Smith recognized his zeal for sorting serial materials as early as 1910, when he offered Harper a temporary job organizing the library of the Alabama Geological Survey. "I know you took a great deal of interest in that," he wrote.[11]

As Harper's collection grew, he stored the papers in his mother's attic in College Point. Planning to move to California in 1922, Bertha pressured him to move the papers out of the rented house on Long Island. "You must think out some plan about that library of yours; you cannot expect me to take it along, should we move far away," she wrote. Oblivious or insensitive to his passion for the southern coastal plain, Wilhelmina and her housemate suggested he move to California as well, take a job as a forester, and put his library in a mountain cabin. "Blanche and I think that's a good idea," she wrote.[12]

The pending loss of the College Point attic was a crisis for Roland. He mentioned the problem in many letters to friends. Several recognized how troubled he was and offered to help. Susan Eppes in Tallahassee suggested that he, Wilhelmina, and Bertha move there, writing, "Tallahassee is a pleasant place to live, rent is not so very high, property can be bought on reasonable terms and to own one's home is a comfortable feeling, then too if you had such a home what would be easier than to put up a building that would hold, not only the books etc., you now have on hand, but also the accumulations of future years?" Charles F. Brooks in the geography department of Clark University in Worcester, Massachusetts, said his department might be able to provide room for Harper's papers. He urged Harper to marry and accept an academic appointment at Clark: "Perhaps you'd better get married, cease your nomadic life (in part), found a home, and put your library in it. There might be room for a good geographer like you right here at Clark University in our department of geography. Of course, this is nothing more than personal suggestion. . . . I doubt whether you will take it seriously, for your nomadic tendencies might make it hard for you to settle down." Louis Moore of Thomasville, Georgia, a soul mate in the matter of hoarding, offered to house Harper's library in his home. "It is my property and I hope to always live there. Should you have to move your library I would be glad to give it space if its proportions allow."[13]

E. Burton Cooke, a landscape architect in Atlanta whom Harper knew in Tuscaloosa as early as 1907, recommended that Harper find a place for the papers in that city, because it was a good central location in the South. Young Walter Jones of the Alabama Geological Survey hinted that Harper should reduce the size of the collection. "I am trying to hold mine down to the very best in the list and to keep out all superfluous volumes." Some friends grasped that Harper's library contained many newspaper clippings as well as scientific materials. DeLoach referred to "your library and clippings" in reporting that C. Stuart Gager at the Brooklyn Botanic Garden offered to store Harper's papers permanently. Gager had invited Harper to consider the Brooklyn garden his "botanical headquarters" in 1914. None of these ideas suited Harper, however. Herman Gunter's brother, Charles Gunter, suggested that as long as Harper was moving from one temporary job to another, he should leave the papers in College Point, if possible.[14] Harper took this advice and arranged to continue renting the College Point attic after Bertha moved to California.

Harper accumulated an enormous new collection in Tuscaloosa once Jones gave him an office in Smith Hall in 1927. David DeJarnette, an engineering student at the university with a part-time job making labels for the natural history museum in 1928, remembered stacks of newspapers two and three feet high on two desks and on the bookshelves in Harper's office. He recalled that Harper would dig through trash baskets in the campus post office to retrieve newspapers that students threw away and circle articles he wanted to clip and save. As time allowed, he clipped the articles and filed them in notebooks on topics such as "demography." He drew a cartoon, "Reading the Funnies," in 1933, in which he poked fun at himself for his habit of saving newspapers to clip, labeling a neat stack of newspapers at the foot of his bed "Last Week's Papers." By the 1940s, he had a serious backlog. Francis's son, Robin, visited Roland in Tuscaloosa then and was amazed by the towering, massive stacks of newspapers in Harper's Smith Hall office.[15]

The problem of the College Point papers arose again in 1938, possibly when the landlady, Anna Mason, finally demanded that Harper remove his belongings from the attic. Under pressure to save his library from the trash bin, Harper cast about again. Francis couldn't take them. He told his brother, "We could accommodate your books in our present house, but there is no telling how long we'll have it." Ironically, Wilhelmina oversaw construction of an entire new library in Redwood City, California, in 1939, thanks to a bond issue, while Roland still struggled to find storage space for his hoard of newspapers, pamphlets, railroad timetables, and other materials. The compulsion to collect and save materials grew stronger as he grew older. In 1962, four years before his death, he was clipping newspapers from the year 1939.[16] His habit became part of the legend of Dr. Harper on the campus of the University of Alabama, where today archivists joke that he dug through trash cans to salvage materials that they now must store as part of his papers in the Hoole Special Collections Library.

His hoard of pamphlets fueled another compulsion, to make lists. Harper practiced list making, a typical obsessive-compulsive habit, as early as 1900, when he made his first car-window notes on a train ride from New York to Georgia. The compulsion was a problem for him even in the Columbia years; when his dissertation advisor, Lucien Underwood, objected to excessive content in Harper's dissertation, he probably was referring to lists of data. Harper's college friend Alfred Akerman also objected to a list in a manuscript early in Harper's career. Ellsworth Huntington at Yale later urged Harper to stop including "great masses of figures" in his articles. While living with Bertha in College Point in October 1909, between periods of working in Tallahassee, Harper noted in his diary that he spent the day in the attic, rearranging "some papers, pictures, boxes, etc.," and then started making a new list of pamphlets he had mailed to friends, spending "several hours on it."[17] Harper also was meticulous about the reference lists in his monographs, which may have made Hugo de Vries' failure to cite Gregor Mendel in his original article about genetic theory, while Harper was at Columbia, particularly galling to the young graduate student. This could explain Harper's strange lack of interest in talking with de Vries when the famous geneticist came to Tuscaloosa in 1912; in his inflexible, judgmental way, he may have believed that the sin of de Vries' omission outweighed the value of his contribution to genetic theory.

Harper's young cousin Anna Tower was the daughter of Bertha's brother, Otto Tauber. Otto had followed his sister from Germany to the United States, eventually changing his name to John Tower. He married, but his wife died when their only child was a year old. Because John's work as a seaman took him away from home for long periods, Bertha took over raising Anna in 1911, when the little girl was four years old. Roland became very fond of his young cousin and accompanied her on a train trip from Cleveland to New York in the fall of 1916 after she had spent a summer with her father on his boat.[18] When Roland stayed with Bertha in College Point, he sometimes sat with the little girl to draw cartoons. Anna gave him two collections of cartoons that she had drawn, the first in 1921. In one, a character she labeled "Maniac" is clipping newspapers with giant scissors while a girl with a doll asks, "Cuttin' clippin's again? Got any cartoons for me?" Another is labeled "The rendezvous of Maniac and Anna Mason in the cellar" and shows a little girl peeking around a door at the Maniac and the College Point landlady. Roland must have told the girl stories about his childhood in Georgia, for another shows "Maniac in 1892 sneaking around the house so he won't have to work in the garden." Anna dedicated the second album, "Maniac Book No. 2 by The Goop," to "the Maniac to remind him of the past and future." After Roland left College Point for another temporary job in 1922, Bertha wrote, "Anna says you took away her inspirations for drawing, and she only can draw when you are around."[19]

Roland took up drawing Maniac cartoons himself, and the pastime eventually became an important way for him to understand and interpret events in the life of the extended Harper family. He copied and carefully colored duplicates of many cartoons and then compiled them in two scrapbooks that he showed to friends and eventually annotated.[20] A May 20, 1926, cartoon commemorated "the arrival of a daughter in the family of the Maniac's youngest brother, an ornithologist, living in Massachusetts at the time. His wife [was] a bobbed blonde, as shown." That summer, he drew a cartoon about "the Maniac's mother and sister [who] live in California. At the time this picture was drawn Sister was in Bakersfield, which is very hot in summer, and she sent her pet bulldog to Mother in Palo Alto, which is much cooler, to keep him more comfortable." After his frightening case of pneumonia in 1929, he drew at least two cartoons about the experience. In annotating the one he drew on Valentine's Day, 1929, which he presented to the nurse Evelyn Smith, he emphasized that his mother "came all the way from California to be with him." The other cartoon depicted his stay with Otto's family in Harlem, Georgia. He probably gave the original cartoon to Otto's children and made a copy to keep. His annotation reads: "While recuperating from pneumonia the maniac spent a few days at the home of one of his brothers, who is a germ fiend. He takes elaborate precautions to defend himself against some comparatively harmless germs, and neglects others that may be more dangerous." In the cartoon, a man sprays a "germosaurus" with "double action" spray while three children run toward him, crying, "Oh Daddy, save us!" In 1931, Roland drew another cartoon about Francis's family, again probably giving the original to the children and keeping a copy. He noted, "The Maniac's youngest brother, a naturalist, spent a few weeks in Okefinokee Swamp in the summer of 1931, with his wife, daughter, and nephew. This picture shows some of the flora and fauna of the swamp, with names more or less imaginary. (The alligator was put up in the tree because there was no room in the water.)" The cartoon shows Francis photographing a woodpecker and saying, "Keep still, William, you'll scare that rare bird away." A boy in a red cap fires a gun at the alligator in the tree. A little girl picks a flower, and a woman says, "Look out, Molly, that might be poison!"

Roland made Francis the star of another cartoon about their trip along Bartram's trail. His annotation: "In the summer of 1939 the Maniac and his youngest brother were trying to trace the route of the naturalist William Bartram through Alabama. This picture shows a creek in Montgomery County, that he is known to have crossed, as it might have looked in 1776 and 1939. The 'grand high forest' that Bartram described is now replaced by smaller trees of the same species, and the animals by smaller ones, and the Indians by negroes." The cartoon is titled "On Bartram's Trail through Alabama 163 Years After." A signpost points to Montgomery and Mobile. Francis drives a car and asks, "What do you see?" of Roland, who stoops beside the road, saying, "Here's his track again!"

Roland also used cartoons to cope with setbacks in his love life. He drew a cartoon on August 29, 1925, commemorating the wedding of a "charming young widow, with three children, who was secretary in the office of the Florida Geological Survey in 1920." He annotated a copy of the cartoon that he preserved: "At the extreme right is the Maniac, who worked in the same office with the widow, and used to bring her comic papers for the children. A copy of this picture was given her two days before the wedding, for a wedding present." The following spring he was disturbed by the woman's decision to cut her hair and depicted her getting the haircut in a February 3, 1926, cartoon. One of her children says, "Wait, Mother, I want to ask the Maniac for that funny paper!" and she responds, "No, Chris, I don't believe he intends to give us any more papers and besides, I must hurry home before too many people see me!"

An August 1927 cartoon seems to be about Olivia Holt of Montgomery. In his annotation of the drawing, Roland explained that a "young lady . . . works in an insurance office in Montgomery, using an old-fashioned high desk. The Maniac used to drop in to chat with her occasionally after having lunch in the neighborhood. One day in August she was busy, and received him rather coldly, and he withdrew crestfallen, and drew this picture." The following month, he drew another cartoon about a second rebuff: "The insurance girl has a first cousin, another office girl, who lives with her mother and sister in a fashionable section of Montgomery. One night when the Maniac was calling on her she was called to the phone by some man, and stayed too long to suit the Maniac." In the cartoon, a woman on a porch swing says, "I would have been glad of an excuse to get away from this boob for a few minutes. . . ." Maniac is eating a slice of watermelon and thinks, "Guess I better beat it when I finish this slice." He called the front porch scene "One Beau Too Many."

In November 1927, he further explored his own obsession with women who cut their hair and alluded to his attraction to the two Montgomery women in yet another cartoon, depicting the Maniac boarding the Georgia, Florida, and Alabama Railroad for Tallahassee while four flappers call out to him. One, labeled "Age 20," waves a rolling pin and says, "I heard what you said about bobbed hair. You better take it back!" Another, labeled "Age 25," says, "I read what you wrote about Montgomery girls being the prettiest. Explain yourself!" A black man with large red lips and kinky hair looks out of a train window and says, "Dem gals sho' layin' fo' somebody." A white man in the next car says, "Look at all the flappers! There must be a female college here."

When a "lady scientist" from Wisconsin came to Tallahassee in 1928 to see longleaf woods, Harper escorted her. Coworkers at the Florida Geological Survey teased him about their "date" by leaving him a poem that alluded to the ongoing problem he had with storing and transporting his ever-growing library and to his longing for a permanent home in the coastal forest. Harper summarized the whole experience in another annotated cartoon: "In March, 1928, a lady scientist from Wisconsin, who is working on turpentine production, visited Tallahassee, and the Maniac arranged with a local botany professor to take her out in the forest to study the trees. . . . On returning to the office late in the day the maniac found on his desk a poem that had been concocted during the afternoon by a gentleman and lady in the office. . . . The first two stanzas represent what the Maniac is supposed to have said to the Turpentine girl, and other two are her reply." The poem suggested that the Maniac asked the Turpentine girl:

> Oh! Do please be mine.
> I've drawn comics for girls in Alabam
> and one in Florida too
> From now on all my comics
> I'll confine to you.

The girl replied:

> A cottage we'll build on the side of a hill
> A room of which your books will fill
> Around this will be a grove of pine
> And I will complete my study of turpentine.

Rejection by the nurse Evelyn Smith, who had cared for him in Athens in 1929, dampened Roland's desire to draw cartoons about the Maniac. Harper wrote this explanation for another cartoon: "From 1929 to 1935 the Maniac was interested in a lady who had helped nurse him through a serious illness in Athens, Georgia. Late in 1935 she wrote him that she was planning to marry the following year, and that gave him quite a shock. This picture gives an idea of how he felt about it. He did not draw many cartoons after that."

Harper often showed the cartoons to friends, so the "Maniac" was clearly an open joke. The cartoons suggest that as early as 1921, when Anna drew him clipping articles with giant scissors, Harper considered himself somewhat mad. His mother made affectionate use of the "Maniac" nickname in 1922, writing that she was glad Roland had made a friend who was "another Main-iac," and in 1928, wrote, "We do enjoy your Maniac cartoons so much, of which we are getting quite a collection."[21] Probably alluding to the cartoon about his outing in the longleaf woods with the "turpentine girl," she commented, "You are getting to be a regular Don Juan in your old days." By 1935, however, she was vicious

about some his idiosyncrasies. As he became more interested in sociological topics, such as the influence of birth order in families, she implied that
he was losing his mind: "I think you are nuts about many of your theories." In another letter, she advised him to abandon his habits of clipping
and hoarding articles, warning, "If you do more such things, I'll begin to
think you are getting queer."[22]

Many members of Harper's family had some combination of obsessive-
compulsive characteristics. In a pattern of behavior that could be considered the moral inflexibility of an obsessive-compulsive personality or
the mood swings and hostility of bipolar disorder, Bertha lavished gifts
and attention on her relatives and acquaintances but could turn on them
angrily when she felt they did not do enough in kind. She wrote disparag-
ingly of her brother Otto and of her sister Fanny and warned Roland not
to invite Fanny to live with him. "With her gypsy appearance and ways,
she would be no credit to you, would mortify you in many ways, and
then, when once down there, you could never get rid of her." She literally
wished Hermina dead in a letter to Roland in 1908, when Hermina asked
the family to help her finance publication of a book. Of her brother's
daughter, Anna, she remarked, "[She] has turned out a regular Hermina
and has really killed my love for her." (While attending Stanford University, Anna began calling herself "Mickie," oddly like Hermina, who had
renamed herself Alice.) Even though she tended to be critical and even
cruel, Bertha cultivated the idea that she was selfless. In Americus, Roland
wrote, she "had more time than ever before to play 'Good Samaritan,' a
congenial role for her. She was always helping neighbors who were sick or
in distress, some of whom unfortunately were ungrateful, and inclined to
look down on her for making a drudge of herself."[23]

Referring to the Tauber line, Bertha told Roland, "[T]his hoarding
of useless things is a great family trait." Franziska, known as Fanny, she
wrote, "still pays for more rooms than she needs in order to accommodate
plunder she preserved since early childhood, like for instance her baby
dresses. . . . When she came to College Point she moved two barrels of
junk from place to place . . . just because she cannot part with anything
she once possessed. You have inherited the same trait."[24]

Bertha's father, Wilhelm Tauber, was an artist of significant ability who
nonetheless failed to sustain a career as a portrait painter in Germany and
ultimately moved with his wife to the United States at Bertha's urging.
She spoke disdainfully of her father's unwillingness to promote his work,
recalling that he "usually would rather have taken a whipping than accept

money for his paintings," perhaps because of an obsessive-compulsive indecisiveness that his work was finished. Alluding to Tauber anonymously painting hands for a more successful portrait painter, Bertha warned Roland not to give assistance to his botanist colleagues without receiving credit. "You'd be a ninny if you did it all for nothing, just like your grandfather was, who contributed to Lembach's fame by painting hands for him which he couldn't paint and got no recognition for it, and no credit," she wrote. Bertha also implied that her father's personality was difficult to understand, once saying that only her granddaughter Charlotte, Otto's child, really understood his legacy.[25]

Bertha's brother, John Tower, who sometimes stayed with her in College Point and later in California, had an unpleasant and volatile personality. "There is much goodness, much helpfulness, lavish presents; but what I have to take along with it, you don't know," Bertha wrote of John to Roland. His daughter, Anna, was always "glad when he [was] out of the house and she [could] study in peace without being continually interrupted by fool talk and card tricks and the like." Wilhelmina observed that John's presence was "a continuous drag" on their mother and that he was "too much for her," "hateful beyond words."[26]

The few hints about Roland's father suggest that obsessive-compulsive personality also could have descended through the Harper line. Bertha observed that her father-in-law, also named William Harper, had the same irrational fear of germs as her son Otto. The job changes that William's sons characterized as "political manipulations" probably stemmed from an inflexible attitude toward school boards and some colleagues. Roland's father attempted to write a book about physics while he was a teacher in Farmington, Maine, and late in life, he began a treatise on sociology "which he had hoped would bring about many reforms in church and society, and would be a lasting monument to him"—but he did not complete either, perhaps because he had a streak of perfectionism.[27]

Bertha, Wilhelmina, and Francis all were concerned at various times about the mental health of Roland's brother Otto, whom the family called "Ging." He was a hoarder who "once had an outbuilding in Georgia filled to the top with old papers he could not part with." He was extremely religious, in his mother's opinion, to the point of contributing money to a "superfluous little church" when his daughter needed financial help to attend college. Bertha seemed to think his faith was an obsession that he could not control. "His narrowest kind of churchiness is so detrimental to him and his family. Poor fellow!" His impulsivity, which is first apparent in his sudden marriage in 1910, caused trouble again in 1914, when he bought a farm at Cuthbert, Georgia, at the same time that his wife had a baby, even though he depended on financial handouts from the other Harpers. He also had an angry temper. Wilhelmina wrote in 1921 that Francis believed that Otto's temper was a sign that he was "mentally unbalanced." Wilhelmina added that Otto's "continued fruitless struggle," apparently to operate the farm in Georgia, "must naturally have a bad effect upon him." "Seems as [though] there ought to be some remedy," she commented and wondered if Otto would ever be financially successful. Bertha "really worried" about Otto, even having bad dreams about him, when Otto's wife, Mary, took the children and left Otto around 1921. Mary could have left Otto because he was financially unsuccessful, or because his neurotic behavior, such as only consuming milk and raw fruit, became intolerable, or possibly because he was physically abusive. While his mother, sister, and brother Francis cast doubts on his sanity and his ability to support his family, Otto sought his older brother's advice and company as well as his financial help, consulting him about the value of kudzu to agriculture and urging "dear Yye" to visit in a note he signed, "With love, Ging." Although an obsessive fear of germs plagued Otto, he rushed to be with his brother when Roland developed the life-threatening case of pneumonia.[28]

As he aged, Otto seems to have been afflicted with indecisiveness, another trait of obsessive-compulsive personality. When he had a chance to trade the farm at Cuthbert for real estate in Napa, California, in 1935, he spent so long trying to decide that the opportunity was lost, prompting Bertha to write, "I would love to set off a fire cracker behind him once in a while. I have no more patience with him." She worried that Otto would lose his job in Napa, a job that his wife seems to have helped him perform. "I am afraid the Napa people are finding it out that he can never come to any decision and how piddling he is, and I really fear they won't keep him. They have already made remarks to the effect that Mary is more efficient in the office. Too bad about these drawbacks of Ot's as otherwise he would be such a fine fellow."[29]

Hermina apparently suffered from a severe, persistent mental illness that manifested itself in her twenties. By the time she was thirty, she was living with her mother and incapacitated by symptoms that family members never clearly described. These symptoms kept her from taking a boat trip with Otto and his bride, Mary, in 1910. After the honeymoon, Mary wrote to Roland, "Mother Harper writes that Hermina is very much better. We are so glad. We were expecting her to take the boat trip on the lakes with us when we got the sad news." Otto and Mary took Hermina to live with them in Georgia the following year, and Bertha reported to Roland, "They don't say much about Hermina. I hope she doesn't make herself disagreeable. Neither does she write. We are only glad she is not here." Later, Hermina moved to North Carolina and married but suffered another mental breakdown of some kind in 1919, apparently after she had a miscarriage and her husband left her. Two buildings where she lived burned in mysterious fires that she claimed to have started; Otto saved her from a possible arson conviction by having her briefly committed to a mental hospital. After divorcing she sometimes lived on charity from the American Red Cross and sometimes supported herself with jobs as a store clerk, with the family sending additional money. Lapsing into broken English, as she often did when distressed, Bertha wrote cryptically in 1922: "[T]he poor soul got to wander again, as she cannot maintain her present abode. She certainly is to be pittied [sic]." Hermina also sometimes went on hunger strikes. Her illness worsened so much in 1927, when she was editing a poetry magazine, that Bertha worried "intensely" and Francis's wife, Jean, urged Roland to help pay for treatment at a psychiatric hospital such as the Phipps Clinic of Johns Hopkins Hospital in Baltimore.[30]

If Hermina went to the Johns Hopkins clinic for treatment, it was not very successful. The next year she told her mother that she was living primarily on produce from a vegetable garden that she struggled to tend by herself and prevailed on Bertha to give her some of the money Roland regularly sent to Bertha. Nonetheless, a writer for the Charlotte Observer was sufficiently charmed by Hermina to describe her as living on an "estate adjoining the old Berry hill place on Tuckaseege road, in a picturesque locality where the charms of the countryside have not yet been entirely destroyed by the expansion of the city." Hermina, who by then used the first name "Alice" and her married name, McFarland, had organized the Poetry Society of the South, a vehicle for her crusade against "the abominable stuff that pose[d] as poetry and [was] accepted as such in many current magazines and anthologies." She wrote an "incoherent" letter to Bertha in 1939, saying she had had a nervous collapse, which Bertha feared was brought on by starvation, a clue that Hermina had anorexia nervosa, another obsessive-compulsive spectrum disorder. She wrote a massive novel called "The Master Race" or "Those Germans," which was not published. She also claimed to have written a biography of Franklin Delano Roosevelt but became involved in a dispute over the manuscript when another woman also claimed to be the author.[31]

Francis sometimes joked that he and Roland were alike, that Roland was "like [him], only more so!" He had the same "note-taking disease" as Roland, keeping field notebooks for every region he explored, including thirty-eight about Okefenokee Swamp. Like Roland and their father, Francis turned from natural history to sociology in his later years and dreamed of writing a comprehensive book about the culture of the Okefenokee Swamp, but never accomplished it. Like Roland, he avoided the commitment of permanent employment; he quit a full-time job with the United States Biological Survey because, he told his brother, he could not "stand any longer the machinations of the gang of bootlickers and hypocrites." He struggled to support his family financially while working on temporary, grant-funded research projects and was sometimes beset by depression, according to Bertha.[32]

In contrast to his brother Otto, whose extreme religiosity was so distasteful to Bertha, Francis rejected organized religion, even after his wife became a Quaker. His son David remembers him as having "no interest in ritualized ceremonies, personalized gods, or biblical quotations. However, he was extremely moral and moralistic." Unlike Roland, who maintained many friendships for decades or even for life, and obviously enjoyed attending dinners, lectures, and other social events, Francis was scornful of many people and never felt "quite comfortable with ordinary society, feeling apart from it," although he deeply admired the people of Okefenokee Swamp, who, he wrote, "have acquired a vast store of intimate knowledge of the life of Okefinokee; they have seen sights in bygone days such as will not be witnessed again; they have opened many pages in the book of nature that remain closed, or at best but half-open, to the zoological visitor." Francis sneered at other scientists whom he considered self-promoters. He despised Germany, in spite of his mother's love for her homeland, and tried to enlist after the United States entered World War II, but was rejected because of his age. In an obituary for Francis in the journal *The Auk*, Ralph S. Palmer wrote, "[H]e divided the 'human race' . . . into categories: the morally degenerate, the grossly unethical, and those not assigned to either of these categories—yet!"[33]

Wilhelmina became the head librarian at the Redwood City (California) Public Library in 1930, and Bertha often reminded Roland of his sister's material and professional success. Francis's children remembered Aunt Willie as the best adjusted of the Harper siblings, able to thrive in her career and eventually to support Bertha, seemingly without the various odd prejudices of her brothers. But she was not immune to the stresses of work. Scrambling to oversee construction of her new library and to give tours of it to groups of librarians who visited during a national conference in San Francisco in 1939, she came near a nervous breakdown and was "under a doctor's care . . . unable to sleep of late without artificial help."[34]

Harper's peculiarities were obsessive-compulsive, but in some ways they fit the nineteenth-century idea of a natural scientist. Summarizing his field observations in the diaries was—and is—good scientific practice. And if Roland read Francis Darwin's 1887 biography of Charles Darwin, he knew that Darwin believed four traits were important to success as a scientist: a love of science, an "unbounded patience in long reflecting over any subject," industrious observation and fact collection, and inventiveness combined with common sense.[35] It probably seemed to him that he was adhering to Darwinian standards by collecting data from newspapers and inventing new ways to interpret the information. Considered altogether, Harper's obsessive-compulsive traits—the compulsions to measure frequencies and abundance of flora, to clip newspaper articles, and to collect and hoard print materials; his frequent criticisms of friends and potential scientific allies; his inflexibility about the kinds of jobs he would accept; his obsession with making lists of data that competed with his scientific responsibility to synthesize his findings; his reluctance to drive, which forced Harper to explore the countryside where friends and colleagues would take him—explain his itinerant career in botany and his failure to produce a scientific masterpiece. His distaste for teaching and his inability to submit to supervision made him unable to accept the sort of academic position that would have given him a place in the center of botany and ecology. The compulsion to save information about the myriad natural and social forces that he believed were interrelated gave him a sense of control over questions that teased, tantalized, and tortured him. These personality traits made statistics, demographics, and sociology almost as appealing to him as botanical discovery. But it was not simply the allure of counting and list making that demography represented, or even the possibilities for greater understanding of interrelated ecological forces, that caused Harper to turn to the subject of demographics. His awareness of his own eccentricities, and, even more significantly, of the entire Harper family's tendency to be peculiar, was like a switch on a railroad track, leading him into the intellectual swamp of eugenics.

CHAPTER TWELVE

A Sacrifice to Science

Although Harper did not record much in his diary about his personal relationships, it is clear that he was fond of children. While boarding with the Marshall family in Tallahassee in 1914, Harper spent time with the Marshalls' children: On a day trip to Lanark in July 1914, he took their two older sons hiking along the shore; they crossed several small branches that emptied into the bay and swam in water that, he carefully noted in his diary, was only about two feet deep. On a similar trip with the Marshall family in July 1920, he rode the train from Tallahassee to Lanark with Mr. Marshall on a Saturday. They met Mrs. Marshall and the children, who had been on the coast since Monday, and Roland went swimming by moonlight that night and the following night with some of the family. Back in Tuscaloosa, Harper sometimes clipped and mailed comics to the Marshall children. The Marshalls were friends with the Bellamys of Tallahassee and may have introduced Harper to them. Harper went hiking on a July evening in 1920 with Raymond F. Bellamy of Tallahassee, a sociology professor at Florida State College for Women, and Bellamy's "little boy Edward." They walked "about two miles out St. Augustine Road, then north by Black Lake to [the] railroad, and back by that." Young Addison Marshall wrote Harper again in March 1922, "I sure do wish you were here. Every time I meet Dr. Bellamy or Mr. Owen they ask about you."[1]

Harper often used gentle humor with children. While visiting Florence Blake and her family at Talladega, Alabama, in 1924, Harper and an assistant from the geological survey took Florence's twelve-year-old nephew along on a mountain hike. Harper found the boy "a quiet little fellow, but he climbed up to the top of the highest mountain with [them] without any trouble." He showed an album of cartoons he had drawn to Florence's five-year-old niece, who "seemed to enjoy it very much." Hiking alone in north Alabama a few years later, he left a pair of worn-out shoes in an empty schoolhouse "to mystify the children when they start back to school." He mused, "If I had been a poet I might have left a message for them, or if I could have found any chalk I might have drawn a maniac picture on the blackboard."[2]

In his fifties, Harper felt a strong grandfatherly affection for Anne and Lyman Findley, whose parents, Herbert and Earline Findley, rented him a bedroom in their house on University Avenue in Tuscaloosa. He drew cartoons for the children and cherished their routine of reading the newspaper "funnies" in the evenings. In "Reading the Funnies Every Night at No. 329," Maniac places an arm around Anne's waist and asks, "What shall I read first?" In the cartoon "The First Day at School," a boy named Rufus torments Anne by tickling her with a feather. A strange and facetiously fearsome creature, with horns like a six-spotted green tiger beetle, peers through the schoolroom window, making threatening "Ggrrr!" sounds toward Rufus. Harper noted in his annotated scrapbook of cartoons, "The creature looking in at the window is the Goopnapper, who carries off naughty children like the boy in the second seat." In a Christmas cartoon, Harper's alter ego, Maniac, Anne and her brother, Lyman, and Santa Claus all are fashioned of prunes and have names like "Pranne" and "Pruniac." Harper depicted five-year-old Anne and a friend at play in "Anne and Emily Having a Lawn Party." In 1935, he left a tiny card, "From Santa Claus," for seven-year-old Anne. "Here's hoping you are as merry as Christmas," was the printed message on the card. Harper added, "From the Sand-man, the Nine-o'clock man, and Santa Claus."[3]

Harper also made pasteboard toys for Anne and Lyman, using cast-off boxes and other scrap materials to create models of the vernacular architecture he often photographed on his treks through the coastal plain. He constructed a two-story, columned plantation house, another large house with a pyramidal hipped roof and shutters hinged at the tops of the windows, several smaller cabins and outbuildings, a church, and a gas station. He made a funny conical building with a roof like a top hat, a round structure from a hatbox, and the pièce de résistance, a ziggurat, a pyramid with a trough instead of staircases around which marbles would roll, disappearing inside the structure and then delightfully reappearing. Dr. Harper, as the Findleys always called him, made the big, round structure to be the centerpiece for Anne's birthday party and hid tiny gifts inside, tying them to ribbons that dangled through the windows, so that each young guest could choose a ribbon to pull and find a surprise. When he sent a photograph to Bertha of Anne and Lyman posing with the houses arrayed on the Findleys' back porch, his mother wrote back, "A pity you are not a daddy yourself; what a good one you would make."[4]

Bertha brutally pressured Roland to find a wife and settle down and encouraged him to court Florence Blake. Harper did correspond with Florence over the years, sending her reprints of some of his publications, and visited her several times. He went to her family's summer home at Erin in Clay County, Alabama, in 1914, making a train trip from Tallahassee around the time of his birthday. Florence met him at the station in a buggy, and he stayed five days. Roland visited Florence again in 1929, after his nine-week hospitalization for pneumonia, while traveling with Bertha from Athens to Tuscaloosa. He may have visited Florence in June 1939, when he explored granite outcrops on the Tallapoosa River in Randolph County. Florence was friendly enough with Roland that she wrote to his mother, who in turn confided that Hermina was suffering from mental or emotional problems. Maybe Harper did propose to Florence, and she turned him down. Or maybe Harper never proposed to Florence, perhaps because she had short hair. He wrote to his old friend J. Walter Hendricks in 1927 that he was waiting to marry after the bobbed hair "fad" ended. His objection was so extreme that Bertha, while she shared his opinion, told him he needed to be less judgmental. "I am afraid you'll have to get used to this bobbed hair foolishness wherever you go."[5]

Bertha could be caustic about Roland's bachelorhood. When he apparently was disappointed that a woman did not visit him, she criticized him for not inviting the woman more clearly. "I suppose you did not give that Wisconsin girl a cordial invitation enough to visit you. Why then should she come, unless one of the bold, forward females?" She nagged him often about his single state, his lack of a steady job, and his lack of a house. Sometimes she combined all of these criticisms in one comprehensive tirade: "[I] wish I could feel [relieved] about you and Hermina and know you [are] established more permanently somewhere. At your age now you ought to have something more steady than floating jobs. You could be learning and expanding just the same and write books and be married, like thousands of others. Now look here, you better spot a girl in the first place; then a more permanent job, as you can't stay a hobo all your life. . . . You get the girl and the job and the home and then write all the books you want." On another occasion, she called him an "OLD baby, with your homelessness, and only half year jobs." She scolded, "Why can't you have a fine job with all your great knowledge . . . like most any other scientist not half as competent as you? . . . Unless you hurry up and find a wife with a little means, and a modest home, I don't know what will become of you finally." Bertha's sister Fanny chimed in: "Roli dear don't you think it would be best [if] you finally got married? I am sure there must be among your numerous friends one nice Lady (short or [long] hair that's very indifferent—as long as she is of good character) who may have some little means too to start a little home—so you would have somebody! . . . If you have salary enough to support a wife, try to get one."[6]

Yet while Roland was smitten time and again, he did not marry until 1943. Perhaps he could not make up his mind which woman to choose. Perhaps he just could not afford to marry. Bertha and the other Harpers badgered him for years to give them money, leaving him little for his own needs, much less for starting a family. Even when he was not fully employed himself, Roland sent money to Bertha and the others when he could. He paid for Wilhelmina to travel by train from Georgia to College Point in July 1910 when she feared she would contract malaria if she stayed in the South. He occasionally sent his mother money to help support his young cousin, Anna. He sent money twice to his brother Otto, after Otto and Mary's second daughter was born in 1914, and fourteen years later paid their older daughter's tuition at Normal School at Statesboro, Georgia, a contribution his mother called "a fine noble thing." He continued sending money to his mother for years after she began living with Wilhelmina and Wilhelmina's companion, Blanche, in California.[7]

The family belittled his unmarried, nomadic lifestyle and used it to justify their demands for money at the same time. When Francis's wife, Jean, asked Roland to send money for medical care for Hermina, she argued that Roland should contribute more than she and Francis. "You have always followed out your own inclinations and ambitions, unhindered by the responsibility of aiding your family in any steady financial way. You have had not family of your own to provide for and, last but not least perhaps, you are the oldest child and a man. All this leads to the simple conclusion—does it not seem right that you should come generously, and steadily so, to the aid" of Bertha and Hermina?[8] Of course, with unsteady employment, Roland was limited in how much he could contribute to the family's support, even though he lived modestly.

His refusal to take a steady job with a bigger salary frustrated the family, principally because supporting Bertha and Hermina was so difficult. Francis alluded to Roland's record of turning down job offers when he heard about Roland's one-year appointment at the University of Georgia. "Such a job seems admirably suited to your needs and peculiarities, but if I should urge you to accept it, it would be just like you to turn it down. I judge that it is now safe to speak." Bertha sometimes mocked Roland's simple lifestyle, as when she wrote, "I suppose you are installed in your bare and gloomy room, living the Piggly Wiggly way again, and thus the New year can't grow into a very happy one, neither for your stomach, nor your mood, nor your self esteem, nor your importance in the world in consequence. . . . I do wish you could get out of this condition. And the first step toward it, is to live respectably." She offered to send him some of her furniture, which she did not want to take with her to California, if he would rent a small house. She suggested that he could occupy a single room and rent the rest to roomers, reversing his customary housing arrangement. At other times, she implored him to move into her and Wilhelmina's home. "You would enjoy this home, and we have a comfortable place for you to make yourself at home."[9]

Roland perhaps avoided marriage and fatherhood rather than risk being unable to support a wife and children if he lost a job, as happened to his father. It must have been evident to him that Wilhelmina was able to support herself and keep demanding jobs as a librarian, first at the Poppenhusen Institute and then in California, while editing books on the side, precisely because she had not married or had children. He clearly felt anxiety about secure employment. When Bertha considered moving to California to live with Wilhelmina, he worried that Wilhelmina would lose her library job and be unable to support their mother, which infuriated his sister. "You are dead wrong about that," she wrote. "I will say for the last and millionth time, that there is no more chance of losing my job than your flying to the moon. . . . For genuine pessimism you are the limit." Meanwhile, his mother's nagging over the decades could not have strengthened his confidence. Bertha steadily berated Roland for his failures and suggested that Francis and Otto were similar failures, Francis for his inability to produce books about his research at Hudson Bay and the Okefenokee, and Otto for his unrealistic dreams of owning a farm and his "churchiness and germ fear."[10]

Perhaps Harper did not settle into a permanent job with a steady salary because he had observed his father's and later Francis's difficulty in answering to supervisors. His inflexibility about the kind of work he would do moved him to turn down seemingly good jobs. He certainly did not want to teach. When Jean Broadhurst, the editor of *Torreya*, suggested he could get a faculty appointment in a college biology department, he told her, "I have no talent for teaching and I prefer to be a producer rather than retailer of scientific facts." Like Francis, he did not want to be part of a bureaucracy, even one devoted to field research. He told Forrest Shreve the same year, "Nobody can make lasting contributions to human knowledge when he is bossed by a bureau chief and not allowed to have any mind of his own." Writing to his mother fourteen years later, he alluded to the same sacrifice of scientific independence that working for a government agency required: "I know of a good many men who used to do pretty good scientific work, and changed their policies to get rich quicker, and soon lost most of their reputation, and became objects of contempt, or almost outcasts. One can't be too careful about such things." He wanted only to "travel and tramp," as Bertha put it.[11]

As he considered whether to marry, Harper may have feared that his own urge to explore the wild places of the coastal plain was drawing him inexorably toward madness. During his miserable stint as a manufacturing worker in New England, he read Thoreau, who wrote: "'When I would recreate myself, I seek the darkest wood, the thickest and most interminable and, to the citizen, the most dismal swamp. I enter the swamp as a sacred place, a *sanctum sanctorum*,'" but American popular culture viewed swamps as places where one explored not just the wilderness of nature but the wilderness of the mind, where there were "possibilities for [mental] regeneration but also . . . psychic disintegration." Perhaps Harper also read *Army Life in a Black Regiment*, by Thomas Wentworth Higginson (1869), who described Civil War service in the coastal plain, including a nighttime swim when, he recalled, "I seemed floating in some concave globe, some magic crystal, of which I was the enchanted centre. With each little ripple of my steady progress all things hovered and changed. The stars danced and nodded above; where the stars ended the great Southern fireflies began; and closer than the fireflies, there clung around me a halo of phosphorescent sparkles from the soft salt water." Higginson lost all sense of time and perspective and became disoriented: "It was as if a fissure opened somewhere and I saw my way into a madhouse." It is impossible that Harper did not know the famous nineteenth-century poem "The Lake of the Dismal Swamp," by Thomas Moore, in which a young man brokenhearted over the death of his true love loses his mind and "hollow'd a boat of the birchen bark / Which carried him off from shore," never to return.[12]

Insanity appears to have weighed on Harper's mind. On his first ramble along the Black Warrior River in Tuscaloosa in 1905, Harper passed the state mental hospital that stood near the bluff. Bryce Hospital was a large Italianate structure located between the university campus and the river.

The hospital was so near the Findley home, where Harper lived in the 1930s, that it must have loomed in his thoughts just as it did at the end of its long straight driveway, visible from University Boulevard. A constant reminder of the ultimate destiny of the hopelessly insane, the hospital admitted more and more patients, its population growing at three times the rate of the state overall, according to its superintendent. Lucien Underwood's suicide in 1907 was a horrific event that Harper could have found a terrifying indication of the unpredictability of insanity: Underwood suddenly attacked his wife and adult daughter, attempting to kill them with a table knife, and then slashed his own throat. Underwood's friends and colleagues were stunned and could imagine no reason for Underwood's sudden mental breakdown, but Nathaniel Britton revealed in an obituary a few weeks later that Underwood "had complained of insomnia and headache at intervals for several weeks"—possibly the early symptoms of an impending manic crisis. In the biographical papers that some of Underwood's colleagues prepared for a memorial session of the Torrey Botanical Club two months later, there were clues that he had experienced intense emotional states, perhaps even mania, throughout his life: deep religiosity as a young man; a tendency to choose the hardest and most laborious course of work, such as "devoting ten extra hours per week to [geology] during the winter term of his junior or senior years, without credit so far as his college course was concerned"; and a charismatic personality and notable talent for leading and inspiring others. Underwood was not the only person in Harper's life to experience mental illness. In 1908, his friend Edward was so undone by depression over a lost love that he told Roland he feared he would "land in the 'bughouse.'" Francis told Roland in 1921 that a mutual acquaintance had become "hopelessly insane," commenting, "It's a great pity."[13]

The Tauber-Harper family was quite familiar with mental illness. In 1864, Bertha's father, Wilhelm Tauber, painted the portrait of "Mad" King Ludwig II that is the most famous image of Ludwig in Munich. Bertha romanticized Ludwig's mania in her memoir—"Ludwig had wonderful ideas of beauty and harmony and gave them shape by erecting the most enchanting castles." Although she demurred at calling the king insane, Bertha came to believe that all three of her sons were unbalanced. "There is something wrong somewhere. . . . When I think of all the talent in the family, of all the hopes we cherished, of all the great integrity and high ideals you all have, and yet how little reward you have reaped! I speak chiefly of you boys," she wrote to Roland in 1922.[14]

Despite having a sanctuary, a relatively steady job at Smith Hall, and his worrisome relatives ensconced a safe distance away in California, Harper sometimes dwelled on madness. He mused in a letter to Paul Finner, the professor of social psychology at Florida State College for Women, in 1937 about the relationship between genius and insanity. Finner replied, "The relationship between insanity and genius raise[s] a knotty problem. The view today seems to tend to a denial of the relationship. Both the defective and the [genius] are the extremes. And the conditions that produce insane behavior seem to be quite the reverse of [those] that lead to creative work." Finner added that finding the roots of insanity would be difficult because "we have no valid definition of the normal." In 1939, a woman friend in Guin, Alabama, a frequent botanizing partner and driver for Harper, was committed to Bryce for at least the second time. Harper made a haunting photograph of the Bryce cemetery on an early spring day in 1940, showing more than a thousand identical gravestones stretching in rows seemingly to the horizon, each marked only with a number, each representing someone lost to history, forgotten and nameless. In 1942, describing a stand of croomia that had been singed by fire, Harper speculated that an increase in arson-caused forest fires was related to an increase in insanity. In 1944, he copied statistics of white and "colored" inmates of jails and mental hospitals. In 1948, he returned to the relationship of genius and madness, writing a commentary on the "development of genius."[15]

Fear that one is becoming insane is a trait of obsessive-compulsive spectrum disorders, but Roland's anxiety deepened as the pseudoscience of eugenics, invented by a cousin of Charles Darwin and promoted by many of England's and the United States' leading intellectuals, promulgated the idea that insanity was inheritable. Sweeping academia, philanthropy, and even government around the turn of the century, eugenics suggested to Harper that he was destined to inherit his family's insanity *and* to pass it on to any heirs. Here is the tragedy of Harper's life: perceiving the Harper lineage of mental "peculiarities," as Francis called them, he sacrificed his own happiness in service to the progressive science of the day, which forbade reproduction by genetically inferior people, including those with mental illness.[16] Avoiding parenthood was a scientific imperative, so Harper resisted the flirtations of several women, decades of nagging by his mother and aunt, and his own strong paternal affection for children, to remain single.

Several trends merged in the early twentieth century to spawn eugenics: the revival of genetic theory, the powerful idea that Hugo de Vries and others reintroduced just as Harper began his doctoral work, and that Edmund B. Wilson and W. S. Sutton pursued at Columbia while Harper was there; the influx of southern European immigrants to the United States; the migration of black southerners from the South to towns and cities in the North; and the increasing pressure on states to provide residential education or care for children and adults with mental retardation, physical disabilities, and mental illness. Eugenics was a popular and credible field with many stellar advocates. Charles Darwin's own cousin, Francis Galton, coined the name "eugenics" for the study of the elimination of hereditary disorders. After the publication of Charles B. Davenport's textbook, *Heredity in Relation to Eugenics*, in 1911, many universities began incorporating eugenics into science curricula, and Davenport became a leading spokesman for the eugenics movement.[17]

Davenport directed the Eugenics Records Office, a hub of eugenics activity. The ERO was a private research effort that merged with Cold Spring Harbor Laboratory, the experiment station of the Carnegie Institution of Washington, where Harper's old friend George Shull worked. (Coincidentally, the ERO considered making Worcester County, Massachusetts, the territory of Harper's great Wachusett Mountain trek in 1898, the site for an analysis of insanity.) Harper met Davenport in the summer of 1905 when Harper visited Cold Spring Harbor. Davenport had some interesting things in common with Harper. Both men had demanding, authoritarian, intensely religious fathers and mothers who found joy in art and natural history. Both men's families were fixated on ancestry. Like Harper, Davenport turned from engineering to biology, although he became a zoologist rather than a botanist.[18] Davenport was, then, a likely figure to impress and influence Harper.

At least five factors influenced Harper to take Davenport's new science seriously. First, the massive movement in the field of biology from natural history to the laboratory science of genetics made Harper's passion for fieldwork seem obsolete within the first few years of the twentieth century, and thus he struggled throughout his career to make his interests and discoveries relevant. Second, his compulsion to clip newspaper articles encouraged him to constantly consider a variety of developments in society and to dwell on how they might be related. Third, his list-making compulsion attracted him to the statistical methods of demographics. Fourth, the Tauber family's preoccupation with lineage and royalty made eugenics, the "science" of ethnicity and inheritance, naturally appealing to Harper. Fifth, and ironically, eugenics fueled another typical obsessive-compulsive trait, the fear that one is becoming insane.

It is not surprising that a person with obsessive-compulsive personality traits, born to a family preoccupied with lineage, raised in a racist society, schooled in proximity to the thrilling new science of genetics, and drawn to the use of statistics—first to interpret phytogeographical observations and eventually to interpret sociological phenomena—would find sense and meaning in eugenics. It was, after all, mainstream science at the time, and statistics was its primary tool. Springing from the new science of genetics and based on the premise that some groups of people were innately inferior to others, eugenics, the study of the relationships of ethnicity to human traits and behavior, was highly respected in Harper's time and in fact seen by many as progressive social policy, the solution to poverty and related problems of the twentieth century. As Edward Larson observes, "[A]pplying turn-of-the-century developments in genetics, scientists offered a means to breed better people just when rising middle-class progressives were seeking to cope with an apparent increase in the number of urban paupers, criminals, lunatics, and so-called 'feeble-minded' persons."[19]

Even if eugenics had not been a growing and respectable branch of science until Hitler's "final solution" became common knowledge, other factors would have contributed to Harper's predisposition to accept the premise of genetic determinism. First, despite the image that Bertha cultivated of compassion for the unfortunate, the superiority of some family lines over others was one of the central tenets of her life. Part of the family legend was that the Taubers in Bavaria, and to a lesser extent the Harpers in Ireland, were members of nobility and had many contacts with nobility. There are many indications of the pervasiveness of this legend in the family. As Bertha told her daughter Wilhelmina, and Wilhelmina later recorded, one of Bertha's grandmothers was a member of the German nobility, living in a castle on the German-French border, and her parents, "well-to-do aristocrats," were killed in the French Revolution. The grandmother, still a child, was brought up by a countess and became a lady-in-waiting to the queen of Bavaria. She married the court architect, named von Tauber, who also was of the nobility. They had one child, Wilhelm von Tauber, who became an artist and "one of Munich's most famous portrait painters."[20] Wilhelm was Bertha's father.

Bertha reminisced about "visits to the king's palace with her father, who had the privilege of copying 'old masters' there." Once, she said, she accompanied her father to the palace but became lost and the king himself led her back to her von Tauber. She often told the heroic story of how, when she was seventeen and working in Sedan, France, as a tutor, she witnessed the Battle of Sedan and "saw the 'brave' Napoleon [III] hiding from his soldiers behind some barrels. He was very pale and stood like a wax image until his soldiers found him and dragged him back to the battlefield to encourage his men.'" Roland recalled her tale this way: "The French emperor, Napoleon III, was in the city with his troops, but when the firing got too hot he took refuge in a cellar, and Mother saw some of his soldiers drag him out and make him face the enemy, who presently took him prisoner." Moving to the United States after marrying William Harper and settling in a small lumber town in Michigan was difficult for Bertha, who told of how "she had always been in circles of nobility, and now she was to live in a small far-away town, with people who were rough and queerly dressed."[21]

The greatness of Bertha's father and the important artists with whom he associated were another important part of the family legend. Bertha told her children that "when she was ten years old her family moved into the house of her father's friend, Dr. Hermann von Lingg, who was one of Germany's great poets." Another aspect of the family ethos was that Germans were superior to people of other nationalities. Roland recalled that when the family moved to Dalton, "one agreeable surprise for Mother . . . was the presence in town or on farms near by, of several good German families. . . . One German family that we became attached to, the Yaegers, lived about seven miles south of Dalton. . . . The wife, a member of an aristocratic family, had eloped with her father's coachman, a good honest man, and they had raised several sturdy sons in Georgia." Again in Americus, the Harper family made "some good friends"; "among them were a few Germans."[22]

Bertha attributed great significance to ancestry. In 1935, she complained that her niece Anna "could never have been congenial or have fitted into [their] family. The traits of such ancestry [were] too pronounced." Anna's father, Bertha's brother John Tower, had married beneath the family and generally associated with lower-class people: "Johnnie always looked down for his associates, instead of up. He must have had an awful inferiority complex. His daughter is the same." Perhaps in conflict with her husband, whose final academic position was superintendent of the school for immigrants in Flushing, New York, and with Wilhelmina, who enjoyed reading stories to immigrant children, Bertha was anti-Semitic and opposed marriages between different ethnicities, believing the world was "overfilled with muts [*sic*]." She mocked an article Roland sent her, which she said consisted of "ridiculous Jew-paper inventions and absurd lies about Germany." Roland's brother Otto absorbed her anti-Semitism and class-consciousness, as he revealed in a letter about his fiancée, Mary Ella Cone. "I don't know whether you got acquainted with any of the Cone family on your visits to Bulloch County, [Georgia,] but it is one of the oldest families in the county. Even though the name has much the same sound as a Jewish family name, there is nothing Jewish about it. Her father is a deacon in the Baptist church and she is a Methodist." Wilhelmina also absorbed at least some of their mother's class-consciousness, considering their grandfather "a true nobleman."[23]

In addition to Bertha Harper's clear belief in genetic superiority, a second factor contributed to Harper's belief in eugenics: He was immersed at a very impressionable age in a culture that depended for its very existence on the premise of racial superiority. When the Harper family moved from New England to Dalton, Georgia, the South's fight to preserve slavery and a legal system of racial inequality was still a sacred cause in the memories of many southerners. Despite his early childhood in New England, Harper came of age believing that the Lost Cause was to be cherished. In the aftermath of emancipation, white culture fostered the idea that blacks were inferior workers who could justifiably be paid less than white workers. By the time Roland graduated from the University of Georgia, the neo-Darwinian "radical mentality" held that the descendants of freed slaves were regressing to a "natural state of savagery and bestiality." Mining and railroad companies were recruiting foreign-born workers to the South to work in the region's mines and to build the region's railroads, generating animosity among native southerners who felt the loss of job opportunities.[24]

The hatred of many white southerners for these ethnic minorities intensified at the same time that eugenics accrued more legitimacy in the United States. The superintendent of the mental hospital in Tuscaloosa, James T. Searcy, whom Harper undoubtedly knew socially, was one of the Deep South's leading proponents of compulsory sterilization for the insane and the developmentally disabled. "Hereditary multiplication of the deficient and defective ought to be discouraged in every way," he declared in 1914. Harper's Tallahassee friend Susan Bradford Eppes romanticized the Old South and the Lost Cause in her books *The Negro of the Old South*

(1925) and *Through Some Eventful Years* (1926). Eppes captured the importance of breeding to social status in the Old South: "Never had we heard it intimated that wealth made one better, or poverty made one less desirable; personality was the criterion; personality and *family* with great stress laid upon this latter qualification." She clearly believed that black slaves, intellectually inferior to whites, were happy with their lot, remembering them as having "smiling black faces and willing hands." During Harper's appointment at the University of Georgia in 1928 and 1929, he also became friends with E. Merton Coulter, a historian there who would become a leading intellectual figure in the defense of the Confederacy. Harper shared his own copy of a paper by his undergraduate friend Ulrich B. Phillips with Coulter in November and chatted with Coulter on a winter evening in December. Coulter visited Harper during Harper's convalescence in February 1929 and apparently gave him a copy of his new book, *College Life in the Old South*, which Harper read while he was still in the hospital. Later that spring, Harper went to his first "talking movie" with Coulter. That same year, Phillips characterized the southern mentality as " 'a common resolve indomitably maintained' that the South 'shall be and remain a white man's country.'" As C. Vann Woodward later described Phillips's interpretation, a belief in white supremacy was " 'the cardinal test of a Southerner and the central theme of southern history.'"[25]

One of the friends Harper made in Tallahassee was the sociologist Raymond F. Bellamy at Florida State College for Women, who lent him the book *Statistics and Sociology*, by Richard Mayo-Smith (1902), a sociologist at Columbia College whose later book *Emigration and Immigration: A Study in Social Science* (1912) examined labor competition and other issues related to immigration. Bellamy also lent Harper *Expansion of Races* (1909) by the anti-Semitic writer Charles Edward Woodruff. In 1921, Harper wrote to Charles Gunter, Herman Gunter's brother, about anti-Semitic articles that Henry Ford had written. Ford's essays did not impress Gunter, and it is not clear that they impressed Harper either. Gunter replied, "You ask if I have read any of Henry Ford's anti-Semitic articles. My brother Carl, who, as you may know, is in Cleveland, sent me a copy or two of the *Dearborn Independent* as well as one or two Jewish replies to these attacks. I have not followed the matter closely and accordingly am not conversant enough to give any opinion. But I am not in favor of persecution. Furthermore, as you intimate, many of the so-called menaces are exaggerated. This I too believe." Gunter added cryptically,

"There are, however, some real menaces; but these are generally ignored by the public and the press."[26]

Increasingly interested in the ideas of the eugenics movement, Harper attended the Second International Congress of Eugenics at the American Museum of Natural History in New York in September 1921, while staying with Bertha at College Point. The speakers included Leonard Darwin, the son of Charles Darwin; Henry Fairfield Osborn, director of the museum; the conservationist Gifford Pinchot; and the inventor Alexander Graham Bell. Harper attended Darwin's speech but did not comment specifically on it in his diary. He examined some of the exhibits at the conference, met the Yale economist Irving Fisher, and saw his old friend George Shull.[27]

Harper believed that ethnicity was a major factor in human potential. In a discussion of demographics in central Florida in a 1921 report for the Florida Geological Survey, he noted changes in immigration between 1880 and 1910, commenting that the "great increase of West Indian and southern European immigration in thirty years indicates quite a deterioration in quality." Perhaps he was thinking of those "good German families" that his mother had found in Dalton and Americus, Georgia, when he observed that earlier immigrants from northern Europe, who tended to become farmers, had better literacy rates than laborers from southern Europe or even than native "whites" in agricultural districts of the South. He also speculated that compulsory education actually stimulated demand for immigrant laborers because schooling enabled native-born children to move up the economic ladder. By 1927, Harper was a subscriber to *Eugenical News*, a publication of the American Eugenics Society and the Eugenics Research Association, which advocated state-sponsored sterilization and other eugenical policies.[28]

Alabama historian G. Ward Hubbs and biologist L. J. Davenport argue that the sociological commentaries that Harper wrote in his later years should be viewed "sympathetically" as reflections of his milieu—a milieu that persisted in the South even though no southern legislature enacted eugenic marriage statutes, as geneticists began to poke holes in eugenical science, and as the public gradually became aware of Hitler's "final solution." Harper recognized that "studies of quality of population" were "very objectionable to a large and growing number of people in practically all civilized countries, who make 'democracy' a fetish; so that it is often necessary to camouflage such studies to get them published at all. One can sometimes express the opinion that some groups or communities are inferior to others, and get away with it; but to prove it statistically arouses resentment."[29] Yet he continued to use demographic and sociological data to demonstrate eugenical ideas about the inferiority of ethnic and racial groups.

Convinced that forces in nature interacted in ways that were not easily perceived and increasingly desperate to make sense of seemingly unrelated facts, Harper wrote to his friends, former colleagues, and even strangers, submitting his ideas and speculations to others whom he hoped would give them credence. In 1926, for example, he wondered whether black and white people had different dietary mineral needs. "I have studied the ages of whites and Negroes in Florida, and reached the conclusion that white people live longest in regions of poor soil and good water, and Negroes vice versa. From this I infer that Negroes need more mineral matter in their diet than white people." He wrote to W. W. Keen, a frequent contributor to the journal *Science*, suggesting that he take up the question. "Although I know very little of medical literature, I suspect that the chemical differences between different races, and people living in different countries, have not been adequately investigated. If so, this ought to be an attractive subject for some of your young colleagues to investigate, in a city like Philadelphia, which has every facility for medical research." Mulling the fact that Philadelphia might have "a scarcity of full-blooded negroes to work on," however, Harper blundered badly, suggesting that Keen begin with experiments involving smaller animals. "Possibly Negroes would be found to resemble monkeys almost as much as they do whites."[30]

As Harper tried to link phytogeographical, biological, and sociological information, he sometimes puzzled his friends. The founding editor of the journal *Genetics* in 1916 and a professor at Princeton University by 1927, George Shull had been analyzing the occurrence of heart-shaped and oval seed capsules in shepherd's purse (*Capsella bursa-pastoris*) to understand how multiple genes can interact to produce particular phenotypes. He asked Harper to collect seed capsules for him in Alabama. Harper obliged but enclosed some cryptic comments concerning college graduates and Episcopalians. Shull was unsure how to respond. "I am not inclined to think that college graduates or members of the Episcopalian Church are likely to carry with them a different form of Shepherd's-purse from what will be found in neighboring communities such as Robinson Springs, where the people are less aristocratic, but still I shall be glad to have collections from every sort of community that you happen to get into."[31]

Charles Davenport asked Harper in 1928 to recommend a location in the South where Davenport could collect data about "crosses between whites and Negroes, on the one hand, and Indians, on the other, also between Negroes and Indians." He inquired, "Do you know of any locality in the Southeast where first generation hybrids between those races might be observed?" He wrote again six weeks later, this time on letterhead of the International Federation of Eugenic Organizations, asking again, "[Would you] inform us if there are areas where widely different races of mankind have recently begun to come in contact in your state or Florida. By races we have in mind not only primary races, like white, Negro, Indian and Orientals but also very dissimilar European races. Especially important would be localities where the first and second hybrid generations can be secured in considerable numbers." It is not clear that Harper actually gave Davenport any leads on race-mixing in Alabama or Florida. The Yale University geographer Ellsworth Huntington, who encouraged Harper to write in a more popular style about the natural history of the South, was another prominent proponent of eugenics who considered non-Nordic immigrants "genuine human weeds."[32] Huntington's coauthor, Leon F. Whitney, was field secretary of the American Eugenics Society; he corresponded with Harper twice in May 1927.

Harper made a trip to New York to participate in the Third International Eugenics Congress in August 1932, which was again at the American Museum of Natural History. This time, Harper presented exhibits on eugenical topics at the conference. He saw Davenport and other eugenics leaders but typically made no note in his diary of his reactions to the ideas exchanged at the conference. He also spent time on botany and with old friends during the conference, going to the library and herbarium at the New York Botanical Garden. He visited Ernest Holt, who was working for the Audubon Society, and saw Charles Gunter, the brother of Herman Gunter of the Florida Geological Survey. He had dinner with John Kunkel Small. He spent one evening with old family friends in College Point. At night in his room at the Hotel Saint Andrew, he clipped newspaper articles as usual. He also made side trips to New Haven, Connecticut, to see Ulrich Phillips at Yale University and to Worcester, Massachusetts, where Ellsworth Huntington's brother drove him to the foot of Wachusett and Little Wachusett mountains. He spent several nights with Francis in Swarthmore. He traveled to New Jersey to explore the pine barrens there and spent a night in Camden with an old friend and another day with Charles Gunter, who lived at New Brunswick.[33]

The proponents of eugenics warned that people of superior intellect should not shirk the responsibility to reproduce merely for reasons of personal convenience. For Harper, then, eugenics was inseparable from the question of whether he should marry and have children. When he sent some calculations about birthrates to Davenport in 1925, Harper commented, "As I am a bachelor, and therefore have really no business fooling with eugenical problems, I feel a delicacy about having my name mentioned in connection with such a study as this." When he attended a college reunion in 1927, he was struck by how many of his classmates were fathers and even grandfathers; he was the only bachelor. One of his classmates, Walter Hendricks, had written to him two years earlier, listing his own four children and commenting, "I am exceedingly sorry to know that you are not making any better progress in matters matrimonial. Your baby brother is doubtless old enough to marry, but perhaps you are not so yet."[34] Harper mused in a letter to his mother in 1927, "Did you ever notice in how many families that have both boys and girls all the boys marry, and some of the girls get left out?" perhaps because in their own family it was he who was "left out."

He became intensely interested in marriage rates and family sizes as they related to social classes and ethnicity and wrote "A Simple Measure of Fecundity Based in Census Figures" that year. He told R. J. H. De-Loach in 1933 that he was studying genealogical records and had "gotten some very interesting results," although little information was available about his own ancestors. Harper feared that a declining birthrate was leading to the breakdown of society and may have felt guilty about his personal contribution to that decline. He commented in a 1943 letter that families tended to die out "when they [got] too brilliant." "[C]hildren in small families are more likely to be spoiled, or emotionally unstable, as the psychologists would say, than those in large families." Like "reckless driving, vandalism, Sunday amusements, profiteering, cheating on examinations, immodesty, immorality . . . and divorce," birth control was a "deplorable condition" that could lead to crime. In a letter to the *Tuscaloosa News* in 1933, he declared, "People who indulge in these things may never become criminals, but they are setting a bad example, to say the least, and making law enforcement difficult. Somewhat less reprehensible, but tending in the same direction, is indulgence in selfish pleasures of many kinds, which need not be specified here." He acknowledged, however, that smaller families were better for struggling farmers and even for the quality of urban life, drawing connections to automobile size and even to parking lots. "[W]e could hardly go back to the good old days of large families even if we wanted to, for it is about all the farmers can do now to support the children they have; and if families should increase in cities, bungalows and automobiles would have to be made larger, and the parking problem would be acute." Although "positive eugenics"—promotion of reproduction by genetically superior individuals—made sense to Harper, he did not agree with compulsory sterilization, warning that laws regulating births to "unfit persons" were "dangerous."[35]

Conflicted over whether his family's superior intellect mandated that he sire children, or his family's "madness" forbade him to do so, Harper made himself a martyr to the eugenics cause: he resisted the desire to have children of his own out of fear that he would pass on the "psychological factors" of his family's numerous odd obsessions and compulsions. Yet Roland kept hoping he would find someone who could give him companionship and comfort. As he entered his sixties, he worried that he would need someone to care for him. He wrote to his old friend George Shull, "Even if you should ultimately become completely incapacitated, you have enough descendants to take good care of you. All this recent agitation for old-age pensions I guess is due mostly to the fact that too many people these days don't have enough children to take care of them."[36]

As the eugenics movement reinforced Harper's fear of insanity and compelled him to remain single, it also fueled his interests in statistics and sociology, pushing him further away from the field where he might have achieved greatness. Like the forestry establishment's dismissal of his theory about fire ecology in longleaf forests, the slights to his "population studies" may have seemed to Harper another example of the academy and government bureaucrats conspiring to suppress his insights. Whereas his ideas about fire eventually received respect and support, his eugenical theories did not. Without children or a major book to carry on his name, with his namesake genus *Harperella* downgraded by the botanist Mildred Mathias in 1936 to a species of the genus *Ptilimnium*, and with Fernald at the Harvard herbarium seemingly determined to minimize Harper's field discoveries, Roland probably feared that his dream of being remembered forever would not come true.[37]

CHAPTER THIRTEEN

Harper's Love-vine

Roland began corresponding with Mary Sue Wigley of Sand Mountain, Alabama, in 1942 after she wrote to ask him for copies of a bulletin. The daughter of a tenant farmer, Mary had been a supervisor of home demonstration agents for the United States Department of Agriculture Cooperative Extension Service for ten years before becoming a full-time lecturer who gave talks on home economics to women's clubs around the country. Harper and she had met once in 1935 when she gave a lecture in Tuscaloosa, coincidentally just after he had been on a botanizing expedition to Sand Mountain. When they resumed their acquaintance, Roland remembered that expedition and perceived a romantic coincidence: "As we passed Noccalula Falls I noticed that my little love-vine (*Cuscuta harperi*) was already in bloom on the rocks there."

Roland was sixty-four; Mary was forty-eight; both were too old to be coy. Roland wrote, "The older we get the faster time goes."[1] Mary was frankly interested in finding a husband. She asked Roland why he was not married. "From the time I was grown until 1931 I hardly ever stayed more than a year and a half at a time in one place, and that wasn't long enough to get well acquainted with any of the fair sex," he replied. "Since 1931 I have been here pretty continuously, in spite of the Depression, etc., but have been too old to make much impression on the fair sex. However, strange as it may seem, I still have a few girl friends."[2]

Roland thought Mary seemed like a good catch and wrote to his mother, "Everything I know about her is good, and she may be what I have been looking for all these years." She was from a genetically isolated section of Alabama where "people come as near being Puritans now as any in Alabama."[3] He went to Birmingham in March 1943 to meet her while she attended a conference. Mary and her sister, Annie Wigley, were staying at the YWCA. Harper called on them there on March 25 and then crossed town to see his old friend H. E. Wheeler, perhaps to talk over his first encounter with Mary. Afterward, he went back downtown to the

Tutwiler Hotel, where a reception for teachers was under way; working his way through the crowd, he found Mary and Annie. They had supper at the YWCA; before leaving for the night, Roland showed them some photographs and "Maniac" cartoons. He rejoined Mary at eight o'clock the next morning and accompanied her to a lecture by the superintendent of the Atlanta schools, who, Roland commented in his diary, was "a good talker, but didn't give much information. Deplored small families of educated people, as usual." The two had lunch at a cafeteria on First Avenue, and then Mary went back to the conference while Roland met Wheeler. He rejoined the Wigley sisters for another evening at the YWCA, spending three more hours getting acquainted. Mary must have left Birmingham the next morning, for Roland spent the day visiting friends in Homewood, a suburban community on the south side of Red Mountain. He left by bus for Cullman in midafternoon and wasted no time in getting to his old friend Brother Wolfgang to talk over his thoughts about Mary.

Roland wrote to Mary almost daily. She wrote almost as often, a fact that pleased him. Mary didn't let Roland think he was the only one with a romantic past, however; in one letter she enclosed part of a missive from another beau, who apparently had told Mary he was unable to have children. Roland was not impressed: "I am surprised that you should have gotten so friendly with a man with such selfish principles as the one part of whose letter you enclosed. (You don't look like such a flirt.)" This unnamed competitor smoked, and Roland speculated that he did so "to help him forget his disappointment when he found that he couldn't have children."[4]

They were getting to know each other. When she received some two-year-old clippings from Roland, Mary asked why. He wrote 838 words to explain, almost four full typed pages, defending his peculiar habit: "I have been cutting clippings since about 1901. At first of course they were relatively few, but as I grew older and my interests broadened I cut more and more. . . . I am now about fifteen months behind with current clippings, and thirteen years behind with papers to be clipped completely and thrown away." Mary was prepared to overlook this strange habit, and they planned another rendezvous, this time at the top of Sand Mountain. Harper suggested that he attend the family's church with the other Wigleys while Mary cooked Sunday dinner, but Mary rejected the idea. He yielded: "I wouldn't insist on going to church Sunday, and will do whatever you say." Before leaving Tuscaloosa, he sent a note to another lady friend in Guin, Alabama, telling her he would be traveling for a couple of weeks but didn't expect to make it to Guin, implying that it was because he had not heard from her lately.[5]

Roland got off the train somewhere in the rugged countryside on the eastern slope of Sand Mountain. Although he was carrying his camera and forty-five pounds of baggage, he dallied, searching a north-facing slope for trailing wakerobin, which he thought the Biltmore botanist Charles Lawrence Boynton had collected in the vicinity in 1906. After finding the wakerobin, which is now endangered, in bloom, as well as an *Erythronium* that he photographed, Roland caught a ride in a passerby's car for about a half-mile and then climbed a ridge, recording every turn in his field notebook.[6] He stopped for lunch before reaching the foot of Sand Mountain and then began the ascent, pausing to rest about every hundred yards. He reached Dawson (elevation: 1,160 feet) after another forty-five minutes and left most of his bags at a store that was also the local post office. Still carrying his briefcase and camera, he walked another mile to catch a school bus for a three-mile ride north. After the bus driver dropped him at the fork of a creek, Roland walked another three miles, passing the town of Liberty, before reaching the Wigley home at four o'clock. Mary's parents, two sisters, niece, and four nephews were waiting with her to meet him.

The following morning, Roland made a pasteboard model of Noah's ark for the children. He went hiking with two of the boys twice on the first day of his visit, with Mary accompanying them in the afternoon. On the second day, he "stayed in [the] house, amusing the children [and] talking with Mary," until after the midday meal. Sometime during this April visit, Roland proposed to Mary, and she accepted. Then Mary, her two sisters, and four of the children crowded into a family car with Roland to drive him back to Dawson, where he caught a bus for Fort Payne to visit his friend J. H. Lester and Lester's wife. The Lesters took Roland to DeSoto State Park on Lookout Mountain. He mailed a note to Mary from there: "I forgot to tell your parents that I thought I had won a wonderful prize when I got you; but you can now convey my sentiments to them. In the next few days and weeks I expect to tell a few intimate friends of my good fortune, but guess I won't divulge your name for the present (except to my mother), for that might possibly complicate some of your plans for the next few months. Affectionately yours, R." Unsure of the protocol for addressing a fiancée, he asked in a postscript, "Is that the proper way to sign myself now?"[7]

In Scottsboro the next day, he mailed a note to his landlords in Tuscaloosa, in whom he had apparently confided his plan to ask for Mary's hand. "I made a deal on Sand Mountain last week, so will have to detour around Guin [where the other lady friend lived] next week. Will tell you more about it when I get back. Nobody else in Tuscaloosa knows anything about it yet." He showed friends in Scottsboro photographs of Mary and the other current "girl friend" and then wrote exultantly to Bertha: "Dada! Here is some exciting news for you, and I hope it won't give you the 'heart-ilitis.' I visited the Sand Mountain girl at her home last week, and am now engaged to her. I will enclose a leaflet showing her picture, and telling everything about her work. She is forty-nine years old, and a willing worker, something like yourself. She has been a teacher and lecturer, but is good at house-work too. She has traveled as much as I have, having been in every state, she says." He closed as he often did in letters to his mother: "Don't worry."[8]

Perhaps to stave off doubts about his future performance as a husband, Roland hinted at his virility to Bertha and in letters to friends, too: "I guess it doesn't happen once in a million times that a man of my age (or any other age) walks eight and a half miles, carrying forty-five pounds of baggage most of the way, to see a girl. But I guess the results justified it." In another letter announcing his engagement, Roland boasted, "The lady lives about twelve miles from the nearest railroad station, and to get there I walked about two-thirds of the way, and carried forty-five pounds of baggage about half way; which I thought was doing pretty well for an old man. (I wonder if your husband could do that?) But the results justified my exertions. I stayed with her about two days, and—believe it or not—we are now engaged." He said much the same to Brother Wolfgang: "I guess not many men my age would want to carry so much baggage so far, and about 450 feet up the mountain in the last mile," noting, too, that Mary was "about fifteen years younger than [him]self."[9]

They planned their wedding at the Wigley home on Sand Mountain in June, and until then they resumed their correspondence, Roland sometimes sending art gum and other small gifts to the Wigley children. The day before his wedding, Roland posed on the steps of Smith Hall, in the same spot where he had posed for photographs in 1913 and 1928. He was a trim 136 pounds, ten pounds less than his bride. His hair was still full and dark, although there was gray in his moustache. He clenched his hands and squinted slightly into the sun as the photographer snapped a picture.[10] The next day, Roland got a marriage license in Fort Payne and rode up the mountain with the Lesters, arriving at about eleven in the morning. Mary was waiting with about eighteen members of her family and Roland's only other guests, Stewart J. Lloyd, a chemistry professor as well as acting director of the geological survey, and his wife. Mary wore a belted dress with a border at the hem, long white gloves, and a broad-brimmed straw hat. Her brother performed the marriage ceremony outdoors a few minutes later, with everyone standing beneath the trees in the front yard, the sun almost directly overhead. Afterward, the newly-weds posed for one photograph by themselves; someone, perhaps Lester or Lloyd, took another of the entire wedding party, before a lunch that included tomatoes and a watermelon Roland had bought in Fort Payne. He and Mary left with the Lesters before one o'clock for a honeymoon at DeSoto State Park.

They spent a week in cabin no. 10; Mary cooked their meals, and Roland took frequent short hikes in the surrounding woods. They picked blackberries and looked down on the west fork of the Little River from a bridge near the park, although they apparently didn't go to DeSoto Falls. They walked to a store to buy buttermilk and lettuce. Roland wrote to Brother Wolfgang and then to numerous Wigley relatives. By the third day of the honeymoon, apparently needing some time to himself, Roland took a three-mile walk without Mary and then clipped some newspaper articles. He observed the opening and closing of Brother Wolfgang's *Talinum*, Menge's fameflower, that was blooming near the cabin, watching small bees pollinating the flowers. After checking out of their cabin on June 30, they returned to the Wigley house, where Roland enjoyed surveying the garden, pasture, and woods. The next week was another new experience for Roland, with lazy days to pick blackberries and visit friends in nearby towns; a "family 'Fourth of July' picnic"; and house and garden chores to perform. He made a pasteboard church for the children and taught two of the boys, Don and Charles, to swim. He prepared an announcement of their marriage for the *Chattanooga Times* and wrote notes to the Findleys and the Gregorys, his current landlords, in Tuscaloosa. Brother Wolfgang had responded immediately to his letter from DeSoto State Park, and Roland wrote to him again.[11] Mary produced some Knoxville newspapers she had saved for him, and Roland promptly clipped some articles from them. He also began making another pasteboard house for the nephews and niece. He noted in his diary that on Sunday he and Mary "went to bed early."

The couple went to Birmingham on July 6 and to Tuscaloosa on July 7; there they walked from a bus stop near Druid City Hospital to the Gregory home, where the Gregorys served dinner to the newlyweds. Afterward, Roland slipped away to his office in Smith Hall to check his mail. Back at the house on Hackberry, he met Mary and took her strolling downtown. They met faculty friends for supper and then attended a lecture by Ernesto Montenegro. They returned to the Gregory house at nine and soon to bed—their first night together in Tuscaloosa. The following day they inspected a possible apartment and the day after that a house for rent in the neighborhood southeast of the campus. They moved in the fall into a small house at 309 Ninth Street in Tuscaloosa, where the university's shrine to the football coach Paul "Bear" Bryant now stands; Harper took two photographs of a stack of wedding gifts in the corner of their bedroom; in one of them two of his neckties can be seen, draped over the dresser mirror.[12]

As Roland and Mary settled into married life, she planted a large vegetable garden in the backyard. They visited often with Judge Herbert and Earline Findley, who lived a block away on University Avenue, and Mary particularly clung to Earline as a friend and confidant. Their families became acquainted; Francis's son Robin Harper visited Uncle Roland and Aunt Mary in Tuscaloosa around 1945 on his way to Deep Springs College in California. He found his uncle reserved but with "a twinkle in his eye [and] a very friendly face." Mary's relatives also visited them in Tuscaloosa.[13]

Roland deeply wanted Brother Wolfgang to meet Mary, telling his friend that he would bring her to St. Bernard and introduce them through Wolfgang's bedroom window.[14] But the couple had no car and little money for bus fare, and years went by without their making a trip to Cullman. Nonetheless, Roland continued to encourage Wolfgang's botanical work, telling him in September 1944, "I believe you still have one more *Talinum* paper to write, including my identification of Dr. Mohr's Bald Rock locality a few years ago. Why not write it up now, and call attention to this locality on limestone, which may be the only one on record?" Roland had another bout with pneumonia in late 1948 or early 1949 and spent nine days in the Tuscaloosa hospital. He wrote to Brother Wolfgang after he had regained his strength. He missed his old friend, telling him, "Take care of yourself, and perhaps I will see you some time this year." He completed another article about *Erythronium* that year, describing five species in Alabama.[15]

Harper's 1943 monograph on Alabama trees was his last major scientific publication, but he continued to work, drafting four articles that year about prairies, three focused on Alabama and the fourth comparing "the

prairies of the Middle West and the pine woods of the Southeast, which
have several species in common, in spite of great differences in soil and climate."[16] In 1945 and 1947, he wrote brief memoirs about his experiences
botanizing in the late nineteenth century for *Torreya* and *Nature Outlook.*
His career was coming to a close, and many of his future trips would be
return visits, with friends and admirers, to sites of his earlier discoveries.

In the meanwhile, the University of Alabama was sharing the scientific
excitement of the postwar years, in part because of the arrival in 1947 of
Ralph Chermock, an entomologist and taxonomist with a doctoral degree
from Cornell who brought the modern synthesis in biology to the university's biology department. Harper probably was interested in Chermock
because the younger man was a relative of the third co-rediscoverer of
Mendelian genetics, Erich von Tschermak. For his part, Chermock could
have heard of Harper while he was still at Cornell, from another gradate
student, Robert Thorne, who had visited Tuscaloosa several times and
found Harper a good field botanist and an interesting character. Young
Edward O. Wilson was an undergraduate who was strongly impressed by
Chermock. "At thirty, Chermock was physically impressive, an amateur
boxer with a compact gymnast's body and thick arms, who occasionally
performed one-arm pushups on his office floor to intimidate his followers." Wilson saw Chermock as helping spread the revolution in systematics
and biogeography that Ernst Mayr promulgated in his groundbreaking
1942 book, *Systematics and the Origin of Species.* Chermock inspired un-
dergraduates to collect specimens in the field. "On weekends and holidays
we struck out across the state, to the farthest corners and back and forth,"
Wilson recalled in his memoir. "We pulled the car over to roadsides and
clambered down into bay-gum swamps, hiked along muddy stream banks,
and worked in and out of remote hillside forests." By promoting botanical collecting, Chermock helped expand the Mohr Herbarium, to which
Harper had contributed several thousand specimens, by thousands more.[17]
It was a busy, hectic time in the biological sciences and on the University
of Alabama campus, where the GI Bill enabled so many veterans to enroll
that the campus was teeming with people and cars. The modern synthesis
restored field biology to respectability and gave it a legitimate connection
to genetics, but the integration of these disciplines occurred too late for
Harper to fully enjoy.

Several persons important to Roland died in the 1940s and 1950s.
Hermina died in October 1945, and Bertha followed in December. Roland wrote fewer letters to Brother Wolfgang in the latter 1940s, but when

he heard in July 1948 that his old friend was ill, Harper contacted one of the priests at St. Bernard to ask if the monk could receive visitors. The last letter from Roland that survived among Brother Wolfgang's papers was dated July 23, 1949. In it, Roland described happy times and a visit by two of Mary's nieces. Brother Wolfgang died September 22, 1950, and Roland wrote an obituary for *Castanea*, paying homage to his friend for his persistent study of the genera *Talinum* and *Erythronium*. In a strange coincidence, Harper's sometime foe at Harvard, Merritt Fernald, died on the same day as Brother Wolfgang. Forrest Shreve, the longtime friend and phytogeographer who focused for most of his career on desert ecology, also died that year.[18]

Still on the payroll of the Alabama geological survey, although he only accepted a very modest salary, Harper continued to keep office hours. He carried on correspondence with interesting scientists and educators around the country, such as H. H. Chase, an elderly authority on diatoms, a type of minute algae. George S. Counts, a prominent, progressive professor of education at Columbia University, sent regards to both of the Harpers in January 1951, assuring Roland that he remembered Mrs. Harper from the time when she was at Columbia. He botanized when he had the opportunity. Thorne, the Cornell graduate student, took Harper into the field at least once, and Harper's car-window technique impressed Thorne, who said almost sixty years later, "He had a habit as we traveled, going fifty miles per hour in the jeep, he was listing all the plants as we went by. On the way back I stopped at some of these spots and sure enough he was correct. He knew what he was saying."[19]

Roland and Mary traveled together as often as they could, spending time at the Wigley home on Sand Mountain and making trips out of state. They may have visited the Chicago Natural History Museum in 1948. A museum employee wrote to Roland in September, "I remember very well your visit of some years ago. I had then never seen you, though you had long been one of my principal sources of information about the state of Florida, and I very much enjoyed the few moments you spent with me. . . . Dr. Julian Steyermark will be in the herbarium, and, I am sure will be glad to see you and to be of all service he can to you. . . . Looking forward to seeing you." The couple enjoyed southern Alabama and went to Gulf Shores, in September 1949 and again in October 1952, probably stopping at Semmes to visit Tom Dodd Jr., a nurseryman who had been a friend of Roland for years. They went to California in 1950, perhaps to visit Wilhelmina in Palo Alto.[20]

In the summer of 1953, Wilbur H. Duncan, a botanist at the University of Georgia, invited Harper to accompany him on a week-long botanizing ramble to some of Harper's early twentieth-century Georgia localities.[21] Harper agreed, probably gathering the relevant journals and field notebooks and some of his early Georgia photographs for reference, and traveled by bus to Columbus on July 29. He waited at the Waverly Hotel for the botanists Duncan and Haskell Venard and a student, Bill Humphreys, who arrived after nine in the evening.[22]

The next morning the group headed northeast on State Highway 85; they passed through Warm Springs, where Harper had called on Franklin Delano Roosevelt in 1929, to reach the 1901 type locality for Harper's yellow-eyed grass at Woodbury in Meriwether County, Georgia. They were disappointed to find the former bog had become "pastured and weedy." (Considered "unquestionably the rarest entity of *Xyris* in the southeastern United States," this plant has never been found again at Harper's type locality and is known only at a very few locations in northwest Florida.)[23] From there, Roland recorded in his diary the group went west "to look for Cedar Rock, described by [the geologist T. L.] Watson in 1902." He noted, "Found what may be it, though there is very little cedar there. It is a big granite outcrop, with some interesting plants." They crossed the Flint River and turned to the southeast, going through Thomaston and Roberta, with Harper making field notes. He wrote in his diary, "[B]efore getting out of Crawford County, [we] stopped to make some notes on sand-hill vegetation." They spent the night in Perry, in Houston County, at a "nice tourist court near [the] middle of town." After supper, Harper paid a call on someone, probably one of his classmates at the University of Georgia, whom he had last seen in 1897.

It was a short trip south into Dooly County the next morning to find the location between Pinehurst and Unadilla where Harper had found *Harperella* growing in May 1904. The "grassy cypress pond" had been partially drained during construction of a railroad, but *Harperella*, or something very similar, still grew there. Harper referred twice in his journal entry to "the supposed *Harperella*," unwilling, apparently, to abandon the genus name given it by Joseph Rose in 1906 despite its downgrading by Mildred Mathias in 1936. He was not sure that the specimens they collected and photographed actually were the same species he had originally found in 1902. Nor was Duncan, who listed "*Harperella*" with a question mark in his field collection book.[24] They also searched briefly for twigrush (*Cladium mariscoides*), another species he had noted in his journal of

1904. Duncan dropped Venard at a bus station so that he could leave for Atlanta that afternoon. After an early supper, the rest of the group went out again in the slightly cooler evening to investigate another cypress pond.

The rare and beautiful Georgia plume was the object of the next day's quest. The botanists drove southwest a few miles from McRae in Telfair County, across Sugar Creek, to Turnpike Creek, to look for a spot where Harper had seen *Elliottia* in July 1903, but without luck. They backtracked to McRae, then turned southeast, passed through Lumber City, and crossed the Little Ocmulgee River to revisit a site where in 1903 Harper had rediscovered pond spicebush (*Lindera melissifolia*, known in 1953 as *Benzoin melissafolium*), a rare species that had not been seen since the mid-1800s. He could not locate the pond where he had found the plant, but they did find "several depressions . . . surrounded by dense bay vegetation, *Nyssa Ogeche* [Ogeechee lime] in river swamp, etc." Reversing course, they drove back through Lumber City and ate a picnic lunch on the side of a road before reaching a railroad cut in the Altamaha Grit formation that Harper had observed from a moving train in 1903. The ponds, the Little Ocmulgee River, and sand hills in the vicinity of Lumber City were rich territory for Duncan, who collected thirty-six specimens there.

Their next stop was Baxley and the home of an acquaintance, George D. Lowe, who went with them "out Nail's Ferry Road . . . to show [them] sand-hills on [the] northeast side of Sellers Big Pond." Returning to town, they turned north and Lowe navigated about ten miles of dirt and paved roads, taking them to a "farm yard" were there was a "peculiar *Gordonia*," or loblolly-bay. When they returned to Lowe's house, Lowe presented a gift to Harper: his personal copy of the 1876 edition of James's *Handbook of Georgia*. Then the band of botanists drove on to Jesup, where they spent the night at a tourist camp.

Harper was a little weary and spent the next morning reading at camp. After lunch in a restaurant, they set out again to explore the sand hills in Long County. Near the tiny community of Ludowici, they "found what seem[ed] to be a *Vernonia recurva*," or tall ironweed, a species Harper had discovered in 1903 in the next county to the south. In the hottest part of the afternoon, they paused to visit the parents of Duncan's wife, the botanist Marion B. Duncan, who lived in the vicinity, and then started the drive back to Jesup. They "went down [a] highway toward Brunswick, a railroad and shipping town on the coast, nearly to Pendavis [and] then turned right and went many miles on smooth dirt roads through unin-habited flatwoods." The woods were second-growth slash pine that had been turpentined. They spent a second night in Jesup.

The group crossed Bartram's trail near Everett in Wayne County the next morning, on a low north-south sand ridge that was an early road. Harper soon noted the dense understory of saw palmetto, gallberry, and wax myrtle that he would later describe to Herbert Stoddard in a let-ter about fire in longleaf. He wrote in his diary that they "crossed the ridge or terrace parallel to [the] coast near [the] line between Glynne and Brantley Counties, but it [was] not conspicuous." They had another early supper, perhaps as an escape from the heat, at a hotel in Nahunta; Harper found it "pretty good" and a bargain at eighty cents plus tax. After eating they continued west, crossing Trail Ridge at a point where Harper found the westward descent "hardly noticeable." Disappointingly, the under-story hid or had supplanted the native flora that Harper had documented during his graduate-school years; Duncan collected only three specimens. As Harper wrote to Stoddard later and probably mentioned to Duncan and Humphreys at the time, "fire propaganda" was probably to blame for the ecological changes. In a roadside ditch beside a swamp southeast of Waycross, Duncan collected a primrose-willow, a species in the *Ludwigia* genus. He was not sure if it was seaside primrose-willow (*L. maritima*), which Harper first collected in a meadow beside sand dunes in Camden County, Georgia, in 1902 and described in *Torreya* in 1904, or shrubby primrose-willow (*L. suffruticosa*), which the planter-naturalist Louis LeConte collected somewhere in Georgia during the first third of the nineteenth century.

They stopped for the night at a tourist camp in Tifton, where Harper strolled about, noting the old post office and the newspaper office. He mailed a card to Mary and dropped off some pamphlets for the local newspaper editor the next morning, and then Duncan accompanied him to the field near the railroad station where Harper had discovered purple-disk honeycombhead and onespike beaksedge on a single day in 1900, only to find the spot covered with kudzu. They found some native spe-cies in a slash pine stand nearby, but they were "mixed with weeds." The locality where Harper had collected a species of *Diodia* that Small de-scribed as a new species, naming it *D. harperi*, or Harper's buttonweed, was "completely destroyed," although Duncan collected one specimen of buttonweed, listing it as *D. virginiana* in his collection book. When Humphreys rejoined Duncan and Harper, the three men drove west out of Tifton. They stopped at a moist pine barren, where Harper showed the others some onespike beaksedge. They stopped again at TyTy Creek, but the creek was stagnant and they found no black titi. Driving on to the southwest, they passed corn, cotton, and tobacco and the town of Norman Park. They spent an hour in Moultrie for lunch around two o'clock. The next stops for the botanists were Ochlocknee Creek, where they hunted unsuccessfully for meadow alexanders (*Zizia arenicola*), a Harper discovery that Fernald had declared was *Z. trifoliata* in 1940, and Camilla, where they wanted to examine a slough. Then they headed north to spend the night in Albany.

Harper called on the local newspaper editor, J. H. Gray, the next morning and gave him a few pamphlets. He left Albany with Duncan and Humphreys before nine o'clock; they drove northeast through pecan country toward Leslie, the town near Americus where the Harper family had good friends in the late nineteenth century and where Harper sometimes stayed during his Georgia botanizing summers. Along the way they stopped for Duncan to collect specimens on Muckalee Creek and in "a small remnant of longleaf pine woods" south of Leslie.[25] Harper guided Duncan and Humphreys east of town to the spring where he had collected the bulrush he described as *Scirpus fontinalis* in 1901. "It is much more shaded now, strange to say, and bordered by pretty thick tangles of Smilax. . . . No sign of the *Scirpus*." Duncan collected a beaksedge there but did not note in his collection book whether it was Harper's onespike beaksedge.[26] They hurried on to Americus, noticing two more remnants of longleaf forest but not stopping to explore them. When they reached the town where the Harper family had spent the years 1892–97, Harper led them to a spot he called Barlow's Mill, where the mill was gone but a pond remained. The pitcher-plant bog he recalled being on the side of the road also was gone, and Harper was at a loss to explain the disappearance. After lunch Duncan and Humphreys waited while Harper made another newspaper stop, leaving more pamphlets with a young assistant editor. They drove on through the afternoon, through Smithville, Cuthbert, Georgetown, and Eufalia, where they took a break to have some ice cream. Afterward, they returned to Georgetown to explore a "deep shaded ravine." Harper did not record whether he had visited the spot before, but he was impressed by its flora: "Found no Croomia there, but some other interesting things, such as *Azalea prunifolia* [plumleaf azalea], *Cornus alterfolia* [dogwood], *Magnolia pyramidata* [pyramid magnolia], and a *Eupatorium* [thoroughwort] with large heads"—the last, he acknowledged in his diary, a species that Duncan recognized first. Then on to Lumpkin, northeast of Georgetown, and through Lonvale, which Harper found "a home-like little place never seen before, though it [was] not far from [Savannah, Americus, and Montgomery] Railroad, and used to have a spur track from Lonvale Junction." Duncan brought them back to Columbus, where he saw Harper checked into the Waverly Hotel again, took him to dinner, and then departed with Humphreys. After picking up two letters from Mary at the local post office and visiting a local bookstore owner, the Reverend Claude Saunders, the next morning Harper took a bus for Birmingham and a second for Tuscaloosa. He arrived there at 5:40 and walked from the stop to their house.[27]

Duncan collected 422 specimens for the University of Georgia herbarium on this botanizing trip. Describing their expedition to Herbert Stoddard, Harper said, "[Duncan] traveled in a station wagon, and brought with him one of his students, and an amateur botanist friend from Atlanta, whom I also knew. . . . We of course did not confine our search to the plants I had discovered, but were on the lookout for other rarities, of which we found several. And Dr. Duncan picked up what may be two new species. . . . The search for my discoveries was rather disappointing, but we did find a few of them. Many of the localities had been destroyed by cultivation or otherwise."[28]

Yale University Press published Francis's annotation of Bartram's *Travels* in 1958 as *Francis Harper's Naturalist Edition*. After the 1939 trip with Roland, Francis had spent almost two decades preparing the book, beginning with a brief article that year about his entire expedition along the Bartram trail for the bulletin of the Garden Club of America. (In 1940, a New York publisher had reissued Van Doren's edition of Bartram's *Travels*, with a new introduction by John Livingston Lowes of Harvard University, the literary scholar who earlier had analyzed Bartram's influence on the poets Samuel Taylor Coleridge and William and Dorothy Wadsworth.) Over the next fourteen years, Francis wrote at least six more articles about Bartram's nomenclature for scientific journals. In 1943, the American Philosophical Society published his annotation of Bartram's report to John Fothergill. Francis noted in it, "Dr. Roland M. Harper, of the Geological Survey of Alabama, has placed at my disposal his extensive knowledge of the vegetation, geography, and geology of the Southeastern States; he has read the comments and annotations in the present publication, making many useful criticisms and suggestions."[29]

The Yale edition included Francis's commentary, an annotated index, a general index, and even an index of Bartram's errors of spelling, punctuation, and grammar. Francis acknowledged Roland numerous times in the book, both for his company and expertise on their June 1939 trip and for his advice on the overall project. "From Montgomery, Alabama, to Tallahassee, Florida, I was accompanied by Dr. Roland M. Harper of the Alabama Geological Survey, whose special knowledge of the vegetation, soils, geography, and geology of that region contributed very materially toward realizing the objectives of the present investigation." Roland, he wrote, "offered many useful suggestions on botanical and geographical matters relating to Bartram's travels in general." He alluded to Roland's own role as a pioneer, pointing out that Bartram missed the Altamaha Grit region that Roland explored in the early twentieth century: "Bartram recognizes and describes some of the major subdivisions of the Coastal Plain of Georgia. . . . It may be of interest to compare his classification with that of R. M. Harper. . . . Bartram's first division . . . apparently comprises both the Coast Strip and the Flat Pine Lands of the modern classification. He omits the Altamaha Grit Region (or Rolling Wire-Grass Country), having barely skirted its northeastern border."[30] Francis dedicated the book to the memory of Arthur Leeds, "a rare and noble spirit who helped to pave the way for a wider and better appreciation of these Quaker naturalists and their works."[31] Concluding his commentary on Bartram's travel narrative, Francis speculated that, by exploring the Deep South, William won his father's approval. One wonders if Francis empathized with the son:

> Those who have taken [William] Bartram's dates literally have believed that he returned to his father's house only to find it bereft of its owner. However, since he returned in *January* (perhaps about the 2d) *1777*, there remained eight full months in which these two rare spirits were able to confer on William's wonderful new experiences and discoveries in the Southland. It is pleasant to believe that the elder Bartram's earlier doubts as to William's worth and ability were at last happily dissolved. For surely, in listening to the tales of persevering endeavor and high adventure among primitive scenes and peoples, and in scanning the field journals brought back, he must have realized that his truly talented son had now attained full stature. His cup would no doubt have been filled to the brim if he had lived to see the publication of the *Travels.*[32]

Perhaps Francis was thinking of his old friend and mentor Arthur Leeds when he wrote these words, or perhaps he was thinking of his own par-

ents, wishing that they had known of his success in annotating Bartram's
Travels.

Roland and Mary visited Francis and Jean in Chapel Hill, North Carolina, when they could; they made a trip in November 1960, probably for
Thanksgiving.[33] He and Francis met once or twice in Savannah, Georgia,
in 1961, where they visited a friend of Francis, Ivan Tomkins. They apparently went to Tybee Island in April, and Tomkins had some sense of the
meaning of the reunion for the brothers, photographing them standing
about five feet apart, facing each other, Francis's binoculars around his
neck, Roland's plant bag over his shoulder. They also went to Savannah
in September, when a local landscape architect, Clermont Lee, and some
other naturalists took them to the site near Bloys where Roland and Walter
Hendricks had rediscovered the lost Georgia plume in 1901. Miss Lee had
been corresponding with Roland since 1958, when the widow of Charles
Cotton Harrold, the Harpers' childhood and college friend, suggested
that Roland write to her. The Harrolds owned land that included a stand
of Georgia plume. "Mr. Roland Harper of the University of Alabama has
recently written me about the *Elliottia*," Harrold's widow wrote. "He is
one of my husband's many queer friends and a lifelong one. He crops up
occasionally and sends me reprints of his writings. In the past he has visited the *Elliottia* . . . and today I get this letter saying that he is going on
a botanizing trip and might go by to see the *Elliottia*."[34]

Inspired to visit Bloys with the rediscoverer of Georgia plume, Lee
and other Savannah plume buffs organized an expedition for the Harper
brothers to *Elliottia* sites on September 2, 1960. The group rode in two
cars, stopping at a bog near the Ogeechee River before reaching the
site at Bloys, with Roland providing directions. Lee remembered that
their reunion was "the first in several years [and] of great importance to
them. . . . Ivan Tomkins teased the Harpers, saying their father must have
been a carpetbagger, coming from New England to Georgia just after the
Civil War. This was too serious an insult for the Harpers to joke about."
She added in 2004, "I mentioned to Dr. R. Harper I had never found
Bartonia virginica [yellow screwstem] or *Burmannia biflora* [bluethread]
in our area. Without moving one step he pointed to both tiny natives. His
knowledge and eyesight amazed me."[35]

In 1963, Alfred E. Schuyler, a young botanist at the Philadelphia Academy
of Natural Sciences, was interested in the relationships among southeast-

ern species of *Scirpus*, including Georgia bulrush and another Harper
species, *S. fontinalis*, which Harper discovered at Leslie, Georgia, during
his graduate school botanizing in 1901. Schuyler wrote to Harper to ask
how to find his type locality for *S. fontinalis*. Harper replied immediately,
telling Schuyler the type locality was at "a large spring on the north side
of the railroad, a quarter of a mile or so east of the station at Leslie." He
told Schuyler that he had revisited the site in August 1953 with Wilbur
Duncan but did not find the plant and suggested Schuyler examine specimens of the plant that he had collected and given to herbaria in New York
and Washington. Harper also referred to specimens of *Scirpus* that Fernald had collected in Virginia, observing snidely that Fernald, "like most
botanists these days, . . . probably did not get very far from a paved highway." He criticized Fernald for describing *S. divaricatus* as having distichous leaves, "oblivious of the fact that a sedge with three-angled stem
could not have distichous leaves." Schuyler followed Harper's directions
to the Leslie type locality of *S. fontinalis* and reported to Harper that he
had found "two small colonies of the plant. They were in about the same
stage of maturity as [Harper's] No. 1012." He asked Harper where he had
deposited the type specimen for *S. fontinalis*. Schuyler also told Roland
that Francis Harper had visited the Philadelphia Academy herbarium "at
least twice since [he had] started working [there] about a year and a half
ago." He remarked, "I was pleased to have the opportunity of meeting
him. I hope that you may stop by for a visit someday." The elderly botanist again replied quickly: "[T]he one at the New York Botanical Garden
might well be considered the type, for I must have had it before me when
I was writing the description." He took another swipe at Fernald, adding, "I never noticed until a few days ago that Fernald, in his last Manual,
1950, extended the range of *Scirpus fontinalis* to Florida, Louisiana, and
Oklahoma. I am entirely uninformed as to whether somebody found it
in those outlying states after the publication of Small's *Manual*, 1933, or
specimens collected earlier turned up in herbaria." Schuyler had an article
about *Scirpus* published in *Bartonia* and sent a copy to Harper, who acknowledged the article and again asked Schuyler about the extension of
Scirpus fontinalis to Florida, Louisiana, and Oklahoma. He commented,
"There should be no danger of confusing *S. fontinalis* with *S. lineatus*
(which I had never seen at the time I described *S. fontinalis*). . . . You
ought to read my original description of *S. fontinalis* again." Once again,
Harper jabbed at Fernald, saying he "blundered badly in his last *Manual*
in describing its leaves as 'distichous,' (which would be impossible with a

three-angled stem)." Harper was interested in Schuyler's analysis of chromosome numbers in *Scirpus*. "I do not remember seeing any chromosome studies of sedges (or grasses) before. I sketched chromosomes in the laboratory at Columbia University in 1899–1900, before anybody knew what their significance was, but I never took much interest in them. And I guess Mr. Fernald never paid any attention to them. But there are over one hundred species of *Scirpus*, and there would not be enough chromosome numbers to go around. So there must be cases of two or more species having the same chromosome number. What would that mean?"[36]

The cold war between Fernald and Harper had continued since the 1939 confrontation in Virginia. In his 1950 edition of Asa Gray's *Manual of Botany*, Fernald ignored Harper's heartleaf. Even though the early nineteenth-century naturalist Constantine Samuel Rafinesque distinguished the genus *Hexastylis* from wild ginger (*Asarum*) in 1825, and John Kunkel Small adhered to Rafinesque's distinction in his *Flora of the Southeastern United States* in 1903, Fernald lumped the heart-leaves with the gingers. In reviewing the entire literature on *Hexastylis* in 1957, however, H. L. Blomquist called Harper's discovery in Alabama "remarkable."[37]

Roland weighed only 124 pounds in November 1964, and he no longer could walk to campus, but he continued to go to his office in Smith Hall every weekday.[38] Sometimes he and Mary called a taxi to take him the few blocks. On other days, one of the Harpers' friends, often Septima Smith, a biology professor at the university, picked him up at their house on Ninth Street in the morning and brought him home in the afternoon. Newspaper clipping was his main activity, and he continued to keep a diary, although the entries became very brief. On November 7, for example, he wrote in faint pencil, "Weather about same. Didn't do much but cut a few clippings, [from the years] 1939 and 1964. Rested much of day."

His memory was a marvel to his friends and admirers. On November 10, a friend dropped by Smith Hall to ask Harper something about trees, and Harper presented him with a 1929 clipping about his marriage, which he had kept nearby for months since finding it in an old newspaper. His discoveries across the coastal plain had become legend, and some scholars sought to get as many details as possible from Harper while there was still time. Joseph Ewan, a botanist and historian of botany at Tulane University, with whom Roland had corresponded since 1950, wrote to ask Harper for a memoir or some information, and Harper sporadically worked at a response in November.

Francis visited Roland and Mary for Thanksgiving. The brothers probably realized they would not see each other again and enjoyed spending time together. Booie arrived by bus on November 24, and he and Roland spent the rest of the day talking in Roland's office and at his house. The next morning he and Francis called a cab to go back to Smith Hall, where they spent the entire day talking while Roland worked a bit, typing some labels for plant specimens he had collected in Florida between 1950 and 1954. A student dropped by to ask for information about salamanders; Roland noted in his diary that Francis gave him more information than Roland could. They also examined Roland's diary record of a one-day trip he had made to Okefenokee Swamp in 1919 to attend a meeting of the Okefinokee Society.[39] Presumably, Mary prepared a special Thanksgiving dinner the next day, but Roland did not mention it in his diary, noting only that he stayed in the house all day, "talking with Booie." The brothers spent full days at Smith Hall on Friday and Saturday, Roland typing some Georgia plant labels and Francis reading more of Roland's Okefenokee diary entries. They stayed at home with Mary on Sunday, again probably having a special dinner, and Booie pitched in on the plant-label project. On Monday, Booie went alone to visit Herbert T. Boschung, an associate professor of zoology. While he was gone, Harper "dug out several old keepsakes to show Booie." They had one more day together, Tuesday, December 1. The brothers went to Smith Hall together by taxi, and after lunch Booie walked to Nott Hall to give a guest lecture. Eugene Smith's son, Merrill P. Smith, picked them up in the late afternoon and after stopping at Roland's house for Francis's luggage, took them to the Trailways station, where Francis departed for Chapel Hill.

By mid-December, Roland was tiring more easily than ever, unable to stay up as late as 7:00 p.m., even to see an eclipse of the moon. On December 20, he "got up late and rested a good deal. Packed up some partly clipped papers. Read and marked some recent papers," but the next day he rallied enough to take a taxi to the office, where he read some magazines and a letter from President Frank Rose of the university. Mary's sisters Annie and Naomi came for a Christmas visit on December 23, and Roland showed them a few of his "boyhood relics" but also "rested a good deal." They spent Christmas Eve and Christmas Day together at home; a friend brought them some grapefruit. Over the next few days, Roland concentrated on clipping "important" articles from some October issues of the *New York Times*, which Septima Smith had brought to him. He restacked September and October newspapers for clipping later.

On December 30, Mary accompanied him to Smith Hall around noon, where he spent a few hours reading magazines. Merrill Smith drove them home at about four in the afternoon.

On December 31, 1964, Harper wrote, "Weather about same, or a little milder. [Took a] taxi [to the office] both ways, with Mary. Got three pamphlets ordered recently from Patrick Henry Group, and spent considerable time reading them. E. Wilson called at office p.m., with his wife and her sister. Renewed subscription to *Milbank Quarterly*, and notified American Eugenics Society of dropping membership, enclosing pamphlets 561 and 566. Read and marked two more November *New York Times*." This is the last diary entry in the Roland McMillan Harper collection in the W. S. Hoole Special Collections Library at the University of Alabama.

Harper died in May 1966 after a continual, slow deterioration of his health; he had been frustrated at his inability to continue working, although what project he yearned to complete is unclear.[40] He was buried in Tuscaloosa. His pallbearers included Judge Herbert L. Findley, Mary's nephews Perry and Charles Wigley, Merrill Smith, Walter Jones, Ralph Chermock, and the entire staff of the Alabama Geological Survey. Joseph Ewan, the historian of botany, praised Harper in an obituary in the *Bulletin of the Torrey Botanical Club*:

> What position will Roland Harper hold in the history of American botany? Certainly his *Altamaha Grit Region*, an ecological classic, will survive the eroding stream of time. His hundreds of plant records, range extensions and new facts about old species—he was fortunate, for example, in finding a new station for the relict *Elliottia*, and photographed it in its vanishing habitat—have provided the new materials for fundamental works like Small's *Manual* and Fernald's *Manual*, local and state floras, and scores of generic revisions.

In a separate tribute to Harper in the journal *Torreya*, the botanist J. T. Baldwin recalled the dramatic occasion when Merritt Fernald challenged Harper in Richmond, Virginia, over the presence of longleaf pine in Virginia, concluding that regarding the matter in dispute, "Harper was correct."[41]

Harper bequeathed all his belongings to Mary, whom he called "my beloved (first and only) wife."[42] Mary may have prepared herself emotionally for his death during his long decline, for she quickly had his enormous collection of newspapers, letters, and other papers moved from their house to the Amelia Gayle Gorgas Library on the University of Alabama campus.[43] The *Tuscaloosa News* reported that summer that she had hired "two helpers" to assist her in sorting and boxing the materials. The newspaper's feature article undoubtedly influenced the local memories of Harper that crystallized in the years to come, images of an eccentric packrat, a curmudgeon on the topics of bobbed hair, cigarette smoking, and race relations. Concerning his papers, the reporter wrote:

> At one time he had filled the barn loft in the back of the Harper home, then filled part of the first floor, filled the chicken house, doubled its size and doubled it again before the overflow expanded to the house. Over the years the materials have gathered dust and become jumbled with transfer from one building to another. Gathered again into separate collections, Mrs. Harper believes they will be valuable to libraries, researchers, historians and rare book collectors. . . . Other boxes full of railroad timetables date back to his early teens.[44]

The very next month, Alfred Schuyler determined that the Georgia bulrush Harper had spotted while rambling outside Athens, Georgia, with his college friend Alfred Akerman in 1897, *Scirpus georgianus*, indeed was "a distinct species from *S. atrovirens*"—despite Fernald's reclassification of the plant as a variety of *S. atrovirens*. By noting on Harper's specimen sheet in the New York Botanical Garden that *S. georgianus* was a distinct species, Schuyler corrected Fernald and vindicated the first species that Harper described.[45]

Schuyler had examined many herbarium specimens at the New York Botanical Garden and elsewhere in the 1960s and found that Fernald had "annotated many herbarium specimens of *S. hattorianus* and *S. georgianus* as *S. atrovirens* var. *georgianus*." Writing in 1967 in the journal *Notulae Naturae*, Schuyler observed that Harper's Georgia bulrush could be "readily distinguished . . . because it either lacks bristles or has 1, 2, or rarely 3 short ones in contrast to *S. hattorianus* which has 5 or 6 bristles." In turn, *S. hattorianus* could be distinguished from *S. atrovirens* because the bristles of the former were usually shorter than those of the latter. He reiterated this in another article the same year: "*Scirpus georgianus* is readily distinguishable from other species which it resembles because it lacks bristles or has up to three short ones." Recalling the restoration of *S. georgianus*, which still stood thirty-eight years later, Schuyler commented in 2004, "It is too bad that [Harper] did not live to see my 1967 paper that discussed its relationships. I think he would have been pleased." Today Harper's Georgia bulrush is listed as endangered in Georgia.[46]

CHAPTER FOURTEEN

Harper's Beauty

One year before Harper died, and three years after the first fire ecology conference at Tall Timbers Research Station, a young botanist spotted something new as he walked slowly along Highway 65 in Franklin County, Florida, scanning the variety of plants growing on the slopes of the ditch on the western side of the road. Sidney McDaniel had presented himself to Robert K. Godfrey at Florida State University some time in the 1960s, declaring that he was there to enter Godfrey's doctoral program in botany. Godfrey, a successor to Herman Kurz at Florida State and also an authority on the plants of northern Florida, replied that there were no openings in the program, but McDaniel insisted that Godfrey allow him to enroll. McDaniel was intensely interested in the botany of the southern coastal plain and possessed a personal library of botany volumes that rivaled the collection of the university's Department of Biology. Impressed, Godfrey eventually admitted him to the program, where McDaniel focused on pitcher plants.[1] In his dissertation on the carnivorous plants, he acknowledged Harper's early work on the beautiful plant predators of the bogs, noting that Harper had reported most of the *Sarracenia* hybrids in nature and that Harper "discussed the historical development of interest in the genus" in 1918. McDaniel also referred to Harper's work on the relationship of fire to *Sarracenia*, observing that "the genus *Sarracenia* is well adapted to moderate fires, at least in the South."[2]

Because they tend to be damp or wet even in dry weather, and because highway mowers often don't penetrate their lowest reaches, roadside ditches can be excellent havens for interesting plants. On May 4, 1965, McDaniel was exploring the side of Highway 65, near Sumatra in Franklin County—a spot about ten miles from the eastern bank of the Apalachicola River that Harper passed on the steamboat *J. W. Callahan, Jr.* in 1909. The highway crossed land that had been heavily timbered and turpentined before its establishment as the Apalachicola National Forest. Looking closely at the tangle of grasses and forbs, McDaniel noticed a delicate, grasslike plant with vivid, almost iridescent yellow flowers at the top of stalks that grew well above the leaves.[3] Although small, the flowers were stunning. Not recognizing the plant, he collected samples and probably first shared them with Bob Godfrey.

McDaniel and Godfrey concluded that the plant was new to science, the first member of a "remarkable" new genus in the lily family. They consulted a Harvard botanist, Carroll E. Wood Jr., who confirmed their suspicion. McDaniel returned to the area near Sumatra on May 11 and collected more blooming specimens in an open bog surrounded by titi and pond pine; he returned again on July 21, when he collected specimens with mature seed capsules. He prepared and sent specimens of the plant, with notations about when and where he had collected them, to the United States National Herbarium in Washington, and to herbaria at Duke University, the University of Georgia, the Missouri Botanical Garden, and other institutions.

McDaniel reported his discovery in an article that he submitted to the journal of the Arnold Arboretum, the late Charles Sargent's preserve at Harvard University. He specifically noted that the plant grew on the edges or slopes of pitcher-plant bogs that were surrounded "by sandy, occasionally burned longleaf pine woods." McDaniel named his discovery *Harperocallis flava*, or Harper's beauty. "It is appropriate to associate with this genus of the Lower South the name of Roland MacMillan [*sic*] Harper (1878–1966) who greatly contributed to an understanding of the vegetation of this area," he wrote. In the brief article, McDaniel speculated that although he had found Harper's beauty nowhere else, it might ultimately prove to have a scattered distribution in the Apalachicola River basin.[4] The article did not appear until 1968, two years after Harper's death.

The bogs and longleaf-wiregrass areas of the Apalachicola National Forest are one of the South's richest areas of biodiversity, possibly because frequent forest fires encouraged the evolution of specialized taxa such as *Harperocallis flava*. In a region with the nation's greatest number of endangered ecosystems, the Apalachicola River basin is the rarest of the rare—and Harper's beauty is its only known endemic genus, that is, a genus that exists nowhere else. The United States Fish and Wildlife Service, the agency that began its existence as the United States Biological Survey and employed Francis Harper for a time, added Harper's beauty to the official federal list of endangered species in 1979. Sites with Harper's beauty became prized finds for naturalists searching Franklin and Liberty Counties. Steven Leonard, a well-known coastal plain field botanist trained in North Carolina, and Wilson Baker, a widely admired self-trained botanist from Tallahassee who worked for many years for Tall Timbers Research Station, spent about three months in 1982 conducting a biological survey of the Apalachicola bluffs and ravines between Bristol and Chattahoochee, Florida, concentrating on selected plants designated as threatened or endangered; they found about three thousand specimens of Harper's beauty. They visited the type locality for Harper's beauty in May of that year, and after seeing a few plants, they decided to "road-cruise," using Harper's car-window technique, in search of more specimens. To their surprise, they spotted approximately six thousand specimens of *Harperocallis* along Route 65 from a point north of Sumatra to just south of Wilma.[5]

Extending the range of different species that Harper described or discovered is a specialized pastime of some coastal plain botanists. McDaniel went to DeKalb County, Alabama, in 1979 to look for Harper's love-vine on rock outcrops. He hunted for Harper's heartleaf in Alabama on two field trips in the summer of 1980. Baker, Steve Orzell, and Edwin L. Bridges found specimens of onespike beaksedge, a species that Harper discovered in pine barrens at Tifton, Georgia, in 1900, in Turner County to the north of Harper's Tifton station in 1991. Surveying power-line easements in Georgia, Maryland, and Virginia to determine if they functioned as refugia for threatened plants, Orzell, Bridges, and Philip M. Sheridan were following Harper's trail and gave him due credit: "One of the early pioneers of this method was the botanist Roland Harper who used railroad rights-of-way as a method for finding rare plant populations."[6]

The botanical illustrator in Georgia, Vicky Holifield, undertook to extend Harper's phytogeographical survey beginning in 1987, surveying most Altamaha Grit sites and compiling a list of more than 150 vascular plants, trees, shrubs, and vines. She established that several rare plants find refuge on the sandstone cliffs and surfaces; that the Altamaha sites tend to have a remarkable diversity of plants, including some that are disjunct, or otherwise found only in distant regions; and that rayless goldenrod, the plant on which Harper discovered his love-vine growing, is a good indicator plant for the Altamaha Grit formation. Holifield also drew many of the illustrations of Harper plant discoveries for *Protected Plants of Georgia*, which the Georgia Department of Natural Resources published in 1995.[7]

For decades, Harper plant aficionados always found Harper's beauty growing on the eastern side of the Apalachicola, in a single very specialized ecological niche, the slopes of seepage bogs that were different from both the level bottoms of the bogs and the wiregrass communities that existed, just a few inches to a few feet higher in elevation, above the rims of the bogs. There grew plants that could survive the low nutrients of the banks, the shortage of oxygen caused by frequently inundated soil, and frequent fires: the pitcher plants, sundews, butterworts, and bladderworts that supplemented the soil's nutrients with insect meals, and their neighbors, showy orchids such as yellow-fringed orchid (*Platanthera ciliaris*), grass-pink (*Calopogon tuberosus*), and rose pogonia (*Cleistes divaricata*).[8] It was in just this kind of narrow ecotone, its boundaries invisible to the untrained eye, that Ed and Lisa Keppner found Harper's beauty.

On a day in May 2003, slogging over boggy ground near Callaway Creek in a slash pine plantation on the outskirts of Panama City, Florida, the Keppners swept long-handled dipnets through the ponds and sloughs, searching the vegetative matter and freshwater creatures they found for the Panama City crayfish (*Procambarus econfinae*).[9] Ed Keppner, a biologist with a PhD from the University of Wyoming, graying, with a dry sense of humor and a penchant for raillery, had spent his career with the National Marine Fisheries Service and the United States Army Corps of Engineers. Lisa, taller and younger than Ed with thick, straight brown hair, was originally from Maryland and had a bachelor's degree in biology; she was an amateur botanist and museum worker. After Ed had retired from the National Marine Fisheries Service in 1996, the Keppners began doing contract survey work for private landowners and public agencies, poking through the Bay County woods and around the edges of lakes, ponds, and creeks to catalog the biological diversity of the county. Ed had played with crayfish, or crawdads, as southerners call them, when he was a boy in Illinois and for years had wanted to rediscover the missing Panama City crayfish. Lisa had been skeptical, but once she found the rare crayfish on her first pond outing, sweeping her new net through the water just three times before turning up one of the crustaceans, she was hooked.[10]

The Keppners had approached the St. Joe Land Company, one of Florida's largest private landowners with vast acreage in timberland and real-estate developments, about surveying its Bay County slash pine plantation for the Panama City crayfish. Persuaded that they should know if and where the rare crayfish existed on their property, company officials issued a request for proposals to various biological field researchers. Determined

to get the contract, the Keppners put in what they hoped was the low bid
for the job and won. They spent a year examining the narrow furrows between twenty-year-old slash pines, pushing back branches of titi that grew
thickly in the damp trenches. Later, they calculated that they received
about three dollars an hour for their crayfish survey.

That day in May, Lisa spotted a small yellow-flowered plant blooming
on the rim of a shallow opening, about twenty feet wide, in the thick
growth of slash pine and titi. Striking for their diamond shape, the shim-
mering yellow petals of the tiny flowers were easy for the experienced field
naturalist to spot. Not recognizing the plant, Lisa collected a specimen
and put it in a plastic bag she had brought in case she found any interesting plants. Then she and Ed continued their search for the Panama City
crayfish.

That night Ed and Lisa spread out the finds of the day in the laundry
room of their stucco house in Panama City. As usual, Ed read the cou-
plets from their favorite botanical key, the *Guide to the Vascular Plants of
the Florida Panhandle*, while Lisa examined the specimens under one of
their microscopes. Having determined that the plant was not woody, Ed
consulted the options for herbaceous plants. Ruling out that the plant
grew underwater, he considered the options for terrestrial plants, and so
on, until he arrived at the family Liliaceae, a group of perennial herbs
with showy flowers and the final descriptive line, "Scapes 1-flowered; te-
pals yellow, about 1 cm long."[11] Lisa paused, looking intently into the
microscope.

"This is *Harperocallis flava*," she said.

"It can't be!" Ed retorted. They both knew that *Harperocallis flava*, a
tiny lily on both the Florida and federal lists of endangered species, was
only known to exist in Franklin and Liberty Counties on the east side of
the Apalachicola River, within the Apalachicola National Forest. For this
plant to be found on the opposite side of the river would be unheard of.

"I'm sure of it," Lisa answered, and she reviewed the key to convince
him. Ed pulled out a copy of the *Field Guide to the Rare Plants of Florida*,
which contained color photographs of all the listed species in the state.[12]
Together, they stared at the picture by Eleanor Dietrich of Harper's
beauty.

"That's it," Ed said.

Realizing they had significantly extended the range of an endangered
Florida endemic species, the Keppners called their friend Linda Chafin,
author of the field guide to rare plants. "We've found *Harperocallis flava*

outside its range," Ed told her. Chafin squealed in excitement over the telephone. "Now, hold on, we might not be right," Ed told her. "Oh, no! Lisa's right! I know she's right!" Chafin said.

The Keppners drove east to Tallahassee the next month to see Loran C. Anderson, a professor emeritus of botany at Florida State University, whom they had met when Lisa took his field botany course. When they entered his office, carrying a briefcase of specimens, the smiling botanist with a fringe of white hair greeted them happily. "You always bring me such interesting things to see," he boomed. Lisa and Ed casually arranged their new specimens, including the Harper's beauty, on Anderson's desk without identifying any of them. He sorted through them, nodding and making comments, until he came to the small lily. Looking up at the Keppners, he asked sharply, "Did you have a permit to collect this?" It is a crime to remove threatened and endangered species from federal lands without a permit from the U.S. Fish and Wildlife Service. "We didn't need a permit. We found that in Bay County," Lisa replied. Anderson leaned back in his chair, clutched his chest dramatically, and exclaimed, "Oh, my goodness!"[13]

Lisa and Ed Keppner had extended the range of one of the rarest plants in the Apalachicola River Basin, a plant named for Roland McMillan Harper. The final answer that I sought was why Harper never noticed the tiny yellow lily growing in the pitcher-plant bogs of Franklin and Liberty Counties, even though from his earliest forays into longleaf country, Harper had been particularly interested in the tiny ecological niches within the longleaf-wiregrass ecosystem.

Why didn't Harper discover *Harperocallis* himself? He visited Franklin and Liberty Counties in 1909, before the establishment of the Apalachicola National Forest, so fire suppression by the Forest Service, while it may have later affected the delicate plant community of the bog rim, cannot explain Harper's oversight. Perhaps the plant did not yet grow in roadside ditches or along the Apalachicola Northern Railroad in Liberty County, where the botanists Leonard and Baker found the rare plant in May 1982.[14] However, it seems likely that Harper missed the endemic lily simply through unlucky timing. Searching the database of Harper photographs in the W. S. Hoole Special Collections Library at the University of Alabama, one finds that Harper visited Bay, Liberty, and Franklin Counties on eleven occasions between 1909 and 1925. Most of those visits lasted two days or longer. Yet few of those visits were actually to pitcher-plant bogs, and none of the bog treks were during the peak May blooming period of Harper's beauty, but rather in late April or early to mid-June. Harper may have tramped around and through other pitcher-plant bogs in the Apalachicola River basin while Harper's beauty was in bloom, but there are no photographs to confirm this. When the lovely yellow flowers are not in bloom, the small plant is almost indistinguishable from the surrounding bog vegetation.[15] Harper himself discussed the difficulty of identifying certain plants when they are not blooming, commenting that "some of them cannot be identified any day in the year as the trees can."[16] It seems, then, that Harper missed discovering *Harperocallis flava* by a week or two.

Fire suppression may not explain why Harper did not discover *Harperocallis flava* himself, but it probably does explain why no one else found it until 1965. The reversal of the Forest Service policy of fire suppression eventually allowed Harper's beauty to become evident in the national forest. McDaniel was right in naming his find for Roland Harper, for it is clear that Harper deserves part of the credit for saving this genus he never saw. As Chapman, the forester at Yale, acknowledged in 1942, Harper was one of the first, and perhaps the very first, of the coastal plain naturalists to perceive the ecological importance of fire in longleaf forests. His advocacy for forest fires triggered a chain reaction of science and policy that may have been the best hope for the fragile biodiversity of the southern coastal plain.

As his career unfolded, Harper did not significantly expand upon his doctoral work on the Altamaha Grit habitat group. In the 1970s, however, a young graduate student in ecology at the University of Tennessee, Hazel Delcourt, became interested in Harper's research on the Altamaha Grit because of the light it shed on presettlement vegetation. She examined his dissertation and concluded that while his interpretation of the Altamaha Grit vegetation reflected the then current ecological ideas of Henry C. Cowles and Frederic Edwards Clements, it anticipated the later approach of F. E. Egler, incorporating all seven aspects of modern vegetation analysis. In an article in the journal *Pioneer America*, Delcourt described Harper's train-window reconnaissance method, his intrepid fieldwork, and his interest in the cultural influences on the coastal plain landscape. "Roland Harper occupies a unique position in history among Southern naturalists. He was an innovator in the field of plant geography, employing what were then unorthodox techniques to the study of vegetation in an early attempt to quantify its structural and compositional attributes," she wrote. "He was at the same time one of the last of the early American botanists privileged to visit and describe examples of original vegetation before disturbance by lumbering and cultivation."[17] Like other Harper buffs, Delcourt collected Harper materials. Her favorite photograph of him was one taken in 1912 by the botanist H. H. Bartlett. Sitting at the base of an enormous pine, Harper contemplated one of the tree's giant cones, two other cones at his feet. He was thirty-four years old, wearing a battered hat, a jacket, and a narrow necktie, his satchel beside him. He smiled slightly, eyes downward, looking as if he intensely wanted Bartlett to capture the moment and his love of the pinewoods.

EPILOGUE

In June 2004, the Keppners took my husband and me to the site of their Harper's beauty discovery. Jim Moyers, a wildlife biologist with St. Joe Land Company, came along. Since the Keppners' discovery, Moyers had developed a management plan for the Harper's beauty sites in Bay County. He planned controlled burns each spring and summer to eliminate the titi understory and to simulate naturally occurring forest fires. To keep foot traffic, which can destroy the tiny plants, to a minimum and to prevent rare plant collectors from poaching specimens of Harper's beauty, he also planned to allow very few visitors to the sites. The day we went to the Keppner site, a red-shouldered hawk screamed from a treetop, southern cricket frogs chorused, and bumblebees buzzed by. Full-size slash pines ringed the bowl-like depression and a single cypress was visible nearby, at the edge of Callaway Creek. Drumheads (*Polygala cruciata*) bloomed, and huckleberry was in fruit. All four carnivorous plant genera—pitcher plants, bladderworts, butterworts, and sundews—grew there. It was easy to imagine Harper tromping through the bog, notebook and pen in hand, camera swinging from his shoulder, perhaps spotting the Harper's yellow-flowered grass (*Xyris scabrifolia*) that he described in 1901.

My last trip along Harper's trail was to the New York Botanical Garden. The conservatory, that fantastic glass palace, is still there; an exhibit inside informs visitors that the NYBG has sent researchers on more than one thousand expeditions since 1897. The massive LuEsther T. Mertz Library, the original museum and herbarium building that was still under construction when Harper first went to the Garden in 1899, stands at the top of a double driveway lined by tulip trees, although the herbarium rooms and library where Harper worked have been remodeled into nonexistence. Botanists still come there to examine specimens Harper collected, sometimes confirming that they were new species, sometimes determining that the original author, Harper or another botanist, was incorrect, as Mildred Mathias did in 1936, when she concluded that Joseph N. Rose of the

National Herbarium was wrong to designate an umbellifer Harper had collected as a new genus, *Harperella*. (Mathias reclassified the specimen as *Ptilimnium nodosum* (Rose) Mathias and her determination withstood further scrutiny by other botanists in 1956 and 1981.)

One of the herbarium curators, Stella Sylva, escorted my husband and me into the locked chamber where specimens are stored. She had pulled the sheets for many of Harper's type specimens, those which he or another botanist had at some time determined were new discoveries. Here Harper's successors have come to examine his finds and reevaluate them in the context of new information. To proffer a new judgment about a specimen's place in botanical taxonomy, they attach a new label to the sheet, summarizing their views, providing a different name if they would reclassify the plant, giving the date, and including a citation if they have published an article on the issue. The labels are evidence of the constant give and take of botany, the bit of immortality that an author can give a collector by designating a plant as a new genus or species, the immortality that another botanist can take away. Harper's original labels, the state and year of collection printed, the name and details of the collection site in his handwriting, hint at his slow, methodical process of classification. For many specimens, one can tell by differences in the ink he used that Harper initially only designated a genus for a specimen and later noted the species. His handwritten names also reflect whether he or another scientist took responsibility for concluding that the specimen was a new discovery; the third part of the botanical name could be Harper, meaning he made the identification himself, or Small, for John Kunkel Small, or Britton, for Nathaniel Britton, or another botanist's name. The NYBG has made digital photographs of many of its specimen sheets and cataloged them in an online collection that visitors can search and view. Examining the tiny photographic prints that Harper attached to some sheets up close, however, reveals more clues: there is no fence evident around the field at Tifton, Georgia, where he photographed purpledisk honeycombhead, and buildings are in the distance, beyond a fringe of trees. Perhaps the Tifton railroad depot was in the pine barren some distance from the center of town.

Edward O. Wilson, who crossed paths with Harper at the University of Alabama during Wilson's undergraduate years, remembered him as "a venerable and legendary figure in the 1940s for his knowledge of plants." He compared Harper to Louis Agassiz, one of history's great naturalists.[1] Agassiz clung to a theist interpretation of creation, not just rejecting

Darwin's theory of evolution but waging intellectual war against it until his death.[2] Harper, too, clung to ideas that were proven wrong—the superiority of Caucasians and particularly northern Europeans, the cultural threat of bobbed hair—but his instincts were good on other subjects, such as the genetic component of mental illness. Eugenics rose and fell as legitimate science during Harper's lifetime, but his intuition that idiosyncrasies such as his were familial was correct. Today, there is new evidence for the genetic basis of human behavior such as Roland's compulsion to make lists and Otto's irrational fear of germs. Genetics counselors advise couples about the risks of passing on particular inherited conditions that DNA tests confirm they possess in their genes. Psychiatrists, like the splitters among taxonomists, distinguish between patients with obsessive-compulsive disorder, who the psychiatrists say are sicker because they do not realize they are sick, and patients with obsessive-compulsive *personality* disorder, who are less sick because they realize they are. The obsession to find new species in the landscape; the compulsions to make lists, to sort through information, to check again and again in the landscape and in libraries and herbaria to confirm his findings, may have been symptoms of an illness, but they were the keys to Harper's success as a scientist.

"Some people know some things that are not so," Harper said.[3] Undoubtedly, he understood that this applied to himself—that some of his new species would later prove to be varieties of previously described species, that his theories of ecological succession and social change were just that, theories subject to review, challenge, and revision by other basic or social scientists. As he wrote in his dissertation, "further study will always bring us nearer the truth," so he continued searching, retracing his own steps as he did those of Bartram, Chapman, Mohr, Small, and others.[4] Behind him came still others: Herman Kurz, who acknowledged Harper's mentoring in the northern Florida woods; Herbert L. Stoddard Sr., who called Harper "the most experienced of all southeastern botanists"; the forester Leon Neel; the expert naturalists Wilson Baker and Angus Kemp Gholson Jr., who liked to think that he had sat on the same bench on a Chattahoochee sidewalk where Harper paused to rest; the botanists Thomas S. Patrick, James R. Allison, and Gregory R. Krakow, who compiled the manual of endangered plants of Georgia that contains many of Vicky Holifield's drawings.

Harper was leery of forming ecological theories, but when George Shull pushed him to join the mainstream of ecological thought in the early twentieth century, he plunged in, proposing two crucial ideas: that wetlands were essential ecosystems and that fire was a necessary element in the preservation of longleaf forest. He wanted most to "travel and tramp," as his mother called his odyssey, tracing and retracing the routes of earlier naturalists, finding the remote places his predecessors had missed, collecting the material evidence of plant diversity. Many of the species that Harper found and described are in danger of extinction today. Harper's yellow-eyed grass, which grows in the same habitats as Harper's beauty, has a global ranking of G3, meaning it is very rare. Harper's love-vine, the parasitic vine he discovered growing on rayless goldenrod on an Altamaha Grit outcrop in Washington County, Georgia, in 1906, is ranked as critically imperiled by the state of Georgia. Harper's heartleaf, the species of *Hexastylis* that he discovered on a farm in Autauga County, Alabama, in 1924, is still only found in central Alabama and thus is considered globally rare; the Nature Conservancy maintains the Roberta Case Pine Hills Preserve in Autauga County in part to preserve Harper's heartleaf. The giant pitcher plant that Harper found on his brief trip into Okefenokee Swamp in 1902 finally received scientific recognition a century later, when the International Carnivorous Plant Society referred to it as *Sarracenia minor* var. *okefenokeensis* Schnell.[5]

Exploring the coastal plain for five decades, compiling records of plant diversity and documenting changes to the landscape, Harper described at least forty new species and varieties and one genus that colleagues agreed were new to science, although some have since been reclassified. What other species are still to be discovered in Harper's coastal plain? Nearly all of the virgin longleaf forest is gone, and many of the rivers have been dammed, destroying the shoals and riverbank vegetation where Harper reveled at species like the Cahaba lily. Yet Harper's descendants keep going, searching for new species and for ways to preserve the biodiversity that scientists have already discovered.

Broxton Rocks, the site in Georgia that Harper visited for a single day in 1906, shelters a refugium, a community of disjunct plants that were neighbors in earlier epochs and other places on the continent, with the greatest diversity of vascular plants and bryophytes of any Altamaha Grit formation. Broxton Rocks is now a preserve of the Nature Conservancy, thanks in large part to a single man who looks back to Roland Harper as a model of the field scientist who visits the same sites over years and in different seasons, each time documenting what he sees. A naturalist whose avocation has been studying and saving Broxton Rocks, Frankie Snow led the campaign to persuade the Nature Conservancy to acquire the property and wrote the management plan for the site, noting that the rare purpledisk honeycombhead thrived in a bog at the headwaters of Rocky Creek, and that Georgia plume, the gorgeous shrub that Harper and Hendricks rediscovered in Candler County, Georgia, in 1901, grew on four unprotected sandstone outcrops near Broxton Rocks.[6] Snow deeply admires Harper and is rather like him, with an extraordinary knowledge of the landscape he loves and little interest in exploring other parts of the world. He has closely studied the plant community at Broxton Rocks, collaborating with Georgia scientists and botanists from the New York Botanical Garden. While Harper merely noted that "common mosses" grew there, Snow and his colleagues have established that the site contains about a quarter of the moss species that occur in Georgia, including some very rare ones. Interested, like Harper, in how plants migrated above or below fall lines, Snow wonders how grit portulaca (*Portulaca biloba*), a species that otherwise grows only in Cuba, managed to become established at Broxton Rocks and speculates that a species of nighthawk, after consuming insects that ate the portulaca's seeds, carried the seeds between Cuba and Broxton Rocks.

Snow and Christopher T. Trowell took my friend Melissa Macdougall and me to Broxton Rocks in March 2004. Following them through the longleaf woods above the creek and down the bank to the streambed, we heard the melodious song of a Bachman's sparrow. Woodpeckers drilled on longleaf trunks, and mosquitoes buzzed at our ears. Rocky Creek spilled over a lovely waterfall into a small pool, frothing because of tannin leached from decaying vegetation, and descended into a widening valley, where over the centuries it had eroded the looming sandstone walls and created an alluvium of Miocene deposits. Harper, Snow said, "documented places that wouldn't otherwise be recorded."

The Keppners' discovery of Harper's beauty to the west of the Apalachicola River demonstrates the importance of field research, to confirm past discoveries and scan the ground again for what might have been missed before. Harper was a visual learner, like Darwin, who Ernst Mayr has observed "got his real education from observing and reading."[7] Harper became "an excellent field man," as the forester and protégé of Herbert Stoddard, Leon Neel, says, "or Mr. Stoddard would not have admired him as he did."[8] Tramping the woods, bogs, and river and creek banks, he found many new species. He did not limit his botanical reconnaissance trips to train rides, but many times walked overland from dawn to dark, collecting plant samples and making running records in his field notebooks that were the raw data of his quantitative reports of vegetation. The products of his compulsion to make lists, his running records or "car-window notes," were an important contribution to field botany. Without the obsession to explore and make new discoveries in the southern coastal plain, without the compulsion to collect, sort, and interpret data, without the "unbounded patience," in Darwin's language, to return to the same places in the landscape again and again, Harper might not have had the breakthrough idea about fire. The biographer Janice Emily Bowers said of Harper's early friend Forrest Shreve—but it describes Harper, too—"He was essentially an innovative researcher in a particular place, and his interests were the ecological problems that place presented."[9] Although botany's lumpers and splitters continue to undo and revise Harper's taxonomic contributions, at this writing his name is still attached to many of his discoveries, as he hoped it would be during his early years in Massachusetts, the years he spent reading Darwin and climbing Wachusett Mountain.

Population genetics rose and fell as a respectable branch of science during Harper's lifetime, and thus his forays into eugenics had disastrous consequences for his reputation among the botanists, geologists, and naturalists who knew him in the latter half of his life. It became "almost impossible, [after] 1933, to discuss eugenics objectively," Ernst Mayr commented in 1982. It was "a dead issue and will remain so until populational thinking is more widely adopted and until we know far more about the genetic component in human characteristics."[10] Harper's urge to apply statistical analysis to the urgent social issues of the day as well as to problems of vegetation studies, and the idea that ecological and population trends were all related, ultimately drove him to attempt too much and thus to achieve too little. He did not complete the masterpiece of phytogeography that seemed to be his destiny. Ironically, the obsessive-compulsive personality that was itself a genetic condition tortured him with irrational fears of disaster, such as being bitten by snakes; of being unable to provide for a family; of contamination by defective genes; of his own madness. The idea that one's ancestry was also one's destiny made his family history of mental illness, most clearly manifested in his sister Hermina and brother Otto, seem like a terrifying prediction of his future. The risk seemed to always threaten him, in the corners of his mind, unless he adhered to routines, like saving and clipping newspapers, which gave him a feeling of mental self-control. It was not only the perceived risk of being unable to financially support a family that caused Harper to avoid marriage but also the fear that he would pass on the mental disease to his progeny, as William and Bertha had done. He sacrificed happiness, forgoing marriage until late in life and fatherhood altogether, to save the population from another generation of Harpers, who, he was convinced by the theories of the eugenicists, were doomed to madness by their genetic makeup. In the terminology of the eugenicists, he performed an act of "negative eugenics" by remaining childless.

While he faltered in his efforts to explore the overlapping fields of biological and sociological phenomena, others persisted. Coincidentally, a young postwar undergraduate at the University of Alabama, who knew of Harper's work as a pioneering phytogeographer but did not study under him, was one of the next generation of scientists to pick up the trail between genetics and human behavior. Edward O. Wilson published *Sociobiology: The New Synthesis* in 1975, attempting "to organize all of sociobiology on the principles of population biology."[11] Wilson was following a new path blazed by a graduate student at Oxford University, William D. Hamilton, who in 1964 redefined natural selection as "inclusive fitness," encompassing "caring for kin who carry copies of your genes in their bodies [so that] an organism can also increase the reproduction of its genes by helping brothers, sisters, nieces, or nephews to survive and reproduce."[12] George C. Williams published *Adaptation and Natural Selection* the year that Harper died, translating Hamilton for lay readers: "Altruism could evolve if the recipients of one's help were one's genetic kin. Parents, for example, might sacrifice their own lives to save the lives of their children, who carry copies of the parents' genes within them. The same logic applies to making sacrifices for other genetic relatives, such as sisters or cousins."[13]

Perhaps Hamilton, Williams, and Wilson can be interpreted to mean that, while Harper had no direct biological descendants, and today few remember his contributions to the modern understanding of the value of wetlands and forest fire, when he retraced Bartram's Alabama passage with Francis, he was not just brother but father to Francis's great work, the annotation of Bartram's *Travels*—or that there is, in one sense, an ancestral link between Roland Harper and the scientists of today.

Harper dreamed as a young man of making botanical discoveries in the virgin forests and bogs of the southern coastal plain, so that he would be "forever famous." In middle age, he mused about his career and his altruistic choice to remain childless: "Doubtless many persons think that it would be a fine thing if geniuses should multiply faster, but is it certain that we have not enough of them now? . . . And history is full of instances of great thinkers who were so far ahead of their times that they were unappreciated, and had great difficulty in making a living for themselves alone, to say nothing of raising families." He hinted at his loneliness but rejected the notion that he had a responsibility to perpetuate his own intellect: "One reads in papers from time to time of 'eugenic marriages' of couples supposed to be perfect physically and mentally, that turned out badly on account of psychological factors that were not taken into consideration. If a superior man or woman marries let it be merely for the sake of companionship or comfort rather than from any hope of improving the race."[14]

In the give and take of botanical taxonomy, some of Harper's plant discoveries have been downgraded from genera to species or from species to varieties. The genus named for him, *Harperocallis*, is one he did not even discover himself. Yet Harper did achieve a kind of immortality—the kind that every scientist achieves as his or her work contributes to the understanding and discoveries of those who follow. Harper lives on in the work of Sidney McDaniel, of Angus Gholson, of Wilson Baker; of Herbert Stoddard's protégé, the forester Leon Neel; of Frankie Snow, the keeper of Broxton Rocks; and of Jim Moyers and Lisa and Ed Keppner, who did not know his name before I met them on Harper's trail.

How many other species and varieties await discovery by the scientists and naturalists who will be lucky enough to explore the right locations at the right times—if the longleaf woods, stone outcrops, river bluffs, and wetlands of the coastal plain survive? So much of the earth is still unexplored, the extent of its biodiversity still undiscovered, while destruction of fragile environmental niches continues, that many species may disappear and, never having been known, not even be remembered.

NOTES

ONE. To Be Forever Famous

1. "Rail Road and Township Map of Massachusetts" (1879), http://memory
.loc.gov/cgi-bin/map_items.pl (accessed Jan. 30, 2004).

2. D. R. Foster, *Thoreau's Country*, 14; R. M. Harper, "Botanizing in Worcester County."

3. Stahle, "Unsung Ancients"; Cogbill and others, *Dynamics of Old-growth
Forests*; R. M. Harper, "Botanizing in Worcester County," 2.

4. Harper to Ed Kasebier (sp?), March 26, 1899; Georgie ? to Harper, February 5, 1886; Otto Tauber to Harper, January 15, 1889.

5. "In Memoriam: William Harper."

6. Butler, *History of Farmington*, 307–8, 326–27.

7. Mallett, *University of Maine at Farmington*; Mrs. H. P. Keyes, *Farmington
Chronicle*, quoted in "In Memoriam: William Harper," 9.

8. "In Memoriam: William Harper"; Traber, "Harper Ancestry"; *Dalton Ar-
gus*, May 21, 1887, in Traber, "Harper Ancestry."

9. Woodward, *Origins of the New South*, 61–62, 120–22; "Early Dalton,"
http://roadsidegeorgia.com/city/dalton.html (accessed Dec. 20, 2003); Flamming, *Creating the Modern South*, 37, 50–51; Grantham, *South in Modern America*, 333.

10. Traber, "Harper Ancestry"; "Early Dalton," http://roadsidegeorgia
.com/city/dalton.html (accessed June 6, 2007); Randy Golden, "The Great Locomotive Chase; The Story of Andrews' Raiders," *About North Georgia*, http://
ngeorgia.com/history/raiders.html (accessed June 6, 2007).

11. Verne, *Mysterious Island*, 17, 24, 37, 59; Clarence H. Knowlton to Harper,
March 6, 1892.

12. Robert Scott Davis Jr., "Andersonville Prison"; Alan Anderson, "Americus" *New Georgia Encyclopedia*, www.georgiaencyclopedia.org (accessed June 6,
2007); R. M. Harper, "Autobiographical Notes"; Clarence Knowlton to Harper,
January 31, 1892; Edward L. Kasebier (sp?) to Harper, January 17, 1893.

13. T. C. Gibson to Bertha Harper (undated); E. Boggs to William Harper,
September 11 and September 15, 1894.

14. Reed, *History of the University of Georgia*; hereafter cited as Reed, *University of Georgia*.

15. DeLoach earned a bachelor's and a master's degree at the university and afterward worked as a botanist for the Georgia Experiment Station and then on the faculty of the Georgia State College of Agriculture, part of the university. After completing a bachelor's degree at the university in 1898, Akerman did graduate work in Germany and at Yale University and was state forester in Connecticut and Massachusetts. He returned to the University of Georgia as a professor of forestry and head of the new forestry school in 1905. Reed, *University of Georgia*.

16. Reed, *University of Georgia*; Francis Harper to Clermont H. Lee, August 9, 1964, Georgia Southern University Special Collection.

17. A graduate student and tutor during part of Roland's undergraduate years, Phillips entered Columbia University in 1900, shortly after Roland did so, earned a doctoral degree in history there, and went on to a significant career as a southern historian. Boney, *Walking Tour*; Reed, *University of Georgia*.

18. Wayne Morgan, "Brownie Dolls and the World of Palmer Cox," http:// home.earthlink.net/~hellerest/VAGABONDSONG.html (accessed Feb. 22, 2004); Francis Harper to Harper, November 2, 1894; Otto Harper to Harper, March 23, 1896.

19. R. M. Harper, "Some 19th Century Recollections"; Alvan Wentworth Chapman, *Flora of the Southern United States*; R. M. Harper, "Notes on the Flora," 333–34, 321.

20. Clarence Knowlton to Harper, July 18, 1895, and January 31, 1892.

21. Clarence Knowlton to Harper, November 24, 1895.

22. Clarence Knowlton to Harper, October 7, 1896; R. M. Harper, "Explorations in the Coastal Plain"; Patrick, Allison, and Krakow, *Protected Plants of Georgia*.

23. Mount, *Reptiles and Amphibians*.

24. William Harper to Harper, February 1, March 19, and November 24, 1895; R. M. Harper, "Condensed Autobiography of Roland Harper."

25. Barry, *Great Influenza*, 31; R. M. Harper, "Studying the Georgia Flora"; R. M. Harper, "Notes on the Flora."

26. Franziska Tauber to Harper, October 1 and October 2, 1898.

27. R. M. Harper, "Some 19th Century Recollections"; Franziska Tauber to Harper, October 2, 1898; Buss, *Evolutionary Psychology*, 7; Larson, *Evolution*, 133; Hooper, *Of Moths and Men*, 30, 36–37; Woodward, *Origins of the New South*, 443–47.

28. R. M. Harper, "Botanizing in Worcester County."

29. Verne, *Mysterious Island*, 69–75.

30. Harper to Ed K?, March 26, 1899.

31. R. M. Harper, "Autobiographical Notes"; Verne, *Mysterious Island*, 452; Harper to Ed K?, March 26, 1899.

TWO. Wonderful Country

1. Lucius E. Ammidown to Harper, Nov. 7, 1899.

2. A native of Vermont, Marshall Avery Howe had earned a degree at the University of Vermont and taught in a Vermont high school and at the University of California at Berkeley before receiving a fellowship at Columbia University, where he studied *Hepaticae* with Underwood and received a PhD in 1898. New York Botanical Garden, "Marshall Avery Howe," http://www.nybg.org/bsci/libr/Howepp.htm (accessed Jan. 22, 2004); www.nybg.org hereafter cited as New York Botanical Garden.

3. McCaughey, *Stand, Columbia*, 207; Clarence Knowlton to Harper, Sept. 2, 1898; Rusby, "Historical Sketch"; Tanner and Auchincloss, *New York Botanical Garden*, 51–54, 128; New York Botanical Garden; R. M. Harper, "Some 19th Century Recollections," 98.

4. Elizabeth Britton spent part of her childhood on a family sugar plantation in Cuba, earned a degree from Hunter College in 1875, became a teacher at Hunter (then called the Normal School), joined the Torrey Botanical Club in 1879, and married Britton in 1885. She was the lone woman among the charter members of the Botanical Society of America in 1893. During the years when Harper was in New York, she helped found the Wild Flower Preservation Society of America (New York Botanical Garden). McCaughey, *Stand, Columbia*, 227, 232; Gleason, "Contributions"; New York Botanical Garden.

5. Rusby, "Historical Sketch," 138–39; Gleason, "Contributions," 41.

6. R. M. Harper, "Some 19th Century Recollections," 99.

7. Hollick and Britton became friends when both were students at Columbia's School of Mines. Hollick worked as a mine supervisor in California and from 1881 to 1891, while he was assistant sanitary engineer of the Board of Health of the City of New York. During those years, he pursued geology as an informal assistant to Professor J. S. Newberry at Columbia. He took over some of Newberry's teaching responsibilities in 1890 and was appointed a tutor in geology on the Columbia faculty in 1893. Two years before Harper entered Columbia, Hollick earned a PhD from George Washington University, while working for the United States Geological Service in Washington, D.C. Britton appointed him assistant curator of the Garden in 1901. New York Botanical Garden.

8. Small studied botany at Franklin and Marshall College in Lancaster, Pennsylvania, and explored some of the mountains of western North Carolina, attracting Britton's attention with submissions to the Torrey Botanical Club's periodical *Memoirs*. He entered Columbia University, conducted field research in Florida in 1901, and contributed descriptions of several families for the first edition of Britton and Brown's *Illustrated Flora*. New York Botanical Garden.

9. Gleason earned a bachelor's and a master's degree from the University of

Illinois, came to Columbia in 1905 to study taxonomy under Britton, and received a PhD the following year (New York Botanical Garden). American Bryological and Lichenological Society (n.d.), http://www.unomaha.edu/~abls/ABLS%20Program2000.htm (accessed Jan. 17, 2004); Willard N. Clute to Harper, Dec. 5, 1898; New York Botanical Garden; John Hendley Barnhart to Harper, 1948; Lentz and Bellengi, "Brief History."

10. R. M. Harper, "Some 19th Century Recollections," 101; New York Botanical Garden.

11. Rusby, "Historical Sketch," 107–8; R. M. Harper, "Some 19th Century Recollections," 100.

12. B. L. Robinson to Harper, Sept. 29, 1899. Harper also made a successful submission to Clute's *Fern Bulletin* in 1899.

13. R. M. Harper, "Some 19th Century Recollections," 101, 103; "Nathaniel Lord Britton; Cornelius Amory Pugsley Silver Medal Award, 1929" (n.d.), http://www.rpts.tamu.edge/pugsley/Britton.htm (accessed Feb. 7, 2004); R. M. Harper, "Synonymy of *Burmannia* and *Gyrotheca*"; Davenport and Hubbs, "Roland Harper."

14. R. M. Harper, "Some 19th Century Recollections," 99; Berg and Singer, *George Beadle*, 29–31; Mayr, *Growth of Biological Thought*, 395–97.

15. Ridley, *Agile Gene*, 232; The Human Genome Project, "Rediscovery of Mendel's Work" (n.d.), http://www.genome.gov/Pages/Education/Kit/main.cfm?pageid=2 (accessed Feb. 4, 2004).

16. Hooper, *Of Moths and Men*, 36–38; Larson, *Evolution*, 158; McCaughey, *Stand, Columbia*, 197–98.

17. David Rose, "Lucien Marcus Underwood Papers; Biographical Note" (New York Botanical Garden, 1999), http://sciweb.nybg.org/science2/libr/finding_guide/underwb2.asp (accessed Feb. 27, 2004); New York Botanical Garden, Virtual Herbarium, http://sciweb.nybg.org/science2/VirtualHerbarium.asp (accessed Dec. 26, 2004). The Garden obscures the locations of some of Harper's plant collections because the species are now so rare. For example, for specimens of longleaf pine that he collected in Chatham County, Georgia, in June 1903 and Coffee County, Georgia, in February 1904, the herbarium notes, "This specimen represents an endangered or threatened species. The specific locality has been removed from the on-line record to protect this species from over-collection. These data may be supplied to researchers on request."

18. Harper diary. Harper also saw Charles Morton Strahan, his engineering professor, and Allen Fort, a member of the class of 1867 who later was elected to the Georgia legislature and served as a judge of the Superior Court and a member of the Georgia Railroad Commission. N. L Britton to Harper, June 2, 1900; Harper diary; Reed, *University of Georgia*.

19. Percy Wilson, a museum aide at the New York Botanical Garden and one of Harper's classmates in an elementary botany course at Columbia, accompanied

him on what may have been Wilson's first expedition on behalf of the Garden; he went on to make trips to the East Indies, Puerto Rico, Cuba, and the Virgin Islands. R. M. Harper, "19th Century Recollections," 103; New York Botanical Garden; R. M. Harper, "*Taxodium distichum* and Related Species"; Harvard University Herbaria, Index of Botanical Specimens, hereafter cited as Harvard University Herbaria; R. M. Harper, "Some 19th Century Recollections," 98.

20. Harper returned to the type localities for purpledisk honeycomb head in 1902, finding that "the locality (a characteristic area of primeval moist pine barrens) [was] so near the center of the city that it [was] in imminent danger of destruction by the encroachments of civilization, but fortunately both species [were] common enough elsewhere in the same and adjoining counties." He saw purple honeycomb head again in 1903 while riding a train through the "nearly flat pine-barrens of Wayne and Pierce counties" and in Coffee and Wilcox counties, and carefully listed the locations. "Traveling from Douglas to Cordele on the 23d [of September], a distance of about 65 miles through the Altamaha Grit region, I noted this plant seventeen times, between different mile-posts, in four counties." R. M. Harper, "Explorations in the Coastal Plain," 15; R. M. Harper, "Phytogeographical Explorations."

21. Bridges and Orzell, "Rediscovery of *Rhynchospora solitaria* Harper (Cyperaceae) in Georgia"; R. M. Harper, "Studying the Georgia Flora," 5; U.S. National Herbarium specimen sheet; R. M. Harper, "Phytogeographical Explorations," 170.

22. R. M. Harper, "*Taxodium distichum* and Related Species," 394; Patrick, Allison, and Krakow, *Protected Plants*; Harper diary.

23. Stoddard, "Use of Fire," 35; Cowdrey, *This Land, This South*, 91.

24. U.S. Fish and Wildlife Service, "Ivory-billed Woodpecker."

25. U.S. Department of Agriculture, "*Sporobolus teretifolius* Harper," *Plants Database* (n.d.), http://plants.usda.gov/cig_bin/plant_profile.cgi?symbol=SPTE4 (accessed Feb. 17, 2004), hereafter cited as USDA Plants Database; R. M. Harper, "Phytogeographical Sketch," 110; R. M. Harper, "Some Vanishing Scenic Features," 200.

26. Hermina Harper to Otto Harper, Aug. 7, 1901; Hermina Harper to Harper, Aug. 5, 1901.

27. Hermina to Otto, Aug. 7, 1901.

28. Hermina Harper to Harper, Aug. 5 and Oct. 15, 1901.

29. "In Memoriam: William Harper"; description of house based on photos taken in 1905 or 1906, courtesy of David Harper; Harper to F. V. Coville, Dec. 12, 1901.

30. Patrick, Allison, and Krakow, *Protected Plants of Georgia*; R. M. Harper, "Phytogeographical Explorations," 141–43; Holifield, "True Grit," 3.

31. R. M. Harper, "Phytogeographical Explorations," 141–42, 147–49, 151–52; Harvard University Herbaria; Harper to ? Cuthbert, Dec. 18, 1904.

32. Harper to ? Cuthbert, Dec. 18, 1904; Lucien Underwood to Harper, May 13, 1905; R. M. Harper, "Condensed Autobiography of Roland M. Harper"; R. M. Harper, "Phytogeographical Sketch."

33. Hollick was Britton's friend Charles Arthur Hollick; Augustin Gattinger was in Tennessee; Smith was Eugene A. Smith, director of the Alabama Geological Survey, and Hilgard was Eugene W. Hilgard, a mentor to Smith.

34. R. M. Harper, "Phytogeographical Sketch," 7–9, 32, 40.

35. New York Botanical Garden, specimen ID 214557.

THREE. A Pioneer or Transient Type

1. R. M. Harper, "Condensed Autobiography of Roland M. Harper"; Rusby, "Historical Sketch," 108; Rogers and others, *Alabama*, 228; "Alabama Museum of Natural History" (museum brochure, undated); Woodward, *Origins of the New South*, 436–40; Cowdrey, *This Land, This South*, 99; Hall and Robb, "Eugene Allen Smith," 13–16.

2. Woodward, *Origins of the New South*, 126–28; Hubbs, *Tuscaloosa*, 56, 60; Clinton, *Matt Clinton's Scrapbook*, 101–2.

3. Hubbs, *Tuscaloosa*, 8–9, 58; Ayers, *Promise of the New South*, 59; Clinton, *Matt Clinton's Scrapbook*, 66–69; Grantham, *South in Modern America*, 27–28; Rogers and others, *Alabama*, 228–29; Woodward, *Origins of the New South*, 178, 311; Flynt, *Poor but Proud*, 60–61.

4. Clay and others, *Land of the South*, 101; Hubbs, *Tuscaloosa*, 8–9; R. M. Harper, "December Ramble"; Bowers, *Sense of Place*, 32; New York Botanical Garden; Davenport, "Nevius and *Neviusia*."

5. R. M. Harper, "December Ramble," 104–7.

6. R. M. Harper, "December Ramble," 104–7; R. M. Harper, "Botanical Bonanza in Tuscaloosa County."

7. R. M. Harper, "Botanical Bonanza in Tuscaloosa County," 155; R. M. Harper, "Some More Coastal Plain Plants," 111, 115; R. M. Harper, "Aquatic Vegetation of Squaw Shoals"; R. M. Harper, *Forests of Alabama*, 100.

8. R. M. Harper, "Some More Coastal Plain Plants"; Owen, "History of Native Plant Communities," 53–54; R. M. Harper, "Vegetation of Bald Knob."

9. Hall and Robb, "Eugene Allen Smith," 13–15; American Association for the Advancement of Science, *Proceedings, 1905*, 362 423; R. M. Harper, "Midwinter Observations."

10. Harper to Mrs. A. P. Taylor, Aug. 19, 1906; Frankie Snow, communication with the author, Dec. 23, 2004; Griffin and Snow, "Broxton Rocks Ecological Preserve"; Frankie Snow, "Broxton Rocks: A Guide" (unpublished manuscript, 2001, courtesy of Frankie Snow), 2.

11. Harper to Mrs. A. P. Taylor, Aug. 19, 1906; R. M. Harper, "Midsummer Journey," 354–58, 364.

12. B. L. Robinson to Harper, Sept. 29, 1906; letter to Harper, Oct. 8, 1906; Forrest Shreve to Harper, Nov. 28, 1906 (unknown author; box 73-009, file 12, Hoole Collection); Clarence Knowlton to Harper, Dec. 20, 1906; E. W. Hilgard to Harper, July 22, 1907; Henry C. Cowles to Harper, Jan. 31, 1908.

13. J. Walter Hendricks to Harper, Feb. 4, 1907; "In Memoriam: William Harper"; R. M. Harper, "Autobiographical Notes"; David Rose, "Lucien Marcus Underwood Papers: Biographical Note," New York Botanical Garden; "Professor Slays Self," *New York Tribune*, Nov. 17, 1907.

14. George H. Shull to Harper, April 25, 1907; Rhoda Amon, "At College Point, Industrialist Conrad Poppenhusen Built a Legacy That Endures," http://www.newsday.com/extras/lihistory/5/hs533a.htm) (accessed Feb. 8, 2004); "Harper Eager for Journey to Wilds," *Brooklyn Eagle*, May 12, 1914, in Traber, "Harper Ancestry."

15. Bowers, *Sense of Place*, 7; Forrest Shreve, "Collecting Trip at Cinchona."

16. Forrest Shreve to Harper, Oct. 8, 1907; R. M. Harper, "Northward Extension."

17. W. L. Sherwood to Harper, March 11, 1907; Edward J. Larson, *Sex, Race and Science*, 41; Reed, *University of Georgia*; R. J. H. DeLoach to Harper, April 26 and June 7, 1907, and Jan. 23, 1908.

18. Henry C. Cowles to Harper, Oct. 12, 1907; E. N. Transeau to Harper, Jan. 20, 1908; C. S. Sargent to Harper, Jan. 10, 1908.

19. Edward W. Berry to Harper, Feb. 15, 1908; Forrest Shreve to Harper, Jan. 16 and Jan. 28, 1908; Reed, *University of Georgia*; Alfred Akerman to Harper, Feb. 3, 1908; William Trelease to Harper, Feb. 13, 1908.

20. Alfred Akerman to Harper, May 27, 1908; C. A. Schenck to Harper, May 30 and June 4, 1908.

21. C. D. Howe to Harper, June 17, 1908; Otto Harper to Harper, June 20, 1908; Edward Berry to Harper, July 8, 1908; J. R. Harper to Harper, July 12 and Aug. 3, 1908.

22. New York Botanical Garden Virtual Herbarium; Bertha Harper to Harper, Aug. 1, 1908; Otto Harper to Harper, Aug. 10, 1908.

23. McGuire, "Living on Longleaf," 52; E. B. Cooke to Harper, April 26, 1908; Bertha Harper to Harper, Aug. 25, 1908; H. D. House to Harper, Oct. 28, 1908.

24. C. Stuart Gager to Harper, Feb. 21, 1908; Rusby, "Historical Sketch," 145; Forrest Shreve to Harper, Aug. 16, 1908.

25. M. L. Fernald to Harper, May 4, 1908.

26. Alfred Akerman to Harper, Nov. 24, 1908.

27. R. J. H. DeLoach to Harper, Aug. 28; Eugene A. Smith to Harper, Sept. 5, 1908; Bertha Harper to Harper, Aug. 25 and Sept. 6, 1908.

28. Eugene A. Smith to Harper, Aug. 17, 1908.

29. R. M. Harper, "Botanical and Geological Trip," 107–8, 117–19.

30. Harper photograph 3.63; Harper diary.

31. H. D. House to Harper, Oct. 28, 1908; William Maxon to Harper, Nov. 2, 1908; R. M. Harper, "Botanical and Geological Trip," 107, 112–19.

32. R. M. Harper, "Botanical and Geological Trip," 109, 112.

33. Clements, *Research Methods in Ecology*, 7–8; Bowers, *Sense of Place*, 58–59; George H. Shull to Harper, March 20, 1908.

34. George H. Shull to Harper, Jan. 20, 1908.

35. Watson School of Biological Sciences, "History of Cold Spring Harbor Laboratory," http://www.cshl.org/gradschool/history.html) (accessed March 1, 2004).

36. A reprint of the memorials for Underwood, which were published in the *Bulletin of the Torrey Botanical Club*, is in the New York Botanical Garden Archive.

37. George H. Shull to Harper, Feb. 5, 1908.

38. R. M. Harper, "Studying the Georgia Flora," 16.

FOUR. In the Footsteps of Croom and Chapman

1. Mueller, *Perilous Journeys*, 252.

2. The botanist George Arnott named the plant in honor of John Torrey in 1838. Hardy and his brother Bryan operated plantations in the area, and Bryan Croom for a time owned the ferry landings on both sides of the river. Hardy Croom had earned a degree from the University of North Carolina in 1817. Rogers and Clark, *Croom Family and Goodwood Plantation*, 17–18, 56–57; Patrick, Allison, and Krakow, *Protected Plants of Georgia*.

3. R. M. Harper, "Phytogeographical Sketch," 149–50.

4. Harper did not identify *Illicium floridanum*, but I deduce it was that species because a group of UNC phytogeographers found it near Bristol in 1997. University of North Carolina, *Proceedings of the Sometimes Annual Phytogeographical Excursion to the Florida Panhandle*, http://www.bio.unc.edu/faculty/peet/lab/PEL/PGE/ (accessed June 9, 2007).

5. Institute for Systematic Botany, *Atlas of Florida Vascular Plants*, http://www.plantatlas.usf.edu; Sargent, *Manual* (1905), 563; Harper to C. S. Sargent, Jan. 23, 1910.

6. Harper's diaries are the source for much of this information.

7. Again, Harper's diaries are the source for much of this information.

8. Mueller, *Perilous Journeys*, 226–28.

9. Willoughby, *Across the Everglades*, 105.

10. R. M. Harper, "Botanical and Geological Trip," 107–26.

11. Owen, "History of Native Plant Communities," 52; Harper to C. S. Sargent, Feb. 3 and Feb. 26, 1910; Harper diary.

12. Federal Writers' Project, *WPA Guide to Florida*, 487; Harper to C. S. Sargent, March 23 and April 30, 1910; Sargent, *Manual* (1905), 666.

13. Harper diary.

14. John Hendley Barnhart to Harper, Sept. 20, 1910; Harper diary; Harper to C. S. Sargent, April 30, 1910.

15. Willoughby, *Across the Everglades*, 107–8; Harper diary; Harper to Sargent, April 30, 1910.

16. Harper diary.

17. Harper to C. S. Sargent, April 30, 1910.

18. C. S. Sargent to Harper, June 13, 1910.

19. R. M. Harper, "River-bank Vegetation."

20. Sargent, *Manual* (1922), 92; R. M. Harper, "*Tumion taxifolia* in Georgia," 121–22.

21. Bowers, *Sense of Place*, 21; Langenheim, "Early History and Progress," 6; Harper diary; Harper to John William Harshberger, Nov. 19, 1910; Collier Cobb to Harper, Nov. 4, 1910.

22. A. M. Henry to Harper, Aug. 24, 1911; Charles E. Rice to Harper, Dec. 5, 1910.

23. H. E. Wheeler to Harper, June 14 and Nov. 24, 1910.

24. Bertha Harper to Harper, Aug. 25, 1908; Harper diary; R. M. Harper, "Few More Pioneer Plants," 217; Harper to Clarence Knowlton, July 3, 1910; Harper to Forrest Shreve, Sept. 6, 1910; Florence Blake to Harper, July 15, 1910; Harper to Florence Blake, Nov. 3, 1910.

25. Eugene A. Smith to Harper, May 27, 1910; Hall and Robb, "Eugene Allen Smith," 16–17; W. S. Hoole Special Collections Library, communication with the author, April 28, 2004; Harper to E. B. Cooke, June 27, 1910; Edward Berry to Harper, May 6, 1910.

26. C. S. Sargent to Harper, Sept. 9, 1910; Eugene A. Smith to Harper, Sept. 16 and Oct. 14, 1910.

FIVE. Harper's Heartleaf

1. Barrington Moore to Harper, Sept. 9, 1920; Wilson Baker, interview with the author, April 30, 2004; C. S. Sargent to Harper, June 11, 1914; Harper diary; Herbert H. Smith to Harper, March 28, 1914; Eugene A. Smith to Harper, April 21, 1914.

2. Davis, "Lamarck's Evening Primrose."

3. De Vries's connections to the network of geologists and botanists in the United States demonstrate how small and close-knit the scientific community was in the first years of the twentieth century. De Vries met with E. W. Hilgard, Eugene Smith's mentor at the University of Mississippi, on his 1904 trip. He also

met with Nathaniel Britton in 1904, probably in June, when he accepted an honorary doctorate from Columbia University.

4. Van Bavel, *Hugo de Vries*, 36–38; Harper diary.

5. M. Keith Causey and Mark Bailey, "Cougar: Alabama's Native Lion," *Alabama Wildlife* (1999), http://www.easterncougarnet.org/Cougar-Alabama's%20Native%20Lion.htm (accessed July 4, 2004).

6. Harper photograph 201.6; Van Bavel, *Hugo de Vries*, 37–38; Harper diary.

7. Harper to Tom Dodd, Sept. 6, 1962.

8. Davis, "Lamarck's Evening Primrose."

9. *Hexastylis speciosa* R. M. Harper specimen sheet, New York Botanical Garden Virtual Herbarium.

10. *Hexastylis speciosa* R. M. Harper specimen sheet, U.S. National Herbarium.

11. Harper diary; U.S. National Herbarium specimen sheet; R. M. Harper, "New Heart-leaf," 80–81.

12. Olivia Holt to Harper, April 29, 1920, Dec. 7 and Aug. 31, 1921, May 19, 1922, Sept. 11 and Oct. 8, 1924; Harper to Olivia Holt, Oct. 10, 1924; Harper diary.

13. Harper to Bertha Harper, Aug. 2, Sept. 18, and Oct. 5, 1927; Harper to Mary Sue Wigley, Feb. 28, 1943.

14. Bertha Harper to Harper, July 9 and Sept. 6, 1928.

15. Harper diary; R. P. Brooks to Harper, July 31, 1928; Alfred Akerman to Harper, Oct. 30, 1928.

16. R. M. Harper, "Mrs. Bertha Tauber Harper."

17. Harper diary; R. M. Harper, "Natural Resources of Georgia."

18. R. M. Harper, "*Asarum* and *Hexastylis*," 71; U.S. National Herbarium; Harper diary. Ernest Holt later worked for the U.S. Soil Conservation Service, having been recommended by the naturalist Aldo Leopold. James N. Levitt, "Innovating on the Land: Conservation on the Working Landscape in American History," presented at "Private Lands, Public Benefits: A Policy Summit on Working Lands Conservation," National Governors' Association, Washington, D.C., March 16, 2001, http://www.nga.org/Files/pdf/INNOVLAND.pdf, 9–10 (accessed Feb. 13, 2007).

19. The Eppes family apparently was acquainted with Charles Sprague Sargent of Arnold Arboretum and communicated with him about Harper. Harper diary; Leon County, Florida Historical Markers Program, http://dhr.dos.state.fl.us/bhp/markers/markers.cfm?ID=leon) (accessed April 4, 2004); Cushman, "Introduction," xvi–xx.

20. Rembert W. Patrick, "Editorial Preface," vi; Eppes, *Through Some Eventful Years*, 19, 30, 38.

21. Harper diary; Susan Bradford Eppes to Harper, Oct. 16, 1921; Bertha Harper to Harper, June 24, 1922.

22. Harper diary; Herman Kurz to Harper, May 16, 1927; Kurz, "Physiographic Study," 79.

23. Harper diary.

24. William Marshall to Harper, Oct. 6, 1920; Addison Marshall to Harper, July 16, 1921.

25. John W. Harshberger to Harper, Aug. 28, 1921; Susan Bradford Eppes to Harper, Oct. 16, 1921.

26. This area was rich in the sort of history that Harper loved. Nearby Quincy had been a base for wealthy planters and politicians since Florida's territorial period; Chapman visited the town in 1840. Federal Writers' Project, *WPA Guide to Florida*, 441–42.

27. Harper to J. A. Avant, Sept. 17, 1927; Avant, *Davis-Wood Family*; Harper diary; David Alonzo Avant III, interview with the author, June 28, 2004; George Avant, interview with the author, June 28, 2004.

28. Louis S. Moore to Harper, Jan. 1, Jan. 26, March 9, and July 23, 1921; Susan Myrick, "Georgia Saga in Private Library," *Macon Telegraph*, March 16, 1930; Louis S. Moore to Harper, Jan. 26, 1921; "Cleaning of Old Vault at Court House Reveals Many Interesting Papers," *Thomasville (Georgia) Times-Enterprise*, Feb. 9, 1931.

29. Louis S. Moore to Harper, Nov. 12, 1921, March 27, 1922, April 8, 1927; Harper diary.

30. Harper photograph 48.

31. Harper photographs 150.1–5, 399.3–4, 413.1–2, 481.5, 481.6.

32. U.S. Geological Survey, "Hale County Soil Survey Map, 1931," http://alabamamaps.ua.edu/historicalmaps/counties/hale.html (accessed June 9, 2007); Harper photographs 482.2–6; Harper diary.

33. Harper photographs 503.5, 504.1–5.

34. Harper photograph 554.1.

35. Harper photographs 554.2–4; Harper diary.

36. The Weather Company, "The Weather Notebook," http://www.theweathercompany.com/cgi-bin/wxnotebook.pl; New York Botanical Garden Virtual Herbarium; Harper photographs 664.5, 697.4–6, 698.1, 698.2–6, 735.1–6, 752.4–6.

37. Harper photographs 754.1–4, 762.5–6, 825.1–6, 833.4–6, 880.4, 934.5; "Alfred Hatch Place at Arcola," National Register of Historic Places, National Register Information System, http://www.nps.gov/history/nr/research/mpslist.htm (accessed Sept. 3, 2007).

38. Harper to Olivia Holt, Sept. 8, 1927; Harper to J. W. Hendricks, Sept. 8, 1927; Harper to William F. Prouty, Sept. 10, 1927; Jones, *History and Work*, 39.

39. Walter B. Jones to the author, Jan. 28, 1975; H. E. Wheeler to Harper, April 20, 1927; R. M. Harper, "Condensed Autobiography of Roland M. Harper."

SIX. A Struggle for Synthesis

1. R. M. Harper, *Economic Botany of Alabama. Part I*; R. M. Harper, "Geography and Vegetation of Northern Florida"; R. M. Harper, "Vegetation Types"; R. M. Harper, "Geography of Central Florida"; R. M. Harper, "Natural Resources of Southern Florida."

2. Simpson, *Out of Doors in Florida*, 136–37, quoted in R. M. Harper, "Natural Resources of Southern Florida," 75.

3. R. M. Harper, "Natural Resources of Southern Florida," 75, 85, 133, 160.

4. R. M. Harper, "Forest Census of Alabama"; R. M. Harper, "Preliminary Soil Census"; R. M. Harper, "'Pocosin' of Pike County," 216–17.

5. R. M. Harper, "Five Hundred Miles"; R. M. Harper, "Cape Cod Vegetation"; R. M. Harper, "Changes in the Forest Area," 448; R. M. Harper, "Forests of Worcester County, Massachusetts," 120.

6. R. M. Harper, "Early Spring Aspects"; R. M. Harper, "A Botanical Cross-section of Northern Mississippi"; R. M. Harper, "Southern Louisiana from the Car-Window"; R. M. Harper, "Phytogeographical Notes"; R. M. Harper, "Some Undescribed Prairies in Northeastern Arkansas"; Forrest Shreve to Harper, Sept. 2, 1910; Bowers, *Sense of Place*, 81; R. M. Harper, "Geography and Vegetation of Northern Florida," 179; R. M. Harper, "Natural Resources of Southern Florida," 77.

7. George H. Shull to Harper, June 14, 1914; Charles F. Brooks to Harper, Nov. 19, 1920.

8. R. M. Harper, "Some Vanishing Scenic Features," 192, 193, 199, 200–201.

9. Ibid., 199, 200–201.

10. Ibid., 194, 196, 202.

11. R. M. Harper, "Some Vanishing Scenic Features," 204; R. M. Harper, "Description of the Natural Features."

12. Barrington Moore to Harper, Sept. 9, 1920; Richard E. Dodge to Harper, Sept. 22, 1920; Alan M. Bateman to Harper, Oct. 27, 1920; Herbert F. Schwarz to Harper, May 19, 1921.

13. R. M. Harper, *Forests of Alabama*; Robert C. Cook to Harper, July 27, 1928; Gilbert Grosvenor to Harper, Jan. 27, 1922.

14. "Roland M. Harper Articles Inventory" (Zach S. Henderson Library Special Collections, Georgia Southern University); R. M. Harper, "Condensed Autobiography of Roland M. Harper"; E. M. Fitton to Harper, Nov. 21, 1928.

15. J. Russell Smith to Harper, May 5, 1921; R. M. Harper, *Resources of Southern Alabama*; R. M. Harper, *Economic Botany of Alabama. Part 2*.

16. Harper to ? Cuthbert, Dec. 18, 1904; "Harper Breaks into the Army," *Flushing Journal* (1917), in Traber, "Harper Ancestry"; R. M. Harper, "Condensed Autobiography of R. M. Harper."

17. R. M. Harper, "High Living Standards in 'Black' Counties," *Montgomery Advertiser*, March 28, 1919; reprint in W. S. Hoole Collection.

18. E. C. Branson to Harper, Aug. 17, 1920; Edwin W. Kopf to Harper, Sept. 23, 1924; William L. Bray to Harper, Oct. 29, 1918; John W. Harshberger to Harper, Aug. 28, 1921.

19. G. G. Lang to Harper, April 27, 1921; Ellsworth Huntington to Harper, April 1, 1922, April 12, 1927, and July 26, 1928; Robin Harper, interview with the author, May 4, 2004.

20. R. M. Harper, "Optimism versus Science," 6, 8, 12.

21. J. Russell Smith to Harper, March 6, 1922; DeLoach, *Rambles with John Burroughs*; Bertha Harper to Harper, June 1, 1928; Simpson, *In Lower Florida Wilds*; Charles Torrey Simpson to Harper, April 7, 1921; Harper diary; Bertha Tauber Harper, *When I Was a Girl*.

22. New York Botanical Garden; Bowers, *Sense of Place*, 47, 91; Ernest Holt to Harper, Sept. 1, 1920, and Feb. 28, 1926; Tom Brahana, "The History of Mathematics at the University of Georgia," Department of Mathematics, University of Georgia, n.d., http://www.math.uga.edu/about_us/history.html (accessed June 8, 2007).

23. "Harper Eager for Journey to Wilds," *Brooklyn Eagle*, May 12, 1914, in Traber, "Harper Ancestry"; Francis Harper, "Mammals of the Okefinokee Swamp," 197; Francis Harper to Harper, Sept. 9, 1913; Harper diary; Harper to Marshall family, April 10, 1919.

24. Brauer, *There to Breathe the Beauty*.

25. Thomas A. Edison to Harper, May 17 and May 27, 1927; "John Kunkel Small Records, Biographical Note" (LuEsther T. Mertz Library, New York Botanical Garden).

26. Kurz, "New and Remarkable Habitat," 91.

SEVEN. A Devotee of Swamps

1. Harper to F. V. Coville, Dec. 12, 1901 (courtesy of C. T. Trowell); C. T. Trowell, "Exploring the Okefenokee: Roland M. Harper in the Okefenokee Swamp, 1902 & 1919" (manuscript, 1988, courtesy of C. T. Trowell), 3.

2. R. M. Harper, "Journal of a Botanical Exploration"; Harper to L. H. Dewey, Aug. 3, 1902 (courtesy of C. T. Trowell); R. M. Harper, "Visit to Okefinokee Swamp."

3. R. M. Harper, "Journal of a Botanical Exploration."

4. Harper's handwritten note, attached to the specimen sheet, is accessible in the Botanical Garden's online herbarium.

5. *Sphagnum portoricense* var. *glaucescens* Warnst., N.Y. Specimen ID 227033, New York Botanical Garden; Francis Harper, *Travels of William Bartram*, 339–

40; R. M. Harper, "Unique Climbing Plant," 21; R. M. Harper, "Catalogue of Plants."

6. Trowell, "Exploring the Okefenokee," 1.

7. R. M. Harper, "Journal of a Botanical Exploration."

8. Trowell, "Exploring the Okefenokee," 11; R. M. Harper, "Visit to Okefinokee Swamp," 156–57; R. M. Harper, "Unique Climbing Plant," 22.

9. R. M. Harper, "Some Neglected Aspects."

10. E. N. E. Klein to Harper, Dec. 23, 1908.

11. Marshall Avery Howe to Harper, Nov. 16, 1908; Foster and O'Keefe, *New England Forests through Time*, 64; Gifford Pinchot to Harper, Nov. 10, 1908; Herbert Osborn to Harper, Sept. 19, 1908.

12. R. M. Harper, "Tramping and Camping," 49; Harper diary; Willoughby, *Across the Everglades*; R. M. Harper, "Natural Resources of Southern Florida," 146.

13. Harper to Bertha Harper, April 11, 1909.

14. Rothra, *Florida's Pioneer Naturalist*, 91; Harper to Bertha Harper, April 11, 1909; Simpson, *In Lower Florida Wilds*; R. M. Harper, "Tramping and Camping," 10, 15 (manuscript in W. S. Hoole Special Collections); Harper to Bertha Harper, April 11, 1909.

15. R. M. Harper, "Tramping and Camping," 152.

16. Harper to Bertha Harper, April 11, 1909.

17. Small had visited the area a second time two months before Harper. He had invited Harper to accompany him, but for some reason Harper was unable to do so.

18. R. M. Harper, "Tramping and Camping" (manuscript, Hoole), 3, 18; R. M. Harper, "Tramping and Camping," 156.

19. Harper and Presley, *Okefinokee Album*, 5; R. M. Harper, "Okefinokee Swamp," 607, 614; Harper diary.

20. Francis Harper, "Mammals of the Okefinokee Swamp," 198–99, 229; Francis Harper to Harper, July 25, 1921.

21. Francis Harper, "Sojourn in the Primeval Okefinokee," 232; Francis Harper to Harper, May 5, 1934; Bertha Harper to Harper, Aug. 6, 1935, and May 25, 1939; C. T. Trowell, "The Search for the Ivory-billed Woodpecker in the Okefenokee Swamp" (manuscript, courtesy of C. T. Trowell, 1998).

EIGHT. On the Bartram Trail with Francis

1. Francis Harper, *Travels of William Bartram*, 17–18.

2. Roland noted as early as 1895 that Bartram had previously passed through an area of Georgia that he had explored. R. M. Harper, "Notes on the Flora," 333; Francis Harper, "Arthur Newlin Leeds"; Harper and Leeds, "Supplementary Chapter on *Franklinia alatamaha*"; Francis Harper to Harper, April 24, 1938.

3. Harper diary; Francis Harper to Harper, May 9, 1910; Harper to C. S. Sargent, May 10, 1910.

4. Francis Harper to Harper, Dec. 8, 1898, Feb. 25 and March 5, 1921.

5. Francis Harper, "Mammals of the Okefinokee Swamp," 208–12; Francis Harper to Harper, May 5, 1934. (Where Roland and Francis used the variant spelling "Okefinokee," I have preserved it.)

6. Francis Harper to Harper, April 30, May 7, and June 5, 1939; Francis Harper, *Travels of William Bartram*, ix; Charles C. Deam to Harper, June 4, 1939; John E. Drewry to Harper, June 7, 1939. Brannon wrote to Roland, "My dear Doctor Harper, . . . suppose you take Hamilton's 'Colonial Mobile' and perhaps therein you can determine the source of Bernard Romans's map which has come into your hands. I do not recall having seen one published as a separate, but the maps of that period are very secure in my mind." Peter A. Brannon to Harper, April 4, 1939.

7. Francis Harper to Harper, May 19, May 27, June 5, and June 12, 1939; Francis Harper to Clermont H. Lee, Aug. 9, 1964 (Georgia Southern University Special Collection). Unless otherwise noted, the facts of Roland and Francis's trip are drawn from Roland Harper's diary.

8. Francis Harper to Harper, June 5, 1939. Jones may have been in Montgomery to ask Governor Frank Dixon to authorize repayment of six thousand dollars Jones had personally contributed to purchase of land for Moundville Archeological Park in Hale County, which had been dedicated the month before. Garrison, "Walter B. Jones and Moundville," 16.

9. Francis Harper to Harper, May 19, 1939; Van Doren, *Travels of William Bartram* (1928); Francis Harper, *Travels of William Bartram*; Peter A. Brannon, *Montgomery Advertiser*, June 25, 1939.

10. William Bartram, in Francis Harper, *Travels of William Bartram*, 251–52. Francis noted that the surveyor Taitt estimated that the river was two hundred yards at the mound site. Francis Harper to Harper, June 5, 1939.

11. William Bartram, in Francis Harper, *Travels of William Bartram*, 252.

12. William Bartram, in Francis Harper, *Travels of William Bartram*, 252, 254, 402.

13. William Bartram, in Francis Harper, *Travels of William Bartram*, 254, 402, 626; Francis Harper, "Bartram Trail," 58; George M. Cheney to Harper, Oct. 3, 1911.

14. Harper to Clare Shackelford, Jan. 23, 1943; Francis Harper, *Travels of William Bartram*, 403.

15. William Bartram in Francis Harper, *Travels of William Bartram*, 255, 403. Roland went back to Little Escambia Creek in March 1948 and collected a specimen of the cedar for the New York Botanical Garden. N.Y. Specimen 16471, New York Botanical Garden.

16. William Bartram, in Francis Harper, *Travels of William Bartram*, 198.

Reflecting on the passage describing slaves cutting longleaf, Francis later briefly noted, with a striking lack of interest in African American culture, considering his fascination with Anglo-Saxon culture in the Okefenokee, "[T]o this day Negroes remain adept at improvising songs as they work." Francis Harper, *Travels of William Bartram*, 381.

17. Since flameflower is the only species in the *Macranthera* genus, Roland may actually have seen scarlet calamint (*Calamintha coccinea*), which in 1928 he himself pointed out resembled flameflower. Francis Harper, *Travels of William Bartram*, 516; USDA Plants Database.

18. William Bartram, in Francis Harper, *Travels of William Bartram*, 257.

19. William Bartram, in Francis Harper, *Travels of William Bartram*, 258; Harper to Wolfgang Wolf, July 1, 1939 (Wolf Collection, Auburn University Special Collections and Archives, hereafter cited as Wolf Collection); R. M. Harper, *Forests of Alabama*, 196.

20. Spornick, Cattier, and Greene, *Outdoor Guide to Bartram's Travels*, 329.

21. Edgar T. Wherry, "Distribution of the North American Pitcher Plants," in Mary Vaux Walcott, *Illustrations of North American Pitcher Plants*, cited in Francis Harper, *Travels of William Bartram*, 407. Wherry was a chemist, mineralogist, and early expert on uranium and radioactivity who also practiced and taught botany at the University of Pennsylvania. Francis Harper, "Bartram Trail," 59.

22. Weston, "Bird Casualties." Francis Harper could have met Francis Marion Weston, a native of Charleston, South Carolina, as early as 1912, when the men shared an interest in loggerhead shrikes, or 1913, when Francis apparently worked at the Federal Fisheries Laboratory at nearby Beaufort, North Carolina.

23. The federal government would give the national forest to the U.S. War Department for adaptation as Eglin Air Force Base almost exactly a year later. Eglin Air Force Base, "History," http://www.eglin.af.mil/history.htm (accessed April 3, 2005).

24. Beidler, "Caroline Lee Hentz's Long Journey."

25. Harper and Leeds, "Supplementary Chapter on *Franklinia alatamaha*," 3; Francis Harper, "Travels in Georgia and Florida," 132; Francis Harper, "Bartram Trail," 55, 59; Francis Harper, *Travels of William Bartram*, vi–vii.

26. American Association for the Advancement of Science, *Proceedings* (1938).

27. R. M. Harper, "Midsummer Journey," 375; Alfred Akerman to Harper, April 17, 1923.

28. Fernald, "Last Survivors."

29. Merritt Lyndon Fernald to Harper, June 27, 1939.

NINE. A Prophet for Fire

1. R. M. Harper, *Forests of Alabama*, 100; Schiff, *Fire and Water*, 98.

2. R. M. Harper, *Forests of Alabama*, 36–37.

3. H. H. Chapman to Harper, Oct. 8, 1942. The assistant state geologist, Stewart J. Lloyd, had already prepared a formal letter of transmittal of the monograph to Governor Frank M. Dixon.

4. Schiff, *Fire and Water*, 23, 109; R. M. Harper, "Phytogeographical Sketch," 32; Harper to J. H. Foster, August 1909 (W. S. Hoole Special Collections; notes courtesy of C. T. Trowell). Harper was in College Point between jobs, when Chapman was in Alabama, and they probably did not meet then.

5. R. M. Harper, "Tramping and Camping" (manuscript, W. S. Hoole Special Collections), 3.

6. R. M. Harper, "Relation of Climax Vegetation," 522–23.

7. Sargent, *Report on the Forests*, 491–93.

8. H. H. Chapman, "Forest Fires and Forestry," 512–17.

9. R. M. Harper, "Historical Notes," 19–20; R. M. Harper, "Defense of Forest Fires"; R. M. Harper, "Geography and Vegetation of North Florida," 185, 203.

10. R. M. Harper, "Relation of Climax Vegetation," 523; Long, *Florida Breezes*, 124, 284; Margaret Louise Chapman, introduction, xvii.

11. R. M. Harper, "Historical Notes," 13, 21.

12. R. M. Harper, "Natural Resources of Southern Florida," 82; R. M. Harper, "Historical Notes," 24; Schiff, 1962, *Fire and Water*, 31, 36; Small, *From Eden to Sahara*.

13. Stoddard, *Memoirs of a Naturalist*, 246–48; Johnson and Hale, "Historical Foundations of Prescribed Burning," 13; Pyne, *Fire in America*, 153–54. Roland's friends in Quincy, Florida, the Davis-Avant family, eventually converted their Gadsden County plantation into a quail hunting preserve, and grandson David Alonzo Avant III, who had a small publishing company, later obtained the rights to reissue Herbert Stoddard's manual on quail management.

14. Stoddard, *Memoirs of a Naturalist*, 246–48.

15. R. M. Harper, "Historical Notes," 23.

16. Harper to S. W. Greene, Dec. 24, 1931, and Sept. 15, 1932.

17. Kilgore, "From Fire Control to Fire Management," 2; Pyne, *Fire in America*, 170; R. M. Harper, "Fire and Forest"; Schiff, *Fire and Water*, 95–96; R. A. Bonninghausen, "Florida Forest Service and Controlled Burning," 49–50; H. H. Chapman, "Fire and Pines," 63–64.

18. Jones, "Roland McMillan Harper," 113; R. M. Harper, "Historical Notes," 25–26.

19. Johnson and Hale, "Historical Foundations of Prescribed Burning," 13; Crofton, "Herbert L. Stoddard, Sr."; Harper to Herbert L. Stoddard, Aug. 10, 1953 (H. L. Stoddard Collection, Tall Timbers Research Station, Tallahassee, Florida; cited hereafter as Stoddard Collection).

20. Herbert Stoddard to Lucien Harris, April 16, 1944 (Courtesy of Leon Neel, Thomasville, Georgia); Harper to Herbert L. Stoddard Sr., May 10, 1955 (Stoddard Collection); Herbert L. Stoddard Sr. to Harper, May 17, 1955 (Stoddard Collection).

21. Harper to Tom Dodd, May 4, 1962; Leon Neel, interview with the author, Greenwood Plantation, Thomasville, Georgia, April 30, 2004, cited hereafter as Neel interview.

22. Neel interview.

23. Tall Timbers Research Station, *Proceedings*, 184; Harper diary. Kurz acknowledged Harper's help in *Trees of Northern Florida*, which was published the same year: "The senior author expresses his thanks to Dr. Roland M. Harper, University of Alabama, who did much to help him learn the tree flora during his early years in the north Florida woods." Kurz and Godfrey, *Trees of Northern Florida*, vii.

24. R. M. Harper, "Historical Notes," 15–17, 19, 29.

25. Harper diary.

26. Schiff also incorrectly identified Harper as affiliated with Alabama Polytechnic Institute, the forerunner of Auburn University, apparently on the basis of oral history interviews with Chapman in the latter 1950s or 1960, when Chapman's memory could have been faulty. Schiff, *Fire and Water*, 18–25, 40; Stoddard, *Memoirs of a Naturalist*, 246–48.

TEN. A Kindred Spirit

1. Harper to Bertha Harper, Oct. 5, 1927.

2. Harper to Wolfgang Wolf, May 18, 1928, and March 4, 1934, Wolf Collection, Auburn University Special Collections and Archives.

3. Alabama Tornado Database (National Weather Service Birmingham Forecast Office, http://www.srh.noaa.gov/bmx/tornadoes/1932.html, accessed May 15, 2005).

4. Harper to Wolfgang Wolf, April 21, 1932, Wolf Collection.

5. Harper to Wolfgang Wolf, June 29, 1932, Wolf Collection.

6. Harper to Wolfgang Wolf, April 13, 1936, Wolf Collection.

7. Harper to Wolfgang Wolf, Dec. 27, 1939, Wolf Collection.

8. Harper to Wolfgang Wolf, April 25, 1928, Sept. 8, 1937, and March 14 and 22, 1938, Wolf Collection.

9. Harper to Wolfgang Wolf, July 19, 1940, Wolf Collection; Baldwin, "Roland M. Harper."

10. "William Willard Ashe" (University of North Carolina Herbarium, http://www.herbarium.unc.edu/Collectors/ashe.htm, accessed May 15, 2005); "*Magnolia magrophylla* Michx. Var. ashei (Weath.) D.L. Johnson," *Atlas of Florida Vascular Plants* (University of South Florida, http://www.plantatlas.usf.edu/main.asp?plantID=1241, accessed May 15, 2005); Harper to Wolfgang Wolf, April 27 and Oct. 22, 1931, Wolf Collection.

11. Harper to Wolfgang Wolf, May 26 and Sept. 8, 1937, Feb. 10, May 1, and Aug. 1, 1938, March 25, April 27, and May 4, 1939, Wolfe Collection; Wolf, "*Ery-*

thronium," 21; R. M. Harper, "Field Notes," Wolf Collection; Clarence Knowlton to Wolfgang Wolf, May 7, 1939, Wolf Collection.

12. Harper to Father Lambert, March 6 and May 5, 1940, Wolf Collection.

13. Wolf, "*Erythronium,*" 22; Clarence Knowlton to Wolfgang Wolf, May 6, 1940, Wolf Collection; Harper to Wolfgang Wolf, May 23 and Sept. 27, 1940, Wolf Collection.

14. Harper to Wolfgang Wolf, March 9 and May 20, 1941, Wolf Collection. (In 1963, C. R. Parks and J. W. Hardin reclassified Harper's dogtooth violet to a subspecies of *E. americanum,* USDA Plants Database.)

15. Harper to Wolfgang Wolf, Aug. 10, 1939, Wolf Collection.

ELEVEN. The Maniac

1. Harper to Bertha Harper, Aug. 28, 1924.

2. Bertha Harper to Harper, Sept. 6, 1908.

3. Penzel, *Obsessive-Compulsive Disorders.*

4. Ibid.; Christensen and Griest, "Challenge of Obsessive-Compulsive Hoarding"; Frost and Hartl, "Cognitive-behavioral Model of Compulsive Hoarding"; Frost, Krause, and Steketee, "Hoarding and Obsessive-compulsive Symptoms"; Frost and others, "Mood, Disability, and Personality Disorder."

5. Charles Darwin, quoted in Bruce, *Launching of Modern American Science,* 69–70; Harper to Florence Blake, Nov. 3, 1910; Harper diary; Frost, Krause, and Steketee, "Hoarding and Obsessive-compulsive Symptoms," 127.

6. David DeJarnette, interview with the author, March 19, 1975, hereafter DeJarnette interview.

7. R. M. Harper, "Natural Resources of Southern Florida," 76; Burton E. Livingston to Harper, Feb. 16, 1922.

8. M. L. Fernald to Harper, May 4, 1908.

9. Harper diary.

10. O. E. Baker to Harper, Nov. 9, 1928; Francis Harper to Harper, Oct. 16, 1928; Harper diary; Molly Harper, interview with the author, April 20, 2004; American Association for the Advancement of Science, *Proceedings, 1934;* Bertha Harper to Harper, June 18, 1935, and May 18, 1938.

11. Clarence Knowlton to Harper, March 21, 1899; Eugene A. Smith to Harper, Sept. 16, 1910.

12. Bertha Harper to Harper, July 28, 1921; Wilhelmina Harper to Harper, Oct. 12, 1921.

13. Susan Bradford Eppes to Harper, Oct. 16, 1921; Charles F. Brooks to Harper, Nov. 10, 1921; Louis S. Moore to Harper, Nov. 12, 1921.

14. E. Burton Cooke to Harper, Dec. 28, 1921; Walter B. Jones to Harper, Feb. 5, 1922; R. J. H. DeLoach to Harper, Feb. 9, 1922; Stuart C. Gager to Harper, Feb. 24, 1914; Charles H. Gunter to Harper, March 7, 1922.

15. DeJarnette interview; Robin Harper, interview with the author, May 4, 2004. (Around this time, Harper paid my teenage mother, Anne Findley, to help him clip articles, sort them by topic, and paste them into scrapbooks.)

16. Bertha Harper to Harper, May 18, 1938; Francis Harper to Harper, April 24, 1938; "History of the Redwood City Public Library" (Redwood City [California] Public Library, www.rcpl.info/services/library_history.html, accessed Dec. 9, 2004); Harper diary (loose entry).

17. Harper diary.

18. R. M. Harper, "Notes on Ann Tower White's Ancestry."

19. "Maniac Book" nos. 1 and 2, Hoole Collection; Bertha Harper to Harper, Feb. 22, 1922.

20. The originals or copies of the cartoons and Harper's comments about them are in Harper Scrapbooks nos. 1 and 2, Hoole Collection.

21. Bertha Harper to Harper, Feb. 22, 1922, and Aug. 1, 1928.

22. Bertha Harper to Harper, Feb. 22, 1922, Aug. 1, 1928, Aug. 26, 1935, and May 18, 1938.

23. Bertha Harper to Harper, Aug. 1, Sept. 6, and Sept. 27, 1928; R. M. Harper, "Mrs. Bertha Tauber Harper: A Tribute," in Traber, "Harper Ancestry."

24. Bertha Harper to Harper, May 18, 1938.

25. Bertha Harper to Harper, June 1, 1928, and May 25 and June 8, 1939.

26. Bertha Harper to Harper, March 29, 1922; Wilhelmina Harper to Harper, March 25, 1921, and April 11, 1922.

27. Bertha Harper to Harper, July 24, 1935; Traber, "Harper Ancestry"; "In Memoriam: William Harper."

28. Bertha Harper to Harper, July 28, 1921, Jan. 13, 1922, May 18, 1938, July 24 and Aug. 6, 1935; Harper to H. E. Wheeler, June 23, 1910; Otto Harper to Harper, Sept. 28, 1914, Nov. 29, 1920, and April 13, 1921; Wilhelmina Harper to Harper, Feb. 22 and May 9, 1921; Traber, "Harper Ancestry."

29. Bertha Harper to Harper, June 18 and Aug. 6, 1935.

30. Mary Ella Harper to Harper, July 20, 1910; Bertha Harper to Harper, Aug. 28, 1911, June 24, 1922, April 23, 1927; Otto Harper to Harper, July 23, 1919; Jean Harper to Harper, April 6, 1927.

31. Bertha Harper to Harper, July 9, 1928 and June 29, 1939; Wallace Stephen, "Charlotte Woman Organizes Poetry Society of the South," *Charlotte Observer*, Aug. 5, 1928, 2; "Inventory of Alice McFarland Papers" (Manuscripts Department, Library of the University of North Carolina at Chapel Hill).

32. David Harper, personal communication with the author, April 3, 2004; Palmer, "Francis Harper"; Delma E. Presley, in Harper and Presley, *Okefinokee Album*, x; Francis Harper to Harper, March 5, 1921; Bertha Harper to Harper, May 18, 1938.

33. David Harper, personal communication with the author, April 3, 2004;

Francis Harper, "Mammals of the Okefinokee Swamp," 261; Robin Harper, interview with the author, May 4, 2004; Palmer, "Francis Harper," 737–38.

34. "History of the Redwood City Public Library"; Bertha Harper to Harper, June 11, 1928, and June 29, 1939.

35. Bruce, *Launching of Modern American Science*, 69–70.

TWELVE. A Sacrifice to Science

1. Harper diary; Addison Marshall to Harper, March 5, 1922.

2. Harper to Bertha Harper, Aug. 8, 1924, and Oct. 5, 1927.

3. Harper cartoon, Hoole Collection; Harper cartoons, Sept. 12, 1934, Nov. 7 and Nov. 3, 1933, private collection of the author; Christmas card in private collection of Anne Findley Shores.

4. Harper photograph, private collection of the author; Bertha Harper to Harper, July 10, 1935.

5. Harper diary; Traber, "Harper Ancestry"; R. M. Harper, "Granite Outcrop Vegetation in Alabama"; Florence Blake to Harper, July 15, 1910; Harper to J. Walter Hendricks, July 5, 1927; Bertha Harper to Harper, May 22, 1927.

6. Bertha Harper to Harper, April 23, 1927, March 9 and June 24, 1922; Franziska Tauber to Harper, Dec. 3, 1936.

7. Bertha Harper to Harper, Aug. 6, 1921, Sept. 6, 1928, and Sept. 19, 1936; Wilhelmina Harper to Harper, July 24, 1910; Otto Tauber to Harper, April 6, 1914; Harper diary; Otto Harper to Harper, Sept. 28, and Oct. 9, 1914; Helen Harper to Harper, Aug. 30, 1928.

8. Jean Harper to Harper, April 6, 1927.

9. Francis Harper to Harper, Oct. 16, 1928; Bertha Harper to Harper, Jan. 4 and Jan. 13, 1922, and May 22, 1927.

10. Wilhelmina Harper to Harper, Feb. 1, 1922; Bertha Harper to Harper, May 18, 1938.

11. Harper to Jean Broadhurst, April 30, 1910; Harper to Forrest Shreve, March 25, 1910; Harper to Bertha Harper, Aug. 28, 1924; Bertha Harper to Harper, Sept. 6, 1928.

12. Miller, *Dark Eden*, 11; Henry David Thoreau, quoted in Miller, *Dark Eden*, 214–15; Thomas Wentworth Higginson, quoted in Miller, *Dark Eden*, 54–55; Thomas Moore, quoted in Miller, *Dark Eden*, 29–30.

13. Larson, *Sex, Race, and Science*, 43; Britton, "Lucien Marcus Underwood"; Edward L. K? to Harper, November 1908; Francis Harper to Harper, March 5, 1921.

14. Bertha Tauber Harper, *When I Was a Girl*, 27; Bertha Harper to Harper, June 24, 1922.

15. P. F. Finner to Harper, Oct. 17, 1937; Harper diary; Harper photograph 786.6; R. M. Harper, "*Croomia* a Member of the Appalachian flora"; R. M.

Harper, unpublished notes, Hoole Collection; "Harper Articles Inventory," Georgia Southern University.

16. De Silva and Rachman, *Obsessive Compulsive Disorder*, 15; Francis Harper to Harper, Oct. 16, 1928.

17. Ludmerer, *Genetics and American Society*, 23; Selden, *Inheriting Shame*, 2; Larson, *Sex, Race, and Science*, 19; Smith, *Eugenic Assault on America*, 2; Daniel J. Kevles, *In the Name of Eugenics: Genetics and the Uses of Human Heredity* (New York: Alfred A. Knopf, 1985), quoted in Larson, "Belated Progress," 47; Larson "Breeding Better Georgians."

18. Larson, *Sex, Race, and Science*, 23, 29; Black, *War against the Weak*, 32–33, 93; Harper to Charles B. Davenport, Sept. 2, 1925 (courtesy of American Philosophical Society).

19. Ludmerer, *Genetics and American Society*, 46; Larson, "Belated Progress," 47.

20. Traber, "Harper Ancestry."

21. Traber, "Harper Ancestry."

22. Traber, "Harper Ancestry."

23. Bertha Harper to Harper, July 24, 1935, May 18, 1938, and June 8, 1939; Otto Harper to Harper, May 26, 1910; Robin Harper, interview with the author, May 4, 2004.

24. Foster, *Ghosts of the Confederacy*, 39; R. M. Harper, "Some Vanishing Scenic Features," 202; Flynn, *White Land, Black Labor*, 156; Grantham, *South in Modern America*, 32–34; Rogers and others, *Alabama*, 283.

25. Grantham, *South in Modern America*, 104; Larson, 1995, *Sex, Race, and Science*, 43; Eppes, *Through Some Eventful Years*, 27, 18; Fred Arthur Bailey, "E. Merton Coulter (1890–1981)," *The New Georgia Encyclopedia* (2003), http://www.georgiaencyclopedia.org/nge/Home.jsp (accessed Jan. 4, 2007); Harper diary; Woodward, *Burden of Southern History*, 9–10.

26. Harper diary; Charles H. Gunter to Harper, Aug. 17, 1921.

27. Mehl, *Brief History*; Harper diary.

28. R. M. Harper, "Geography of Central Florida," 235–39; Leon F. Whitney to Harper, May 2 and May 13, 1927; Selden, *Inheriting Shame*, 44. Harper also was elected that year to the National Council of the National Economic League, to represent the state of Florida. The league's aim was to give "expression to the informed and disinterested opinion of the country regarding economic, social, and political problems." The executive council of the league included Charles E. Hughes, the Republican presidential nominee in 1916 and secretary of state from 1921 to 1925; Frank O. Lowden, a former governor of Illinois; James Rowland Angell, president of Yale University; the merchant Edward A. Filene; Charles M. Schwab, chairman of the board of Bethlehem Steel Corporation; Nicholas Murray Butler, president of Columbia University; and A. Lawrence Lowell, president of Harvard University. National Economic League to Harper, June 21, 1927.

29. Davenport and Hubbs, "Roland Harper," 25; Larson, *Sex, Race, and Science*, 100; R. M. Harper, 1930, "Optimism versus Science." The *Tuscaloosa News* reported on April 20, 1945, that my grandfather, Herbert L. Findley, urged the Tuscaloosa County delegation in the Alabama legislature to support compulsory sterilization for the mentally ill and mentally retarded. Findley told the delegation, " 'There are at present a number of girls who are patients at the Partlow State School who could be released from the institution but for the threat that they might bear children.' As inferior court judge, Judge Findley has to deal with numerous cases involving juvenile delinquency and other domestic problems." Findley made these comments just five days before Soviet troops surrounded Berlin and ten days before Hitler committed suicide.

30. Harper to W. W. Keen, June 30, 1926.

31. "George Harrison Shull Papers," *A Guide to the Genetic Collections*, American Philosophical Society, www.amphilsoc.org/library/guides/glass/shull.htm (accessed Jan. 4, 2007); Shull, "Duplicate Genes"; George H. Shull to Harper, May 10, 1927.

32. Charles B. Davenport to Harper, Sept. 28 and Nov. 14, 1928; Ludmerer, *Genetics and American Society*, 27.

33. Harper diary.

34. C. C. Peters, *Foundations of Educational Sociology* (New York: Macmillan, 1930), quoted in Selden, *Inheriting Shame*, 93; Harper to Charles B. Davenport, Sept. 2, 1925 (courtesy of American Philosophical Society); Harper to R. J. H. DeLoach, June 24, 1927; J. Walter Hendricks to Harper, June 12, 1923; Harper to Bertha Harper, July 16, 1927.

35. "Harper Articles Inventory," Georgia Southern University; Harper to R. J. H. DeLoach, July 13, 1933, Georgia Southern University Special Collections; Harper to Mary Sue Wigley, March 7, 1943; R. M. Harper, Letter to the editor, *Tuscaloosa News*, Oct. 12, 1933, Hoole Collection.

36. Harper to George Shull, March 8, 1943.

37. Mathias, "Studies in the Umbelliferae V.," 244.

THIRTEEN. Harper's Love-vine

1. Harper to Mary Sue Wigley, March 7, 1943. Much of the material in this chapter is taken from Harper's diary.

2. Harper to Mary Sue Wigley, Feb. 20, 1943.

3. Harper to Bertha Harper, March 7, 1943; Harper to Mary Sue Wigley, March 7 and 12, 1943.

4. Harper to Mary Sue Wigley, April 8, 1943.

5. Harper to Mary Sue Wigley, Feb. 28 and April 11, 1943; Harper to Edna Shelton, April 15, 1943.

6. Looking through references after returning to Tuscaloosa, Harper found

his memory was incorrect: Boynton actually discovered the species of trillium on Sand Mountain near Collinsville in 1901. U.S. National Herbarium Type Specimen 00784900, http://ravenel.si.edu/botany/types//fullRecords.cfm?myFamily (accessed April 30, 2005); Harper to Wolfgang Wolfe, May 12, 1943.

7. Harper to Mary Sue Wigley, April 20, 1943.

8. Harper to Mr. and Mrs. J. B. Gregory, April 21, 1943; Harper diary; Harper to Bertha Harper, April 22, 1943.

9. Harper to Bertha Harper, April 22, 1943; Harper to Mrs. F. C. Stewart, May 12, 1943; Harper to Wolfgang Wolf, May 12, 1943, Wolf Collection.

10. Harper photograph 860.1.

11. Harper to Wolfgang Wolf, July 3, 1943, Wolf Collection.

12. Mary Sue Wigley Harper to the author, Jan. 3, 1972; Harper photograph 970.5.

13. Robin Harper, interview with the author, May 4, 2004; Harper photographs 927.1, 934.5.

14. Harper to Wolfgang Wolf, March 21, 1944, Wolf Collection.

15. Harper to Wolfgang Wolf, Sept. 7, 1944, and March 7 and June 15, 1945, Wolf Collection; R. M. Harper, "Fifth Species of *Erythronium*."

16. Harper to George H. Shull, March 8, 1943.

17. Robert Thorne, interview with the author, Dec. 17, 2004; Wilson, *Naturalist*, 108–13; "University of Alabama Herbaria," *http://www.as.ua.edu/biology/scf/Herbarium.html* (accessed April 30, 2005).

18. Traber, "Harper Ancestry"; Harper to Father Lambert, July 31, 1948, Wolf Collection; Harper to Wolfgang Wolf, July 23, 1949, Wolf Collection; "Collectors of the University of North Carolina Herbarium," University of North Carolina Herbarium, http://www.herbarium.unc.edu/Collectors/wolf.htm (accessed Feb. 13, 2005); "Papers of Merritt Lyndon Fernald, 1893–1934: A Guide," Gray Herbarium Library, Harvard University Herbaria; Bowers, *Sense of Place*, 54–55.

19. H. H. Chase to Harper, Aug. 9, 1950; George S. Counts to Harper, Jan. 23, 1951; Robert Thorne, telephone interview with the author, Dec. 17, 2004.

20. B. E. Dahlgren to Harper, Sept. 19, 1948; letters from V. L. Corey to Harper, Hoole Collection; *Chrysopsis lanuginose* Specimen Sheet, New York Botanical Garden; Mary Sue Wigley Harper to the author, Jan. 27, 1975; Charles C. Deam to Harper, July 29, 1950.

21. Much of the material about the trip with Wilbur Duncan is from Harper's diary.

22. Duncan and Venard had rambled Georgia together before; they made the first Georgia discovery of a rare coastal plain species, Oconee bells (*Shortia galacifolia*) in Rabun County in 1949. That species was the only one in a genus otherwise found in eastern Asia. Patrick, Allison, and Krakow, *Protected Plants of Georgia*.

23. Godfrey and Wooten, *Aquatic and Wetland Plants*, 493.

24. Wilbur Duncan collection book (courtesy of the University of Georgia Herbarium).

25. Duncan collection book.

26. Ibid.

27. Harper diary.

28. Harper to Herbert L. Stoddard Sr., Aug. 10, 1953, Stoddard Collection.

29. Francis Harper, "Bartram Trail"; Van Doren, *Travels of William Bartram*, with an introduction by John Livingston Lowes (1940) ; Francis Harper, "Travels in Georgia and Florida," 133.

30. Francis Harper, *Travels of William Bartram*, x, 341.

31. Ibid., xii.

32. Ibid., 422.

33. R. M. Harper, "Studying the Georgia Flora," 3.

34. Mrs. Charles Cotton Harrold to Clermont Lee, Aug. 1, 1958 (courtesy of Clermont Lee).

35. Clermont H. Lee to Richard W. Lighty, Jan. 14, 1994, Georgia Southern University Special Collection; Clermont H. Lee to the author, March 24, 2004.

36. *Scirpus fontinalis*, N.Y. 51639, New York Botanical Garden, http://sweet gum.nybg.org/vh/specimen.php?irn=164882 (accessed Jan. 5, 2005); Alfred E. Schuyler to Harper, March 8, 1963, and Feb. 24, 1964 (courtesy of Alfred E. Schuyler); Harper to Alfred E. Schuyler, March 12, 1963, and March 2, 1964 (courtesy of Alfred E. Schuyler); Schuyler, "Notes on Five Species"; Harper to Alfred E. Schuyler, Oct. 7, 1964 (courtesy of Alfred E. Schuyler).

37. Blomquist, "Revision of *Hexastylis* of North America," 256.

38. This section is based primarily on Harper's diary.

39. Harper to Florence Blake, June 20, 1919.

40. Jean Sherwood Harper to Clermont Lee, Feb. 15, 1973 (courtesy of Clermont Lee).

41. Ewan, "Roland McMillan Harper"; Baldwin, "Roland M. Harper," 235.

42. Marie Parsons, "Legacy to a 'Beloved' Wife," *Tuscaloosa News*, Aug. 14, 1966.

43. She left her own papers to Auburn University in Alabama.

44. Parsons, "Legacy to a 'Beloved' Wife."

45. "*Scirpus georgianus*," Missouri Botanical Garden Nomenclatural Data Base, http://mobot.mobot.org/cgi-bin/search_vast (accessed Jan. 5, 2005). Describing an expedition to Nova Scotia in the journal *Rhodora* in 1920, Fernald had erroneously determined that Harper's species should be a variety of *Scirpus atrovirens*. While reporting Georgia bulrush on the shore of Grand Lake, Fernald renamed Harper's species as *S. atrovirens* var. *georgianus*, and stated that it was "a common New England bulrush." Fernald, "Gray Herbarium Expedition

to Nova Scotia"; *Scirpus georgianus*, N.Y. Specimen 51641, New York Botanical Garden, http://sweetgum.nybg.org/vh/specimen.php?irn=89807 (accessed Jan. 5, 2005).

46. Schuyler, "Taxonomic Revision"; Alfred E. Schuyler, communication with the author, Dec. 28, 2004; USDA Plants Database.

FOURTEEN. Harper's Beauty

1. Angus Gholson, interview with the author, June 22, 2004.

2. McDaniel, *The Genus* Sarracenia *(Sarraceniaceae).*

3. McDaniel, *"Harperocallis."*

4. McDaniel, *"Harperocallis,"* 36.

5. Owen, "History of Native Plant Communities," 54–58; Engstrom, Kirkman, and Mitchell, "Natural History of the Fire Forest"; Utech and Anderson, "Genus *Harperocallis*"; U.S. Fish and Wildlife Service, *Endangered and Threatened Species*; Leonard and Baker, "Additional Populations of *Harperocallis flava* McDaniel"; Wilson Baker, personal communication with the author, Nov. 7, 2004.

6. U.S. National Herbarium; Bridges and Orzell, "Rediscovery of *Rhynchospora solitaria*"; Sheridan, Orzell, and Bridges, "Powerline Easements," 451.

7. Holifield, "True Grit"; Patrick, Allison, and Krakow, *Protected Plants of Georgia.*

8. Engstrom and others, "Natural History of the Fire Forest," 16.

9. The State of Florida considered the Panama City crayfish a "species of special concern" under the terms of the state Endangered Species Act. A species discovered by H. H. Hobbs Jr. in 1938, the crayfish had only been found within a forty-three-square-mile area of Bay County and had not been seen in years.

10. Edwin J. Keppner and Lisa A. Keppner, interview with the author, June 2004.

11. Clewell, *Guide to the Vascular Plants*, 177.

12. Chafin, *Field Guide.*

13. Loran C. Anderson, personal communication with the author, November 2004.

14. Leonard and Baker, "Additional Populations of *Harperocallis flava* McDaniel," 151.

15. The U.S. Fish and Wildlife Service observes that the leaves of Harper's beauty are "almost identical to those of *Narthecium* and some species of *Tofieldia*, and in the vegetative condition identification would be difficult, even if the plants could be distinguished from surrounding grasses." U.S. Fish and Wildlife Service, *Endangered and Threatened Species*, http://www.fws.gov/endangered/i/q/saqOq.htm (accessed Sept. 5, 2007).

16. R. M. Harper, "Geography of Central Florida," 79.

17. Delcourt, "Roland McMillan Harper, Recorder of Early Twentieth-century Landscapes in the South," 37.

Epilogue

1. Edward O. Wilson, interview with the author, Oct. 11, 1995.

2. Dobbs, *Reef Madness*.

3. Jones, "Roland McMillan Harper," 113.

4. R. M. Harper, "Phytogeographical Sketch," 40.

5. "Special Concern Plant Species in Georgia," Georgia Department of Natural Resources, http://georgiawildlife.dnr.state.ga.us/ (accessed June 9, 2007:); Flora of North America Editorial Committee, *Flora of North America*; International Carnivorous Plant Society, "*Sarracenia minor.*"

6. Frankie Snow, "Broxton Rocks Preserve Design," manuscript, 2004, courtesy of Frankie Snow.

7. Mayr, *Growth of Biological Thought*, 395–97.

8. Leon Neel, interview with the author, April 30, 2004.

9. Bowers, *Sense of Place*, 149–51.

10. Mayr, *Growth of Biological Thought*, 623–24.

11. Wilson, *Naturalist*, 323.

12. Wilson, *Naturalist*, 315–21. William D. Hamilton, "The Genetical Evolution of Social Behaviour," *Journal of Theoretical Biology* 7 (1964), 1–52, quoted in Buss, *Evolutionary Psychology*, 12.

13. George C. Williams, *Adaptation and Natural Selection; A Critique of Some Current Evolutionary Thought* (Princeton, N.J.: Princeton University Press, 1966), quoted in Buss, *Evolutionary Psychology*, 12–32.

14. R. M. Harper, "Some Problems of Eugenics."

BIBLIOGRAPHY

American Association for the Advancement of Science. *Proceedings of the American Association for the Advancement of Science, 1905, New Orleans, Louisiana*. Washington, D.C.: American Association for the Advancement of Science, 1905.

———. *Proceedings of the American Association for the Advancement of Science, Berkeley, California, 1934*. Washington, D.C.: American Association for the Advance of Science, 1934.

———. *Proceedings of the American Association for the Advancement of Science, Richmond, Virginia, 1938*. Washington, D.C.: American Association for the Advance of Science, 1938.

Anderson, L. C. "Stalking the Pygmy Bladderwort (*Utricularia olivacea*), Lentibulariaceae." *Carnivorous Plant Newsletter* 29 (2000): 73–74.

Avant, Fenton Garnett Davis. *The Davis-Wood Family of Gadsden County, Florida, and Their Forebears*. Easley, S.C.: Southern Historical Press, 1979.

Ayers, Edward L. *The Promise of the New South: Life after Reconstruction*. New York: Oxford University Press, 1992.

Baldwin, J. T., Jr. "Roland M. Harper (1878–1966) and *Jamesianthus alabamensis*." *Bulletin of the Torrey Botanical Club* 96 (1969): 232–35.

Barry, John M. *The Great Influenza: The Epic Story of the Deadliest Plague in History*. New York: Penguin, 2004.

Beidler, Philip D. "Caroline Lee Hentz's Long Journey." *Alabama Heritage* (Winter 2005): 24–31.

Berg, Paul, and Maxine Singer. *George Beadle, an Uncommon Farmer: The Emergence of Genetics in the 20th Century*. Cold Spring Harbor, N.Y.: Cold Spring Harbor Laboratory, 2003.

Black, Edwin. *War against the Weak: Eugenics and America's Campaign to Create a Master Race*. New York: Four Walls Eight Windows, 2003.

Blomquist, H. L. "A Revision of *Hexastylis* of North America." *Brittonia* 8 (1957): 255–81.

Boney, F. N. *A Walking Tour of the University of Georgia*. Athens: University of Georgia Press, 1989.

Bonninghausen, R. A. "The Florida Forest Service and Controlled Burning." In Tall Timbers Research Station, *Proceedings*, 43–52.

Bowers, Janice Emily. *A Sense of Place: The Life and Work of Forrest Shreve.* Tucson: University of Arizona Press, 1988.

Brauer, Norman. *There to Breathe the Beauty.* Dalton, Pa.: Norman Brauer Publications, 1995.

Bridges, E. L., and S. L. Orzell. "The Rediscovery of *Rhynchospora solitaria* Harper (Cyperaceae) in Georgia." *Phytologia* 72 (1992): 369–72.

Britton, Nathaniel L. "Lucien Marcus Underwood." *Columbia University Quarterly* (December 1907): 67–69.

Bruce, Robert V. *The Launching of Modern American Science, 1846–1876.* Ithaca, N.Y.: Cornell University Press, 1987.

Buss, D. M. *Evolutionary Psychology: The New Science of the Mind.* Boston: Allyn and Bacon, 1999.

Butler, Francis Gould. *A History of Farmington, Franklin County, Maine, from the Earliest Explorations to the Present Time, 1776–1885.* 2nd ed. Somersworth, N.H.: New England History Press, 1885.

Chafin, Linda G. *Field Guide to the Rare Plants of Florida.* Tallahassee: Florida Natural Areas Inventory, 2000.

Chapman, Alvan Wentworth. *Flora of the Southern United States: Containing an abridged description of the flowering plants and ferns of Tennessee, North and South Carolina, Georgia, Alabama, Mississippi, and Florida, arranged according to the natural system.* 3rd ed. Cambridge, Mass.: Cambridge Botanical Supply Company, 1897.

Chapman, H. H. "Fire and Pines: A Realistic Appraisal of the Role of Fire in Reproducing and Growing Southern Pines." *American Forests* 50 (1944): 62–64, 91–95.

———. "Forest Fires and Forestry in the Southern States." *American Forests* 18 (1912): 510–17.

Chapman, Margaret Louise. Introduction to *Florida Breezes; or, Florida, New and Old,* by Ellen Call Long. Gainesville: University of Florida Press, 1962.

Christensen, Daniel D., and John H. Griest. "The Challenge of Obsessive-Compulsive Hoarding." *CNS Spectrums* 5 (2000): 79–86.

Clay, James W., Paul D. Escott, Douglas M. Orr Jr., and Alfred W. Stuart. *Land of the South.* Birmingham, Ala.: Oxmoor House, 1989.

Clements, Frederic Edwards. *Research Methods in Ecology.* Lincoln, Neb.: University Publishing, 1905.

Clewell, Andre F. *Guide to the Vascular Plants of the Florida Panhandle.* Gainesville: University of Florida Press, 1988.

Clinton, Matthew W. *Matt Clinton's Scrapbook.* Tuscaloosa, Ala.: Portals, 1979.

Cogbill, Charles, David Foster, John O'Keefe, and David Orwig. *Dynamics of Old-growth Forests on Wachusett Mountain (Princeton, MA).* Cambridge, Mass.: Harvard University Harvard Forest, 1997.

Cowdrey, Albert E. *This Land, This South: An Environmental History,* Revised ed. Lexington, Kentucky: University of Kentucky Press, 1996.

Crofton, Elizabeth W. "Herbert L. Stoddard, Sr.: King of the Fire Forest." In Georgia Wildlife Federation, *Fire Forest*, 40–41.

Cushman, Joseph D., Jr. Introduction to Eppes, *Through Some Eventful Years.*

Davenport, L. J. "Nevius and *Neviusia.*" *Alabama Heritage* 57 (2000): 46–48.

Davenport, L. J., and G. Ward Hubbs. "Roland Harper, Alabama Botanist and Social Critic: A Biographical Sketch and Bibliography." *Alabama Museum of Natural History Bulletin* 17 (1995): 25–45.

Davis, Bradley Moore. "Was Lamarck's Evening Primrose (*Oenothera Lamarckiana* Seringe) a Form of *Oenothera grandiflora* Solander?" *Bulletin of the Torrey Botanical Club* 39 (1912): 519–33.

De Silva, Padmal, and Stanley Rachman. *Obsessive Compulsive Disorder: The Facts.* New York: Oxford University Press, 1992.

Delcourt, H. R. "Roland McMillan Harper, Recorder of Early Twentieth-Century Landscapes in the South." *Pioneer America* 10 (1978): 36–50.

DeLoach, R. J. H. *Rambles with John Burroughs.* Boston: R. G. Badger, 1912.

Dobbs, David. *Reef Madness: Charles Darwin, Alexander Agassiz, and the Meaning of Coral.* New York: Pantheon Books, 2005.

Engstrom, R. Todd, L. Katherine Kirkman, and Robert J. Mitchell. "The Natural History of the Fire Forest." In Georgia Wildlife Federation, *Fire Forest: Longleaf Pine-Wiregrass Ecosystem*, 5–17.

Eppes, Susan Bradford. *Through Some Eventful Years.* 3rd ed. 1845. Reprint, Gainesville: University of Florida Press, 1968.

Ewan, Joseph. "Roland McMillan Harper (1878–1966)." *Bulletin of the Torrey Botanical Club* 95 (1968): 390–93.

Federal Writers' Project. *The WPA Guide to Florida.* New York: Pantheon, 1939.

Fernald, M. L. "The Gray Herbarium Expedition to Nova Scotia, 1920." *Rhodora* 23 (1921): 89–111, 130–52, 153–71, 184–95, 223–45, 257–78, 284–300.

———. "Last Survivors in the Flora of Tidewater Virginia." *Rhodora* 41 (1939): 465–504. Cited in "Fernald's Ecstacy! Fernald's Chagrin!" by Cecil C. Frost and Lytton J. Musselman, in *From Blue Ridge to Barrier Islands: An Audubon Naturalist Reader*, edited by J. Kent Minichiello and Anthony W. White, 241–48. Baltimore: Johns Hopkins University Press, 1997.

Flamming, Douglas. *Creating the Modern South: Millhands and Managers in Dalton, Georgia, 1884–1984.* Chapel Hill: University of North Carolina Press, 1992.

Flynn, Charles L. *White Land, Black Labor: Caste and Class in Late Nineteenth-Century Georgia.* Baton Rouge: Louisiana State University Press, 1983.

Flynt, Wayne. *Poor but Proud: Alabama's Poor Whites.* Tuscaloosa: University of Alabama Press, 1989.

Flora of North America Editorial Committee, eds. *Flora of North America North of Mexico.* New York: Flora of North America Editorial Committee, 1993–.

Foster, D. R. *Thoreau's Country: Journey through a Transformed Landscape.* Cambridge, Mass.: Harvard University Press, 1999.

Foster, D. R., and J. F. O'Keefe. *New England Forests through Time.* Cambridge, Mass.: Harvard University Press, 2000.

Foster, Gaines M. *Ghosts of the Confederacy: Defeat, the Lost Cause, and the Emergence of the New South.* New York: Oxford University Press, 1987.

Frost, R. O., and T. L. Hartl. "A Cognitive-behavioral Model of Compulsive Hoarding." *Behaviour Research and Therapy* 34 (1996): 341–50.

Frost, R. O., M. S. Krause, and G. Steketee. "Hoarding and Obsessive-compulsive Symptoms." *Behavior Modification* 20 (1996): 116–32.

Frost, R. O., G. Steketee, L. Williams, and R. Warren. "Mood, Disability, and Personality Disorder Symptoms in Hoarding, Obsessive Compulsive Disorder, and Control Subjects." *Behavior Research and Therapy* 38 (2000): 1071–82.

Garrison, Ellen. "Walter B. Jones and Moundville." *Alabama Heritage* (Summer 2001): 6–17.

Georgia Wildlife Federation. *The Fire Forest: Longleaf Pine-Wiregrass Ecosystem.* Covington: Georgia Wildlife Federation, 2001.

Gleason, H. A. "Contributions of the Torrey Botanical Club to the Development of Taxonomy." *Torreya* 43 (1943): 35–43.

Godfrey, Robert K., and Jean W. Wooten. *Aquatic and Wetland Plants of Southeastern United States: Monocotyledons.* Athens: University of Georgia Press, 1979.

Grantham, Dewey W. *The South in Modern America: A Region at Odds.* New York: HarperCollins, 1994.

Griffin, Dana, and Frankie Snow. "Broxton Rocks Ecological Preserve." *Tipularia* (1998): 23–28.

Hall, John C., and Frances Osborn Robb. "Eugene Allen Smith and the Geological Survey of Alabama." *Alabama Heritage* (1994): 8–18.

Harper, Bertha Tauber. *When I Was a Girl in Bavaria.* Boston: Lothrop Lee and Shepard, 1932.

Harper, Francis. "Arthur Newlin Leeds." *Journal of Mammalogy* 20 (1939): 282–83.

———."The Bartram Trail through the Southeastern States." *Bulletin of the Garden Club of America* 7 (1939): 54–64.

———. "The Mammals of the Okefinokee Swamp Region of Georgia." *Proceedings of the Boston Society of Natural History* 38 (1927): 191–396.

———. "A Sojourn in the Primeval Okefinokee." *Brooklyn Museum Quarterly* 2 (April 1915): 226–44.

———, ed. "Travels in Georgia and Florida, 1773–74: A Report to Dr. John Fothergill, by William Bartram." *Transactions of the American Philosophical Society* 33 (1943): 121–242.

———, ed. *The Travels of William Bartram: Francis Harper's Naturalist Edition.* Athens: University of Georgia Press, 1998.

Harper, Francis, and Arthur N. Leeds. "A Supplementary Chapter on *Franklinia alatamaha.*" *Bartonia* 19 (1938): 1–13.

Harper, Francis, and Delma E. Presley. *Okefinokee Album*. Athens: University of Georgia Press, 1981.

Harper, R. M. "The Aquatic Vegetation of Squaw Shoals, Tuscaloosa County, Alabama." *Torreya* 14 (1914): 149–55.

———. "*Asarum* and *Hexastylis* in Alabama and Neighboring States." *Castanea* 1 (1936): 69–76.

———. "Autobiographical Notes." 1954. Manuscript courtesy of Christopher T. Trowell.

———. "A Botanical and Geological Trip on the Warrior and Tombigbee Rivers in the Coastal Plain of Alabama." *Bulletin of the Torrey Botanical Club* 37 (1910): 107–26.

———. "A Botanical Bonanza in Tuscaloosa County, Alabama." *Journal of the Elisha Mitchell Scientific Society* 37 (1922): 158–60.

———. "A Botanical Cross-section of Northern Mississippi, with Notes on the Influence of Soil on Vegetation." *Bulletin of the Torrey Botanical Club* 40 (1913): 377–99.

———. "Botanizing in Worcester County in the 90s." *Nature Outlook* 5 (1947): 14–15, 17.

———. "Cape Cod Vegetation." *Torreya* 21 (1921): 91–98.

———. "Catalogue of Plants Collected in Georgia within 60 Miles of Okefinokee Swamp in the Counties of Pierce, Ware, Charlton, Glynn, Camden, Clinch and Echols in August, 1902." N.d. Manuscript courtesy of C. T. Trowell.

———. "Changes in the Forest Area of New England in Three Centuries." *Journal of Forestry* 16 (1918): 442–52.

———. "Condensed Autobiography of Roland M. Harper." Sept. 22, 1946. Manuscript courtesy of Mary Wigley Harper.

———. "*Croomia* a Member of the Appalachian Flora." *Castanea* 7 (1942): 109–13.

———. "A December Ramble in Tuscaloosa County, Alabama." *Plant World* 9 (1906): 102, 104–7.

———. "A Defense of Forest Fires." *Literary Digest* 47 (1913): 208.

———. "Description of the Natural Features of Alabama, by Regions." In *Naturalists' Guide to the Americas*, 446–53. Baltimore, Maryland: Ecological Society of America, 1926.

———. "Early Spring Aspects of the Coastal Plain Vegetation of South Carolina, Georgia, and Northeastern Florida." *Bulletin of the Torrey Botanical Club* 38 (1911): 223–36.

———. *Economic Botany of Alabama. Part 1*. Monograph 8. Tuscaloosa: Geological Survey of Alabama, 1913.

———. *Economic Botany of Alabama. Part 2*. Monograph 9. Tuscaloosa: Geological Survey of Alabama, 1928.

———. "Explorations in the Coastal Plain of Georgia during the Season of 1902." *Bulletin of the Torrey Botanical Club* 31 (1904): 9–27.

————. "A Few More Pioneer Plants Found in the Metamorphic Region of Alabama and Georgia." *Torreya* 10 (1910): 217–22.

————. "A Fifth Species of *Erythronium* in Alabama." *Castanea* 14 (1949): 49–52.

————. "Fire and Forest." *American Botany* 46 (1940): 5–7.

————. "Five Hundred Miles through the Appalachian Valley." *Torreya* 13 (1913): 241–45.

————. "A Forest Census of Alabama by Geographical Divisions." *Proceedings of the Society of American Foresters* 11 (1916): 208–14.

————. *Forests of Alabama.* Tuscaloosa: Alabama Geological Survey, 1943.

————. "Forests of Worcester County, Massachusetts." *Torreya* 18 (1918): 119–20.

————. "Geography of Central Florida." *Annual Report of the Florida Geological Survey* 13 (1921): 71–307.

————. "Geography and Vegetation of Northern Florida." *Annual Report of the Florida State Geological Survey* 6 (1914): 163–437.

————. "Granite Outcrop Vegetation in Alabama." *Torreya* 39 (1939): 153–59.

————. "High Living Standards in 'Black' Counties." *Montgomery Advertiser,* March 28, 1919.

————. "Historical Notes on the Relation of Fire to Forests." In Tall Timbers Research Station, *Proceedings,* 11–29.

————. "Journal of a Botanical Exploration of Okefinokee Swamp and Adjacent Territory in the Counties of Ware, Pierce, Charlton, Wayne, Glynn, Camden, Clinch, Echols, and Lowndes in Georgia and Portions of Nassau and Baker in Florida during the Month of August, 1902." N.d. Manuscript, Botany Library, Smithsonian Institution, courtesy of C. T. Trowell Collection.

————. "A Midsummer Journey through the Coastal Plain of the Carolinas and Virginia." *Bulletin of the Torrey Botanical Club* 34 (1907): 351–77.

————. "Midwinter Observations in Southeastern Mississippi and Eastern Louisiana." *Torreya* 6 (1906): 197–205.

————. "Mrs. Bertha Tauber Harper: A Tribute by Her Surviving Children." In Traber, "Harper Ancestry."

————. "The Natural Resources of Georgia." *Bulletin of the University of Georgia* 30 (1930): xi, 105.

————. "Natural Resources of Southern Florida." *Annual Report of the Florida Geological Survey* 18 (1927): 27–206.

————. "A New Heart-leaf and Other Interesting Plants from Autauga County, Alabama." *Torreya* 24 (1924): 77–83.

————. "Northward Extension." 1907. Manuscript, W. S. Hoole Special Collections Library, University of Alabama, Tuscaloosa.

————. "Notes on Ann Tower White's Ancestry." 1965. Manuscript, W. S. Hoole Special Collections Library, University of Alabama, Tuscaloosa.

————. "Notes on the Flora of Middle Georgia." *Bulletin of the Torrey Botanical Club* 27 (1900): 320–41.

————. "Okefinokee Swamp." *Popular Science Monthly* 74 (1909): 596–614.

————. "Optimism Versus Science: Georgia's Problem." *Georgia Alumni Record* (1930): 1–16.

————. "Phytogeographical Explorations in the Coastal Plain of Georgia in 1903." *Bulletin of the Torrey Botanical Club* 32 (1905): 141–71.

————. "Phytogeographical Notes on the Coastal Plain of Arkansas." *Plant World* 17 (1914): 36–48.

————. "A Phytogeographical Sketch of the Altamaha Grit Region of the Coastal Plain of Georgia." *Annals of the New York Academy of Science* 17 (1906): 1–415.

————. "The 'Pocosin' of Pike County, Alabama, and Its Bearing on Certain Problems of Succession." *Torreya* 41 (1914): 209–20.

————. "A Preliminary Soil Census of Alabama and West Florida." *Soil Science* 4 (1917): 91–107.

————. "The Relation of Climax Vegetation to Islands and Peninsulas." *Bulletin of the Torrey Botanical Club* 38 (1911): 515–25.

————. *Resources of Southern Alabama: A Statistical Guide for Investors and Settlers, with an Exposition of the General Principles of Economic Geography.* Geological Survey of Alabama, Special Report 11. University of Alabama: *Geological Survey of Alabama*, 1920.

————. "The River-bank Vegetation of the Lower Apalachicola, and a New Principle Illustrated Thereby." *Torreya* 11 (1911): 225–34.

————. "Some 19th Century Recollections of New York and Its Botanical Activities." *Torreya* 45, no. 4 (1945): 97–103.

————. "Some More Coastal Plain Plants in the Palaeozoic Region of Alabama." *Torreya* (1906): 111–17.

————. "Some Neglected Aspects of the Campaign against Swamps." *Southern Woodlands* 2 (1908): 46–67.

————. "Some Problems of Eugenics." Sept. 30, 1921. Manuscript, W. S. Hoole Special Collections Library, University of Alabama, Tuscaloosa.

————. "Some Undescribed Prairies in Northeastern Arkansas." *Plant World* 20 (1917): 58–61.

————. "Some Vanishing Scenic Features of the Southeastern United States." *Natural History* 19 (1919): 192–204.

————. "Southern Louisiana from the Car-window." *Torreya* 20 (1920): 67–76.

————. "Studying the Georgia Flora and Some Red-letter Days in the Life of a Botanist." *Castanea* 32 (1967): 1–17.

————. "Synonymy of *Burmannia* and *Gyrotheca*." *Torreya* 1 (1901): 33–34.

————. "*Taxodium distichum* and Related Species, with Notes on Some Geological Factors Influencing Their Distribution." *Bulletin of the Torrey Botanical Club* 29 (1902): 383–99.

———. "Tramping and Camping on the Southeastern Rim of the Everglades." *Florida Review Illustrated* 4 (1910): 44–49, 51–55, 147–57.

———. "*Tumion taxifolia* in Georgia." *Torreya* 19 (1919): 119–22.

———. "A Unique Climbing Plant." *Torreya* 3 (1903): 21–22.

———. "The Vegetation of Bald Knob, Elmore County, Alabama." *Plant World* 9 (1906): 265–69.

———. "Vegetation Types." *Annual Report of the Florida State Geological Survey* 7 (1915): 135–88.

———. "A Visit to Okefinokee Swamp in Southern Georgia." *Torreya* 2 (1902): 156–58.

Holifield, Vicky. "True Grit: Georgia's Other Outcrops." *Tipularia* (Spring 1989): 2–8.

Hooper, Judith. *Of Moths and Men: An Evolutionary Tale.* New York: W. W. Norton, 2002.

Hubbs, G. Ward. *Tuscaloosa: Portrait of an Alabama County.* Northridge, Calif.: Windsor Publications, 1987.

"In Memoriam: William Harper, 1843–1907." Anonymous manuscript, W. S. Hoole Special Collections Library, University of Alabama, Tuscaloosa.

International Carnivorous Plant Society. "*Sarracenia minor* Walt. var. *okefeno-keensis* Schnell: A New Variety." *Carnivorous Plant Newsletter* 31 (2002): unpaginated.

Johnson, A. Sidney, and Philip E. Hale. "The Historical Foundations of Pre-scribed Burning for Wildlife: A Southeastern Perspective." In *The Role of Fire in Nongame Wildlife Management and Community Restoration: Traditional Uses and New Directions, Proceedings of a Special Workshop.* Washington, D.C.: United States Department of Agriculture General Technical Report NE-288, 2000.

Jones, Walter B. *History and Work of Geological Surveys and Industrial Develop-ment in Alabama.* University, Alabama: Geological Survey of Alabama, 1935.

———. "Roland McMillan Harper." *Journal of the Alabama Academy of Science* 38 (1967): 111–13.

Kilgore, B. M. "From Fire Control to Fire Management: An Ecological Basis for Policies." In *Transactions of the 41st North American Wildlife and Natural Re-sources Conference.* Washington, D.C.: Wildlife Management Institute, 1976.

Kurz, Herman. "A New and Remarkable Habitat for the Endemic Florida Yew." *Torreya* 27 (1927): 90–92.

———. "A Physiographic Study of the Tree Associations of the Apalachicola River." *Proceedings of the Florida Academy of Sciences* 3 (1938): 78–90.

Kurz, Herman, and Robert K. Godfrey. *Trees of Northern Florida.* Gainesville: University of Florida Press, 1962.

Langenheim, Jean H. "Early History and Progress of Women Ecologists: Emphasis upon Research Contributions." *Annual Review of Ecology and Systematics* 27 (1996): 1–53.

Larson, Edward J. "Belated Progress: The Enactment of Eugenic Legislation in Georgia." *Journal of the History of Medicine and Allied Science* 46 (1991): 44–64.

———. "Breeding Better Georgians." *Georgia Journal of Southern Legal History* 1 (1991): 53–79.

———. *Evolution: The Remarkable History of a Scientific Theory.* New York: Modern Library, 2004.

———. *Sex, Race and Science: Eugenics in the Deep South.* Baltimore: Johns Hopkins University Press, 1995.

Lentz, David L., and Marlene Bellengi. "A Brief History of the Graduate Studies Program at the New York Botanical Garden, 1925–1940." *Brittonia* 48 (1996): 404–12.

Leonard, S. W., and W. W. Baker. "Additional Populations of *Harperocallis flava* McDaniel." *Castanea* 48 (1983): 151–52.

Long, E. C. *Florida Breezes; or, Florida, New and Old.* Floridiana Facsimile and Reprint Series. Gainesville: University of Florida Press, 1962.

Lowes, John Livingston. *The Road to Xanadu: A Study in the Ways of the Imagination.* New York: Houghton Mifflin, 1927.

Ludmerer, Kenneth M. *Genetics and American Society: A Historical Appraisal.* Baltimore: Johns Hopkins University Press, 1972.

Mallett, Richard P. *University of Maine at Farmington: A Study in Educational Change, 1864–1974.* Portland, Maine: Bond Wheelwright, 1974.

Mathias, Mildred E. "Studies in the Umbelliferae V." *Brittonia* 2 (1936): 239–45.

Mayr, Ernst. *The Growth of Biological Thought: Diversity, Evolution and Inheritance.* Cambridge, Mass.: Harvard University Press, 1982.

McCaughey, Robert. *Stand, Columbia: A History of Columbia University.* New York: Columbia University Press, 2003.

McDaniel, Sidney. *The genus* Sarracenia *(Sarraceniaceae).* Tallahassee, Fla.: Tall Timbers Research Station Bulletin no. 9, 1971.

——— "*Harperocallis*, a New Genus of the Liliaceae from Florida." *Journal of the Arnold Arboretum of Harvard University* 49 (1968): 35–40.

McGuire, John P. "Living on Longleaf: How Humans Shaped the Piney Woods System." In Georgia Wildlife Federation, *Fire Forest*, 43–53.

Mehl, Barry. "A Brief History of the European and American Eugenics Movements of the 1930s: Excerpts from a History of the American Eugenics Movement." Ph.D. diss., University of Illinois, 1988. http://www.ferris.edu/isar/arcade/eugenics/movement.htm (accessed May 16, 2004).

Miller, David C. *Dark Eden: The Swamp in Nineteenth-Century American Culture.* Cambridge: Cambridge University Press, 1990.

Mount, Robert H. *The Reptiles and Amphibians of Alabama*. Tuscaloosa: University of Alabama Press, 1996.

Mueller, Edward A. *Perilous Journeys: A History of Steamboating on the Chattahoochee, Apalachicola, and Flint Rivers, 1828–1928*. Eufala, Ala.: Historic Chattahoochee Commission, 1990.

Owen, Wayne. "The History of Native Plant Communities in the South." In *Southern Forest Resource Assessment*, edited by David N. Wear and John G. Greis, Forest Service, Southern Research Station Gen. Technical Report. SRS-53, 47–61. Asheville, N.C.: U.S. Department of Agriculture, 2002.

Palmer, Ralph S. "Francis Harper." *The Auk* 90 (1973): 737–38.

Patrick, Rembert W. Editorial preface to Eppes, *Through Some Eventful Years*.

Patrick, T. S., J. R. Allison, and G. A. Krakow. *Protected Plants of Georgia*. Social Circle: Georgia Department of Natural Resources, 1995.

Penzel, Fred. *Obsessive-Compulsive Disorders*. New York: Oxford University Press, 2000.

Pyne, Stephen J. *Fire in America: A Cultural History of Wildland and Rural Fire*. Princeton, N.J.: Princeton University Press, 1982.

Reed, Thomas Walter. *History of the University of Georgia*. Athens: University of Georgia, 1949. Online at http://dlg.galileo.usg.edu/cgi-bin/ebind2html .pl/reed_cii?seq=24 (accessed Feb. 8, 2004).

Ridley, Matt. *The Agile Gene: How Nature Turns on Nurture*. New York: HarperCollins, 2003.

Rogers, William Warren, and Erica R. Clark. *The Croom Family and Goodwood Plantation: Land, Litigation, and Southern Lives*. Athens: University of Georgia Press, 1999.

Rogers, William Warren, Robert David Ward, Leah Rawls Atkins, and Wayne Flynt. *Alabama: The History of a Deep South State*. Tuscaloosa: University of Alabama Press, 1994.

Rothra, Elizabeth Ogren. *Florida's Pioneer Naturalist: The Life of Charles Torrey Simpson*. Gainesville: University Press of Florida, 1995.

Rusby, H. H. "Historical Sketch of the Development of Botany in New York City." *Torreya* 6 (1906): 101–11, 133–45.

Sargent, Charles Sprague. *Manual of the Trees of North America*. 2nd corrected ed. New York: Dover, 1905.

———. *Manual of the Trees of North America (Exclusive of Mexico)* 2nd ed. New York: Dover, 1922.

———. *Report on the Forests of North America (Exclusive of Mexico)*. Washington, D.C.: U.S. Government Printing Office, 1884. Excerpted in "History with Fire in Its Eye: An Introduction to Fire in America," by Stephen J. Pyne, in *Nature Transformed: The Environment in American History* (Research Triangle Park, N.C.: National Humanities Center, n.d.). http://www.nhc.rtp.nc.us/tserve/ nattrans/nattrans.htm (accessed April 23, 2005).

Schiff, A. L. *Fire and Water: Scientific Heresy in the Forest Service.* Cambridge, Mass.: Harvard University Press, 1962.

Schuyler, Alfred E. "Notes on Five Species of *Scirpus* in Eastern North America." *Bartonia* 33 (1964): 1–6.

———. "A Taxonomic Revision of North American Leafy Species of *Scirpus.*" *Proceedings of the Academy of Natural Sciences of Philadelphia* 119 (1967): 295–323.

Selden, Steven. *Inheriting Shame: The Story of Eugenics and Racism in America.* New York: Teachers College Press, 1999.

Sheridan, P. M., S. Orzell, and E. Bridges. "Powerline Easements as Refugia for State Rare Seepage and Pineland Plant Taxa, February 24–26, 1997." In *Sixth International Symposium on Environmental Concerns in Rights-of-Way Management,* edited by J. R. Williams, J. W. Goodrich-Mahoney, J. R. Wisniewski, and J. Wisniewski, 451–60. Oxford: Elsevier Science, 1997.

Shreve, Forrest. "A Collecting Trip at Cinchona." *Torreya* 6 (1906): 81–84.

Shull, G. H. "Duplicate Genes for Capsule-form in *Capsella bursa-pastoris.*" *Zeitschrift für Induktive Abstammungs- und Vererbungslehre* 12 (1914), 97–149.

Simpson, Charles Torrey. *In Lower Florida Wilds: A Naturalist's Observations on the Life, Physical Geography, and Geology of the More Tropical Part of the State.* New York: G. P. Putnam's Sons, 1920.

———. *Out of Doors in Florida: The Adventures of a Naturalist, Together with Essays on the Wild Life and the Geology of the State.* Miami: E. B. Douglas, 1923.

Small, John Kunkel. *From Eden to Sahara: Florida's Tragedy.* Lancaster, Pa.: Science Press, 1929.

Smith, J. David. *The Eugenic Assault on America: Scenes in Red, White, and Black.* Fairfax, Va.: George Mason University Press, 1992.

Spornick, Charles D., Alan R. Cattier, and Robert J. Greene. *An Outdoor Guide to Bartram's Travels.* Athens: University of Georgia Press, 2003.

Stahle, David W. "The Unsung Ancients." *Natural History,* February 2002, 48.

Stoddard, Herbert L., Sr. *Memoirs of a Naturalist.* Norman: University of Oklahoma Press, 1969.

———. "Use of Fire in Pine Forests and Game Lands of the Deep Southeast." In Tall Timbers Research Station, *Proceedings,* 31–42.

Tall Timbers Research Station. *Proceedings of the First Annual Tall Timbers Fire Ecology Conference, March 1–2, 1962, Tallahassee, Florida.* Tallahassee, Florida: Tall Timbers Research Station, 1962.

Tanner, Ogden, and Adele Auchincloss. *The New York Botanical Garden: An Illustrated Chronicle of Plants and People.* New York: Walker and Company, 1991.

Traber, Lucy Harper. "Harper Ancestry." 1993. Unpublished compilation of materials, courtesy of Lucy Harper Traber.

U.S. Fish and Wildlife Service. *Endangered and Threatened Species of the South-eastern United States.* Washington, D.C.: U.S. Fish and Wildlife Service, U.S. Dept. of the Interior, 1991.

———. "Ivory-billed Woodpecker." In *Multi-species Recovery Plan for South Florida,* 4:465–70. Atlanta: U.S. Fish and Wildlife Service, 1998.

Utech, F., and L. C. Anderson. "The Genus *Harperocallis.*" *Flora of North America* 26 (2002): 58–59.

Van Bavel, Cornelius. *Hugo de Vries: Travels of a Dutch Botanist in America, 1904–1912.* Kerrville, Tex.: Herring Printing, 2000.

Van Doren, Mark, ed. *Travels of William Bartram.* New York: Macy-Masius, 1928.

———, ed. *Travels of William Bartram.* Introduction by John Livingston Lowes. New York: Barnes and Noble, 1940.

Verne, Jules. *The Mysterious Island.* New York: Penguin Group, 1986.

Weston, F. M. "Bird Casualties on the Pensacola Bay Bridge (1938–1949)." *Florida Naturalist 39* (1966): 53–54.

Willoughby, Hugh L. *Across the Everglades: A Canoe Journey of Exploration.* Port Salerno: Florida Classics Library, 1992.

Wilson, Edward O. *Naturalist.* New York: Island Press, 1995.

———. *Sociobiology: The New Synthesis.* Cambridge, Mass.: Belknap Press of Harvard University Press, 1975.

Wolf, Wolfgang. "*Erythronium,* a Neglected Genus in Alabama." *Castanea 6* (1941): 21–27.

Woodward, C. Vann. *The Burden of Southern History.* Baton Rouge: Louisiana State University Press, 1960.

———. *Origins of the New South, 1877–1913.* Baton Rouge: Louisiana State University Press, 1951.

INDEX

Abbot, John, 31

Abercrombie, John William, 34

Academy of Natural Sciences, 113, 141

African Americans, Harper's view of, 96–97, 178

Agassiz, Louis, 212

Agassiz Association, 24

Akerman, Alfred, 14, 18, 27, 43, 45, 47, 63, 78, 148, 153

Alabama Academy of Science, 140

Alabama Department of Archives and History, 115

Alabama Forestry Commission, 137

Alabama Geological Survey, 2, 73, 88, 89, 99, 115, 119, 200

Alabama Museum of Natural History, 34, 71

Alabama Natural History Society, 73

Aldrich, T. H., 48

Allison, James R., 213

Altamaha Grit region (Altamaha Formation), 29, 59, 195, 204, 214; dissertation on, 32–33, 96, 129, 135, 136, 208; habitats in, 113, 115; longleaf in, 141; 1903–6 exploration of, 30–33; mentioned, 39, 191

American Association for the Advancement of Science, 38, 51, 107, 126, 141, 150

American Botanist, 134

American Bryological and Lichenological Society, 24

American Eugenics Society, 177, 178

American Forestry Association, 133

American Forests, 131

American Museum of Natural History, 23, 40, 71, 114, 177, 179

American Optical Company, 8,

American Philosophical Society, 115, 194

American Scenic and Historic Preservation Society, 94

Americus, Ga., 13, 16–17,

Ammidown, Lucius E., 19, 22

Anderson, Loran C., 207

Andersonville, Ga., 13

Andrews, E. F., 132

Annals of the Association of American Geographers, 95

Apalachicola, Fla., 4, 57–59, 65–66

Apalachicola Bay, 58

Apalachicola National Forest, 6, 57, 59, 202; diversity of, 203–4

Apalachicola River basin, 6, 69; ecology of, 81

Appalachian Plateau, 1

Archer, Allan F., 142

Arnold Arboretum, 36, 64, 203

Ashe, William Willard, 143

Aspalaga Bluff, Fla., 54–57, 130

Audubon Society, 179

Avant, David, 82–83

Avant, Fenton Garnett Davis, 82–83

Baker, Wilson, 204, 213

Balduina atropurpurea (purpledisk honeycombhead), 27, 212

Baldwin, J. T., 142, 200